BETTER LIBRARIES MAKE
BETTER SCHOOLS

CONTRIBUTIONS TO LIBRARY LITERATURE
John David Marshall, Editor

BOOKS, LIBRARIES, LIBRARIANS, Selected by
John David Marshall (with Wayne Shirley and Louis
Shores), 1955. #1

OF, BY, AND FOR LIBRARIANS, Selected by John
David Marshall, 1960. #2

AN AMERICAN LIBRARY HISTORY READER,
Selected by John David Marshall, 1961. #3

BETTER LIBRARIES MAKE BETTER SCHOOLS,
Selected by Charles L. Trinkner, 1962. #4

BETTER LIBRARIES MAKE
BETTER SCHOOLS

Contributions to Library Literature #4

Selected by
CHARLES L. TRINKNER

Introduction by
JOHN DAVID MARSHALL

THE SHOE STRING PRESS, INC.
HAMDEN, CONNECTICUT
1962

Copyright 1962 by The Shoe String Press, Inc.

July 1963

Library of Congress Catalog Card Number: 62-16835
Printed in the United States of America

Dedicated to
Marian, the Librarian

CONTENTS

TABLE OF CONTENTS

TABLE OF CONTENTS

Part III: THE LIBRARY AND READER SERVICE

TABLE OF CONTENTS

x

ACKNOWLEDGMENTS

The editor thanks the authors and publishers with whose permission the articles in this book have been reprinted. The following information includes bibliographic data which would otherwise be supplied in footnotes or in a separate list.

1. Gladys L. Potter. "Our School Libraries and Librarians," ALA Bulletin, 49:56-57, February, 1955. Reprinted by permission of author and publisher.

2. Mary Peacock Douglas. "How Well Will the School Library Serve," High School Journal, 43:47-51, November, 1959. Reprinted by permission of author and publisher.

3. Helen R. Sattley. "The School Library," Bulletin of the National Association of Secondary School Principals, 40:131-134, October, 1956. Miss Sattley's article first appeared in ALA Bulletin, 50:373-376, June, 1956. Reprinted by permission of author and publishers.

4. Frances H. Adams. "Librarians Work at their Problems," California Journal of Secondary Education, 35:309-313, May, 1960. Reprinted by permission of author and publisher.

5. Fay J. Buttle and June Berry. "Core Curriculum and the Library," High School Journal, 41:9-13, October, 1957. Reprinted by permission of authors and publisher.

6. Josephine Wortham. "The Library — A Classroom Must," ALA Bulletin, 49:58-60, February, 1955. Reprinted by permission of author and publisher.

7. Donald E. Strout. "Are Librarians Censors?", The Nation, 189:379-381, November 21, 1959. Reprinted by permission of author and publisher.

8. Mary L. Tarbox. "Some Challenges We Face," Wilson Library Bulletin, 31:164-167, 169, October, 1956. Reprinted by permission of author and publisher.

ACKNOWLEDGMENTS

9. Benjamin C. Willis. "School Librarian: Coordinator," ALA Bulletin, 51:92-94, February, 1957. Reprinted by permission of author and publisher.

10. Robert L. Amsden. "Characteristics of Effective School Library Service," Bulletin of the National Association of Secondary School Principals, 43:55-58, November, 1959. Reprinted by permission of author and publisher.

11. Irving E. Lane. "An Administrator Looks at the Library," Bulletin of the National Association of Secondary School Principals, 43:58-61, November, 1959. Reprinted by permission of author and publisher.

12. Christopher A. Legge. "Policies and Programs of a Small College Library," Junior College Journal, 29:412-413, March, 1959. Reprinted by permission of author and publisher.

13. Ben M. Harris. "Put Your Elementary Library to Work," School Executive, 78:64-65, February, 1959. Copyright 1959, Buttenheim Publishing Corp., New York, and reprinted by permission of author and publisher.

14. Eleanor E. Ahlers. "How Will the New School Library Standards Affect High School Libraries?", High School Journal, 43:42-46, November, 1959. Reprinted by permission of author and publisher.

15. Felix E. Hirsch. "New Horizons for Junior College Libraries," Library Journal, 85:2372-2375, June 15, 1960. Reprinted by permission of author and publisher.

16. Felix E. Hirsch. "New College Library Standards," Library Journal, 84:1994-1996, June 15, 1959. Reprinted by permission of author and publisher.

17. "School Library Bill of Rights," Library Journal-Junior Libraries, 80:1929, September 15, 1955. Reprinted by permission of publisher.

18. Elizabeth Hodges. "Book Selection Practices in the Nation's Schools," School Libraries, 6:11-13, 15, March, 1957. Reprinted by permission of author and publisher.

19. David McAllister. "Aids to Book Selection," National Elementary Principal, 35:145-150, September, 1955. Reprinted by permission of author and publisher.

ACKNOWLEDGMENTS

20. Bertha D. Hellum and Albert J. Biggins. "Cost-Saving in Book Cataloging," Library Journal, 82:1729-1730, July, 1957. Reprinted by permission of authors and publisher.

21. Veda Fatka. "Cost of Cataloging Versus Printed Cards in the School Library," Wilson Library Bulletin, 33:239, November, 1958. Reprinted by permission of author and publisher.

22. Edward C. Werner. "Cutting Cataloging Costs in the Small Library," Library Journal, 82:32-33, January 1, 1957. Reprinted by permission of author and publisher.

23. Lawrence R. Huber. "Materials and Methods in Book Finishing and Repairing," ALA Bulletin, 49:326-330, July-August, 1955. Reprinted by permission of author and publisher.

24. Raymond G. Erbes, Jr. "Microfilm in the High School Library," Wilson Library Bulletin, 33:302-303, December, 1958. Reprinted by permission of author and publisher.

25. "Lettering Without Pain," Library Journal-Junior Libraries, 81:209-212, January 15, 1956. Reprinted by permission of publisher.

26. Sylvia Ziskind. "Why Count the Circulation?", Wilson Library Bulletin, 31:625, 627, April, 1957. Reprinted by permission of author and publisher.

27. Lois E. Wrisley. "Student Staff Assistants," Wilson Library Bulletin, 31:626-627, April, 1957. Reprinted by permission of author and publisher.

28. Roy D. Baker. "An Organized Club of Student Library Assistants," School Activities, 30:119-122, December, 1958. Reprinted by permission of author and publisher.

29. I. T. Littleton. "Training Circulation Assistants," Southeastern Librarian, 6:82-85, Summer, 1956. Reprinted by permission of author and publisher.

30. Julie Silagyi. "Library Assistants' Self-Evaluation," Wilson Library Bulletin, 31:178, 182, October, 1956. Reprinted by permission of author and publisher.

31. Frances Perske. "Overdues: A Positive Approach," Wilson Library Bulletin, 34:423-424, February, 1960. Reprinted by permission of author and publisher.

ACKNOWLEDGMENTS

32. Stanley D. Truelson, Jr. "But I Returned That Book Long Ago!", Wilson Library Bulletin, 34:208-209, November, 1959. Reprinted by permission of author and publisher.

33. Gerald Raftery. "Why Kids Steal Books," Library Journal-Junior Libraries, 84:1639-1641, May 15, 1959. Reprinted by permission of author and publisher.

34. Bernard Poll. "The Unconscious Motivation of Library Fines," Wilson Library Bulletin, 34:422, February, 1960. Reprinted by permission of author and publisher.

35. Joseph F. Shubert. "Developing Interest in the School Library," Wilson Library Bulletin, 30:172-173, October, 1955. Reprinted by permission of author and publisher.

36. Jean Parriss. "The Librarian as Persuader," Wilson Library Bulletin, 32:490-491, March, 1958. Reprinted by permission of author and publisher.

37. James H. Cherry. "What Librarians Have to Sell," School Libraries, 6:33-35, May, 1957. Reprinted by permission of author and publisher.

38. Johnnie Givens. "The Small and Medium Sized College Library," Southeastern Librarian, 7:12-15, Spring, 1957. Reprinted by permission of author and publisher.

39. Virginia Tozier. "What Motivates Secondary School Voluntary Reading?", Wilson Library Bulletin, 30:166-169, October, 1955. Reprinted by permission of author and publisher.

40. Alma N. Stanlis. "Promotion Aids for the High School Librarian," Wilson Library Bulletin, 34:492-493, March, 1960. Reprinted by permission of author and publisher.

41. "What Makes a Book Talk Good?", Library Journal-Junior Libraries, 81:2410-2414, October 15, 1956. Reprinted by permission of publisher.

42. Helen B. Baldwin. "Library Activities for an Elementary School," Wilson Library Bulletin, 33: 142-145, October, 1958. Reprinted by permission of author and publisher.

43. Lynn L. Solomon. "Anyone Can Tell Stories . . . Including Student Assistants," Wilson Library Bulletin, 34:661, May, 1960. Reprinted by permission of author and publisher.

44. Walter R. Lund and John C. Roman. "The Library: Key to

Curriculum Cooperation," Wilson Library Bulletin, 30:769, 771, June, 1956. Reprinted by permission of authors and publisher.

45. Amy Fenner. " 'Catchy' Captions," Library Journal-Junior Libraries, 81:213, January 15, 1956. Reprinted by permission of author and publisher.

46. Philip S. Ogilvie. "Library Orientation," Library Journal-Junior Libraries, 82:1081-1084, April 15, 1957. Reprinted by permission of author and publisher.

47. Violet E. Peterson. "Library Instruction in High School," Wilson Library Bulletin, 30:180, October, 1955. Reprinted by permission of author and publisher.

48. Bess Gray. "Teaching Library Skills in Elementary School," Library Journal-Junior Libraries, 83:2457-2459, September 15, 1958. Reprinted by permission of author and publisher.

49. Helen Wheeler. "The Teaching of Library Skills and Attitudes," High School Journal, 43:52-57, November, 1959. Reprinted by permission of author and publisher.

50. Dorothy Roche. "The School Library: Each Teacher's Responsibility," Wilson Library Bulletin, 31:630-631, April, 1957, by permission of author and publisher.

51. Louise L. Klohn. "Six Pointers for Teachers," Library Journal-Junior Libraries, 83:2461-2462, September 15, 1958. Reprinted by permission of author and publisher.

52. Georgetta Merritt [Campbell]. "Library Orientation for College Freshmen," Library Journal, 81:1224-1225, May 15, 1956. Reprinted by permission of author and publisher.

53. Georgia Rankin Cole. "Classification for the Non-Librarian," Library Journal-Junior Libraries, 85:1637-1638, April 15, 1960. Reprinted by permission of author and publisher.

54. George R. Ridge and Davy S. Ridge. "Cross References Make Cross Readers," Southeastern Librarian, 9:166-170, Winter, 1959. Reprinted by permission of author and publisher.

55. Mary L. Connor and Ruth Ault. "Fourth-Graders Go to the Library," National Elementary Principal, 35:160-162, September, 1955. Reprinted by permission of authors and publisher.

56. Emily Harris and D. Richard Bowles. "Our Library is a Center

ACKNOWLEDGMENTS

for Recreational Reading," National Elementary Principal, 35: 140-144, September, 1955. Reprinted by permission of authors and publisher.

57. Virginia Musselman. "Playground Fun in Storyland," Library Journal-Junior Libraries, 3:2434-2435, October 15, 1956. Reprinted by permission of author and publisher.

58. Delta Jack. "Guiding Children's Reading," Wilson Library Bulletin, 33:355-356, 358, January, 1959. Reprinted by permission of author and publisher.

59. Elizabeth Hodges. "The Art of Reading," ALA Bulletin, 51: 90-91, February, 1957. Reprinted by permission of author and publisher.

60. W. Ambrose Kincaid and Mamie Ingram. "Central Library on a Low Budget: With Tips on Planning, Staffing — and Sharing," School Executive, 78:62-63, February, 1959. Copyright 1959, Buttenheim Publishing Corp., New York. Reprinted by permission of author and publisher.

61. Mildred P. Frary. "The Elementary School Library and the Gifted," ALA Bulletin, 52:100-101, February, 1958. Reprinted by permission of author and publisher.

62. Edith W. Dahlgren. "The School Library Helps the Gifted Child," Wilson Library Bulletin, 33:140-141, 145, October, 1958. Reprinted by permission of author and publisher.

63. Reba Burtis. "The Role of the Librarian in the Reading Program," Wilson Library Bulletin, 30:330, December, 1955. Reprinted by permission of author and publisher.

64. Marianne Schmidt. "Building a Vocational Information File," Wilson Library Bulletin, 33:231-232, 238, November, 1958. Reprinted by permission of author and publisher.

65. Aurelia Davis. "The Librarian and the Guidance Program," ALA Bulletin, 49:60-62, February, 1955. Reprinted by permission of author and publisher.

66. Helen F. Faust. "Cooperation of Counselor and Librarian," School Libraries, 8:9-11, 33, October, 1958. Reprinted by permission of author and publisher.

67. Virgil M. Howes. "Guidance Through Books," School Libraries, 9:9-11, May, 1959. Reprinted by permission of author and publisher.

ACKNOWLEDGMENTS

68. Richard L. Darling. "Mental Hygiene and Books: Bibliotherapy as used with Children and Adolescents," Wilson Library Bulletin, 32:293-296, December, 1957. Reprinted by permission of author and publisher.

69. M. Elizabeth Leonard. "Small Fry Need Good Books," Wilson Library Bulletin, 33:357-358, January, 1959. Reprinted by permission of author and publisher.

70. John A. Ratliff. "Junior High School Libraries Must Be Different," Bulletin of the National Association of Secondary School Principals, 43:61-65, November, 1959. Reprinted by permission of author and publisher.

GENERAL INTRODUCTION

The book you now hold in your hand is a practical one — a collection of short, helpful essays and articles in the craft of school librarianship. It has been assembled principally with the library school student and the beginning librarian in mind. For these, it can serve several uses — as a volume of supplementary readings for course work, as a "handbook" of useful information to be carried into the field, or simply as a morale-builder. The more experienced librarian should, however, find its contents of no mean interest.

Three facts about librarianship have suggested the inclusion of Better Libraries Make Better Schools in the "Contributions to Library Literature Series": (1) a large number of both library school students and beginning librarians will be spending their professional lives in some kind of school; (2) the special problems that the new school librarian confronts will be greatly simplified by the knowledge which more experienced librarians have shared with their colleagues through the printed page; and (3) the published articles containing this knowledge lie buried in a great variety of large, heavy volumes from which only the more assiduous graduate students could ever hope to extract them.

The shame of a good many professions — librarianship among them — is that their literature is inaccessible to the persons who need it most. The "Contributions to Library Literature Series" is an attempt on the part of the compilers, the general editor of the series, and the publisher to make certain essays and articles from the literature of librarianship more readily accessible.

The unseasoned librarian — one, say, who has difficulty solving the problem of overdues in his own library — may have no idea where to locate a possible solution . . . if, indeed, he suspects that one may exist in print. "Overdues: A Positive Approach" by Frances Perske might contain the answer to this problem, and it might solve the problem in advance for the student of librarianship who takes the time to read it or who enters his profession with a photostat of the article in his briefcase. But Mrs. Perske's essay, along with sixty-nine others of its kind, is included in <u>Better Libraries Make Better Schools</u> — the the only book, to my knowledge, which attempts to bring together between the covers of one volume some of the large and diffuse body of literature that directs, supports, and instructs the school librarian in his quest for a more effective professional life.

An anthologist, almost by definition, is a person incapable of satisfaction — which is what keeps him at his post. No good anthologist ever claims that his work is finished. No anthology is ever made "complete" — at least not without the sacrifice of a precious amount of order and direction. It need hardly be said then that an anthology represents both the taste and the literacy of only a few men, that its contents are always the subject of small controversies, and that essays could be added and subtracted with ease from the published book, depending on the preferences of its individual purchasers or readers. Articles and essays, advocating this or that solution to a multitude of library problems, will continue to appear; and anthologies, containing a selection of them, will doubtless continue to be assembled. But the measure of value represented in this first in-gathering of the professional knowledge of school librarianship is one which is unlikely to be erased soon — if ever.

JOHN DAVID MARSHALL
General Editor, Contributions to
Library Literature Series

PREFACE

The purpose of this anthology is to bring together in one volume the chief "working" concepts of school librarianship as an aid to progressive librarians responsible for building better libraries. This guide to better libraries contains 70 articles, drawn from library literature, representing practical approaches to on-the-job problems by successful library personnel and administrators in the nation's educational system. The articles were carefully selected within the framework of elementary and secondary school and college levels.

The arrangement of the material under three main headings with sub-topics shows the extensive breadth and depth of the main theme — Better Libraries Make Better Schools. The organization is directed toward capitalizing on ideas, stimulating re-thinking, and advancing the cause of school librarianship. A combination Author-Title index locates the individual article or author.

The book is designed to be a ready-reference handbook focusing and reflecting various viewpoints and outlooks for improving library service in the years ahead. It is hoped that it will provide encouragement, techniques, re-orientation, and challenges for the prospective as well as the practicing librarian.

The school librarian has varied duties and responsibilities both to the school system and to the nation. Top-ranking is service coupled with teaching. Effective librarianship includes the guidance of the youngster's exploring, learning, thinking, research, reading, and searching for the truth.

Library services vary widely between two extremes, both of which may be found in the United States. At one extreme a very meager collection may be found, whereas at the other extreme the librarian has a large collection with added materials available. Of course the latter case permits fitting the material to the particular needs of the child thus leading him to more satisfying experiences.

In the last two decades emphasis has been placed on the

PREFACE

broad aspects of school library service. A new trend in school library services is beginning to appear in the American educational process. New patterns for better libraries use terms such as "individual service to individual children through reading guidance," "social functions," "pupil behavior and library use," and "cumulative guidance records." Today's specific services include such projects as developing good study habits, strengthening curriculum development, supplying occupational and career materials, building bibliographies, furnishing individual reference aid, promoting effective reading, and solving emotional, social, spiritual and personal problems through reading.

As a service agency, the library exists for the students and faculty. No greater service can be singled out than that service provided by the genuine librarian. It is within the power of every librarian to provide this service; that is, to provide guidance, understanding, and interest in terms of the student's needs, drives, and emotional well-being. It is the aim of this volume to aid the librarian in doing so.

Building better libraries builds a better America. Libraries set the pace for progress and national growth. The growth and use of our library resources is in direct relation to the growth of our nation. Libraries and librarians must provide genuine leadership and constructive guidance for today's readers and tomorrow's leaders.

Acknowledgments are due the authors and publishers who have given their permission to reprint material; to Professor Delbert McGuire, Director, Journalism Department, Texas A & M, College Station, Texas, for his sharing of journalistic ideas; to Florida librarians who have made the decision to build better libraries for a better state; to the wonderfully patient staff of The Shoe String Press; to the Louisiana State University Library School under the excellent direction of Professor Florinell Morton, ALA President, for training better librarians for better schools; and to Florida's Dr. Louis Shores for his leadership and contributions to the field of librarianship.

Special acknowledgment is due Mr. John David Marshall, University of Georgia Libraries, and general editor of the Contributions to Library Literature Series, for his keen "library insight" and editorial skills.

PREFACE

Finally, thanks are due my wife, who is a librarian, counselor, and Dean of Girls in the Florida school system, for providing patience, understanding, loyalty, faith, and compassion throughout the project.

CHARLES L. TRINKNER
Pensacola, Florida
January, 1962

Part I: THE IDEAL SCHOOL LIBRARY

1. OUR SCHOOL LIBRARIES AND LIBRARIANS

Gladys L. Potter

School libraries are always an item of concern to school administrators. They are expensive to build, to equip, and to staff and to maintain. The administration must be constantly alert to insure the most effective use of money invested. In general there is no question in the minds of administrators that libraries are essential — as essential as gymnasiums or cafeterias. There is no question in the minds of thinking men of the growing importance of the library in the education of children and youth in a shrinking world. It is evident that wider sources of information are needed today than were needed yesterday. The wise administrator is aware of these things, but he must be sure that he gets his money's worth from his investment. He needs evidence that the library serves as the greatest of all aids to teaching, "fanning sparks that pass from teacher to student." This is its purpose. He must be sure that classroom teachers, as well as the librarians, know the material in the library and use it assiduously for their own growth as well as the growth of their students.

Henry Lash, in the May, 1953, Wilson Library Bulletin, objected to indicating that the library was the "heart of the school." "Heart of the school — my foot!" says Mr. Lash. But if we don't call the library the heart of a school we must at least accept the fact that a good library with a good librarian is indispensable to an efficient school. It is a service agency, a teaching agency, and a materials center as well as a reading center. President Eisenhower in addressing the ALA indicated that the library served "the precious liberties of our nation: freedom of inquiry, freedom of spoken and written word, and freedom of exchange of ideas." And he adds that democracy depends for its very life on these principles. What a responsibility is carried by the school librarian! Much depends on him. If he does not have insight into the values of good library service, the library will not function as the "heart of the school" and the investment of the district will be a loss.

The librarian is more important than the building, the materials, the equipment — everything else. He is the person that makes the library. Without him the library is an ivory tower.

What kind of person must this school librarian be in order to carry out these vital responsibilities?

There's a feeling prevalent in many quarters that librarians are a bit removed from the activities of the common man. They have beautiful, quiet quarters where they devote themselves to cataloging and book selecting. They are themselves a bit aloof and ungracious and chose librarianship as a profession because they wanted a sheltered life where pressures and tensions did not touch them. The average run of the mill patron is a little frightened of this type of librarian who is a custodian of books.

All librarians would vigorously deny such an appraisal of the members of their profession. It should be denied because, of course, on the face of it, it is not a true picture of the librarian of today. But because 25 years ago this picture was more true than it is now, and because there are still some remnants of this conception of a librarian, the picture needs to be examined.

Where did such an idea get started? Do some librarians think more of books than of people? Are they better satisfied to have more books on the shelves than in circulation? Are they sometimes aloof and protective of "their" libraries and the demands made upon them? School librarians, because of the very nature of their assignment and the fact that they chose this branch of service, are probably further removed from the implied criticism than some other types. But some of them may tend to think of "their library" as a hallowed place — a thing apart from the hubbub of a busy school.

It is the school librarian's job to bring books and people together. He cannot be aloof and isolated. It is his job to understand and participate in the needs and problems of the school. This means he must attend faculty meetings, participate in curriculum work, and volunteer for committees. He should know the results of the school testing program. He should consider it as one of his duties to contribute to the im-

provement of these results. It is a part of the school program
and thus a part of the library program. It should be the school
librarian who is quick in discovering youngsters with reading
difficulties and be ready to deal with these difficulties and to
help other teachers to deal with them, too. He should be alert
to the study habits of youngsters and work on the improvement
of these habits. Because he knows books as well as people, he
will be alert to the activities of the world and be constantly relating books and magazine articles to the happenings of everyday life. With the help of other teachers, rather than alone,
the school librarian should make his selection of books since
in no better way can the needs and interests of the school be
served. The social guidance given during the story hour, the
discussions, the insights, the security given should not be
overlooked as a library service, nor the splendid guidance
given to very superior youngsters who reach out hungrily for
wider fields to conquer!

The library as the coordinating agency of the school should
represent a place where both students and teachers are helped.
The evaluation of the library service, Mr. Administrator,
should be in terms of improved pupil achievement, improved
teaching, and richer, fuller living for both teachers and students. If you have these, you have your money's worth.

A large order you say. Are the responsibilities outlined
too much to expect of the able, well-trained school librarian?
The picture we have drawn is quite different from the one of
the aloof person working in a solitary, quiet atmosphere with
silent printed materials. Is the alert administrator expecting
too much of the school librarian? I am not sure. It is evident
that the school librarian needs recognition as a teacher. Too
frequently he is not thought of as a teacher and does not call
himself a teacher. He must be well trained in library techniques but also versed in the techniques of instruction. He
should have an extra-curricular assignment just as other
teachers do. In such a way his acquaintance with young people
grows and deepens. Rather than thinking of the library as "his"
the wise librarian knows it to be a workshop, a gathering place,
a laboratory, a source of materials — a vital part of the school
belonging to everyone. If not the heart, Mr. Lash, the library
is the pulse of the school, perhaps, when we list the important
functions it serves in an efficient and effective program.

2. HOW WELL WILL THE SCHOOL LIBRARY SERVE

Mary Peacock Douglas

A recent study of the use of the school library in secondary school teaching[1] has brought to the forefront the need for formulating more definite plans within each school for practicing reference and research skills which are admittedly essential for an educated individual. The responsibility for increased library usage in connection with any subject course lies first of all with the classroom teacher, but the librarian and the administrator have responsibilities too. Working together, analyzing strengths and weaknesses, planning for improvements, and putting plans into operation, they can provide for pupils experiences which should result in developing each student toward his potential.

This first nationwide study of the secondary-school teacher and library services brought out these facts:

"Virtually all, 99 percent, of the teachers in urban secondary schools are teaching in schools that have central libraries.

Secondary-school teachers are almost unanimous in the belief that learning how to use various library resources should be a fundamental part of the education of all boys and girls, and a substantial majority of teachers believe that they have a personal responsibility for helping to develop library skills.

A majority of secondary schools have well-organized programs for developing student skill in the use of library material.

A majority of teachers recognize library services as either essential or important to effective teaching in their subject areas.

Teachers of the various subjects appear to be divided
into three rather distinct groups according to the extent to which they utilize library services. Teachers
of English, social studies, and science are the <u>major</u>
<u>users</u> of library services. Teachers of business edu-
cation, industrial arts, and mathematics are the
<u>minor users</u>. Teachers of art, foreign languages,
<u>household</u> arts, music, and health and physical edu-
cation are <u>potential major users</u>.

The school library today not only serves the curriculum
needs of students and teachers, but it also provides
materials for the professional growth of teachers."[1]

The recognition of the library as a service center as well
as a materials center is emphasized in another publication
based on a careful and extensive study of good school libraries.
The New National Standards[2] for school libraries, soon to be
published by the American Library Association for the American Association of School Librarians is a document which all
school persons should read, study, and ponder. Its real purpose is to portray a positive <u>program</u> for school libraries and
to indicate the essentials for carrying out that program. Now
is the time to evaluate the impact of the library in each school.

The forward looking school

Provides, in sufficient abundance and variety, the
many resources needed for teaching and learning.

Has these materials easily accessible for use in the
school and in the home.

Supports a well-planned school library program that
provides for the careful evaluation and selection of
materials, for the efficient organization of materials,
and for the guidance and assistance desired by faculty
members and students in selecting and using materials.

In your school does the library effectively serve to further this

7

educational ideal? Does it provide the materials, funds, and staff needed so that students can

Derive the fullest benefit from their classroom instruction.

Extend the boundaries of their knowledge and experience.

Pursue self-directed learning of all kinds.

Explore and satisfy their many curiosities and interests.

Find enjoyment in the rich stores of the imaginative expressions of creative artists.

Learn how to use libraries and to evaluate the materials of communication.

Obtain materials that meet their individual needs and abilities.

Establish intellectual habits that last for life.

Does it provide materials, funds, and staff needed so that teachers and counselors can

Achieve their instructional objectives to the fullest degree.

Enrich course content.

Prepare assignments that provide for the needs and abilities of individual students.

Motivate students to use materials for curricular and noncurricular purposes.

Have the materials needed in counseling students in many aspects of guidance work.

HOW WELL WILL THE SCHOOL LIBRARY SERVE

Use materials directly with students in the classroom.

Teach students how to use materials and libraries.

Keep abreast with the best ideas and practices in education.

Use materials to broaden their own knowledge and to derive personal enjoyment.

Have materials easily accessible and efficiently organized so that time is not wasted in locating materials for examination and use.

The realization of these potentialities may not be easy to achieve, but very few worthwhile things have been achieved easily. The American Association of School Librarians in its study arrived at certain conclusions as to what materials, personnel, funds, quarters and equipment would be required to provide the services which are indicated. It must be realized that these essential elements are inter-locking and interdependent. No one quantitative measure can be considered valid of itself; each is closely related to all others.

The Collection of Materials should

Provide a wide variety, covering many subjects.

Provide a wide variety, covering many reading levels.

Provide for extensive reference and research.

Include many types of materials, including books, periodicals, pictures, pamphlets, maps, recordings, films, filmstrips, slides, models, regalia, and others.

Include at least 6,000-10,000 books for schools with 200-999 pupils with emphasis upon quality rather than proportion in relation to size of enrollment. Schools of 1,000 or more should average at least 10 books per pupil.

9

Provide a collection of professional materials for the school faculty of books, periodicals and other instructional materials.

The Library Personnel should

Include a staff of trained librarians and clerical helpers for the program to be administered.

Include staff members administering the audio-visual program if it is part of the library responsibility.

Be assigned for central cataloging and organization.

Include a supervisor or director of library services for the school system.

Have time to appraise and cooperatively select materials for purchase, to work with individual pupils, to work with teachers, to work with class groups, to organize materials, to prepare bibliographies, to teach the use of books and libraries.

Include at least one full-time certified librarian for each 300 pupils up to 900 and one certified librarian for each 400 pupils thereafter.

Include one half-time clerical worker for each 300 pupils.

Increase the staff by 50% if the library has full responsibility for the audio-visual materials and program within the school.

The Library Quarters should

Provide a suite of rooms to include reading rooms, work room, storage space, conference rooms, classroom (for larger schools), office (for larger schools), listening and viewing areas.

Provide reading rooms seating not fewer than 45-55 in schools with 550 pupils or fewer and ten per cent of the student enrollment in schools having 551 or more students; provide multiple reading rooms, each seating not more than 75 and each under the direction of a trained librarian, in large schools.

Provide 30 to 35 square feet per reader in the reading room.

Provide adequate shelving for present need and future growth.

Should be suitably and attractively furnished and equipped.

Should be centrally located and easily accessible.

The Library Budget should

Provide funds for needed personnel.

Provide funds for regular library books of $1,000 to $1,500 annually in schools having 200-249 pupils; provide $4.00 to $6.00 per student in schools having 250 or more pupils.

Provide additional funds for other printed materials.

Provide funds for the purchase of audio-visual materials of $2.00 to $6.00 per pupil.

Provide funds for professional materials for teachers.

Provide additional funds to bring the library up to standard.

Provide funds for keeping the materials collection in good physical condition.

Provide for supplies and equipment as needed.

11

These are recognized as high standards, but not high for the service which is needed, and expected in many communities, from the library. When the first national standards for secondary school libraries were projected by a National Education Association Committee headed by C. C. Certain in 1917, the committee stated ". . . a schedule of systematic library development should be outlined, with definite annual goals to be attained, until all standards have been achieved. It is estimated that not more than five years should be required for the complete achievement of standards given in this report."[3] That challenge holds again today. The challenge of new standards is set before schools in an age that measures speed by sound, not by the plodding turn of a wooden wheel. How fast the development of communication and transportation in a decade; how slow the means of sharing the wisdom of the ages and the swiftness of man's scientific genius through the guided use of print!

Will schools accept the challenge? How well will each library serve?

3. THE SCHOOL LIBRARY

Helen R. Sattley

In articles and discussions concerning the school library the trend is toward the library as a materials center – a center which will organize, maintain and service slides, films, recordings and tapes as well as books and magazines. Some would include the school textbooks and the museum exhibits.

For most school libraries this materials center is still in the article and discussion stage. There are very few, by comparison to the total number of libraries, already in existence. However, so much has been written and discussed about this hypothetical center that librarians are beginning to take this development as a matter of course, even though so often they, themselves, can see little likelihood of being able to carry on this extended program in their own libraries.

The ideal of such a materials center is certainly a worthwhile goal, but too much of the discussion concerning it is hypothetical and impractical. It is asking too much of the school librarians involved and—what is even more important—is asking for a curtailment of book programs in our schools at the very time in our cultural development when books are meeting their greatest challenge.

It is time we stopped and looked at the obstacles and objections to this development. It is time we took stock of the school libraries in the country to see if they have had the personnel and the time necessary to develop the programs on which they are already embarked before setting before all of them impossible goals which, in the end, may weaken to a critical degree any contribution they may be able to make to their schools.

Perhaps the most important thing is to examine goals, first. What is it we want our school libraries to be—storehouses and servicing agencies or dynamic teaching agencies? There are many of us who believe that the latter is the more important and that the organizing and servicing of materials is the framework on which we base our teaching programs.

It is right here that we must emphasize our differences from the college libraries and stop lumping remedies and plans which are "good" for the one and "inevitably" good for the other. We are dealing, here, with two distinct kinds of programs. Although college libraries are doing more teaching today than they have in the past, their teaching function is not one of their foremost reasons for being—and to many elementary and secondary school librarians, teaching is one of their foremost reasons. (By "teaching" is meant the formal and informal teaching—work with classes in the library and in the classroom; work with individuals for research and reading guidance; work with individual teachers so that complete integration with class work results; work with curriculum committees and subject chairmen; in fact, a dynamic program which makes the library a real part of most activities of the school.)

If the school librarian is to take over the cataloging and maintenance and servicing of slides, films, recordings and tapes as well as textbooks (this last has invariably become

13

mere clerical checking and has been astutely avoided by alert librarians for many years) and add these to an already full book cataloging and maintenance and servicing job, where will time come from for the teaching program which is so essential? If besides the cataloging and maintenance, the selection of the audio-visual materials is added to the selection of books and magazines and pamphlet material, how will we make a 12 hour day stretch out into 24, 36, and 40? (Have you ever <u>counted</u> the hours it takes during a school year to keep a pamphlet file current?)

Let us face the fact that all the way across the country school libraries are in such a pioneer era that one librarian is servicing 1000, 2000, 3000, 4000 students and doing his own cataloging besides. Of course, there "should be" central cataloging, but it is coming slowly. Of course, there "should be" clerical help, but it is usually easier to sell a school system an additional professional position than a newly created clerical one. Of course, there "should be" time off for the librarian to do his book selection and his book order, but in school after school, the librarian does even his cataloging at a reference desk in the main reading room with one eye cocked for the student who will need his help and both ears alert to the general atmosphere of the room.

In line with a philosophy of the librarian as teacher comes the need for the library schools to add to the training program or prerequisites of the school library student courses in curriculum, psychology of children and adolescence, and practice teaching in classrooms and libraries. Thus to an already full schedule of courses, more essentials are added. But the time for library training is still the same, at most, a fifth of a five-year program or a full fifth year, and some very definite prerequisites in education. Fortunately, there are often, today, basic requirements in audio-visual courses in many education schools and departments, thus enabling most students who enter a library school with a minor or concentration in education to be well grounded in an understanding of audio-visual programs. Moreover, in many of the library schools, instruction in audio-visual materials and equipment is a part of many different library school courses. Thus school librarians should be quite well prepared to understand and cooperate with any audio-visual program being carried on in their schools.

Again, however, this is additional subject matter added to the library school curriculum. That more time for specific courses in audio-visual materials and instruction can be spared from one year of library school training is questioned by many of us who have been concerned with library school training within the past 5-10 years. As more "essentials" are added to the library school courses, it is too often the book courses which get crowded out.

Isn't it quite ironic that at the very time that well trained audio-visual specialists are beginning to be available for the schools that school librarians' book knowledge is being dissipated?

Here, then, are some very definite obstacles inherent in our existing school libraries and training programs which hamper the development of school libraries into materials centers: (1) the impossibility of having, in most existing libraries, the cataloging, maintenance, and servicing of slides, films, recordings, tapes (not to mention equipment), textbooks, library books, magazines and pamphlets and have time left over for the teaching program; (2) the impossibility of having an intelligent and thorough selection and ordering of all such materials done by the present school library staffs who usually have a full schedule of classes and students; (3) the recognition that book programs must not be sacrificed as other responsibilities are added to the school library; (4) the impossibility of adding indefinitely to the training courses of the prospective school librarian; and (5) the very imminent danger that the librarian soundly based in book knowledge will be lost to our school systems and to succeeding generations of school children.

These are the obstacles at the present time and they will be with us for a long time to come. We must be aware of them as we move forward and see that the best of our present library programs are preserved and protected as our responsibilities are increased.

But as we move forward, there are, also, some objections. The first ties up with the first obstacle and is that too often in the trend toward materials centers, the emphasis of the school library is on the organization and maintenance function rather than on the teaching function. Enough has been said above concerning this.

15

A second objection is that not enough recognition is given to the audio-visual specialist who is emerging as an important helpmate. He believes that his is a teaching function and that the audio-visual program is a dynamic one, just as we believe our library program is dynamic. We should be two special teachers working together for the good of the school. Co-operation will differ from city to city, even from school to school. In many school systems, there is need of two thoroughly developed fields, the library and the audio-visual ones, and these systems should be encouraged to finance and develop both. For either group to be anxious about the boundaries of the other's territory and to try to set up a single field where two really exist, is to act defensively – is to ask for curtailment of services we should not expect or tolerate in education today. Two highly developed fields should be expected in such school systems.

If it is practical for both fields to be combined into one materials center the librarian needs to rely upon the audio-visual specialist for selection of materials in his own fields. If the librarian can rely upon him, one of the great obstacles to the development of a materials center can be met to a great extent. If, further, the audio-visual specialist can assume responsibility for the organization of his materials, as well as the maintenance of his equipment, the library teaching program will not need to be sacrificed so that the audio-visual teaching program may flourish. The teaching program of the one is as important as the other. Here are areas where the give and take will have to be based on good will, but the positive programs which will result when each field is reinforcing the other will be worth the effort.

A third objection is the possible trend toward a deadly library environment for school children – one which threatens to outdo our most dreadful memories of stuffed owls on top of bookcases and every other book a frightening tome which dampened young readers' enthusiasm. Are we, in our enthusiasm for a functional materials center, sometimes getting a curriculum center for teachers mixed up with a functioning center for children?

The school library has an important future. But let us be aware of the pitfalls as we move toward our goals.

4. LIBRARIANS WORK AT THEIR PROBLEMS

Frances H. Adams

As school librarians in California read and hear comments
from other parts of the nation concerning library problems,
they realize that their difficulties are far from unique. At the
same time, they see certain circumstances as combining to
bring them so severe a situation that it is imperative to tell
their story outside their own associations and their conference
groups.

The general population increase has brought whole new
communities into existence which need funds not only for
schools but for every sort of community service. Since the
crest of the population growth is now at the adolescent level,
the special pressure point becomes the senior high school.
And the library, as the heart of the school, seems sometimes
to be the steam gauge which sounds the warning that there are
many problems which must be met.

The Need for People

The senior high schools need more trained librarians who
have triple skills – in maintaining the library, in helping teachers, in understanding adolescents. They commonly need more
library assistants than they have, more hands to do better the
jobs which ought to be done.

The Need for Space and Materials

As schools expand and enrollments increase, libraries
ought to grow too. Even if enrollments stood still, library
collections should expand year by year, for a balanced collection to serve a large high school does not come in a package.
But room for pupils to do research or browse, conference
space, shelf space, storage and service areas – all are at a
premium in newer high schools as well as in the older ones.
In California the library not bulging at the seams is rare.

ADAMS

The Need for Understanding
Larger school staffs and student bodies often mean less
communication among people. Librarians today are seeking
ways to help the principal and the superintendent see the library's problems. They share techniques for aiding teachers
to make better uses of the library's facilities in their classroom teaching and in meeting varying pupil needs. They try
to modify their own procedures in terms of the changing curriculum and newer teaching methods.

The Need for Better Community Relations
School libraries are finding that they need to take the initiative in numerous ways in their own communities. They are
working with the local public library to establish harmonious
relationships through these procedures:

1. Sharing curriculum materials and book lists so that
   the public library may know the school's program
   better.

2. Encouraging student leadership in developing codes
   of conduct in public library situations so that the
   community library—which has its own problems in
   serving larger populations—may be as efficient as
   possible in meeting pupil needs.

3. Helping to ease situations as peak hours in the public
   library by finding school people who can serve as
   part-time personnel.

In some communities, too, school librarians work with
youth councils—recognizing that when pupils use school or
community libraries as purely social centers to a degree that
seems to lessen their usefulness for others, the condition is
often a symptom of need for additional suitable places of activity for adolescents and an indication that the problem needs to
be considered by a civic group.

The Need for Sharing Practices and Progress
School librarians meet many teachers and students in the
course of a single day. One librarian who serves a student

18

population of 2,500 in one large high school indicates that on a busy day there will be at least 500 individual pupil visits to the library, without counting any of the people who come in before or after school. On a run-of-the-mill day at least 250 young-sters will come in during the time that classes are in session.

And yet in another sense the librarian is alone. In a school where everybody else has a different sort of job, she must seek ways to help the staff know the library and know her. Of-ten, even though she would like to keep the library open for additional time after school, it is important to close and to attend faculty meetings so that teachers realize she is one of them.

She invites a cross section of the faculty to participate on book-selection committees, and on committees to decide what materials should be discarded. One librarian has persuaded the principal of the school to be chairman of the library com-mittee – which has brought added status and better understand-ing to the work of the group.

The school librarian, wherever space is at all available, welcomes the use of the library at suitable hours for commit-tees or for meetings of the total staff, knowing that increased contacts mean better relationships within the school. Book-jacket displays in hallway cases, brief announcements in the school bulletin of particularly interesting new books, main-tenance of a professional library for faculty, a policy of clip-ping reviews of special materials and sending these to the right people – all are goodwill builders which many librarians use.

Some school districts have extended to librarians as well as to teachers the policy of hiring a substitute so that visits for the purpose of observation in other districts may be made. Only by such procedures can promising practices and ideas be fully shared. Here, however, is the statement of one librar-ian[1] concerning growth and change in her own district's prac-tices:

> In our district within the last year we have present-ed to the Board of Education a colored slide review of the use of materials in our district. This was a thirty-minute presentation showing the use of books from kindergarten through the activities in a high school li-brary, and it touched every area of the curriculum.

We are sure, as a result of that program, that our
Board is more informed as to the need for good materials and for centers in which to house them. At our
Superintendent's meeting with his principals last week,
one of the items on his agenda was a review of school
library usage. Prior to this meeting we called the principals in each school and talked over with them the
scope of the item so they could talk with their librarians and come prepared for the discussion.

In one of our schools the library committee, composed of a member of each department and the librarian,
is chaired by the principal. The purpose of this committee is to discuss the problems that concern the library and to develop the understanding that every
department has a responsibility for the school library's
development and use. It meets only a few times a year
but has been most effective in its action. We hope our
other schools will soon have such a committee activated.

We would be concerned if the librarians in our
district went to the principal with complaints. We
believe we go to him with problems and with several
suggestions for solutions. This gives a positive approach to the interview and involves him in decision-
making. We need to make him aware of the many fine
activities that are going on in our department.

One problem which librarians face is that teachers
make unrealistic assignments in relation to the availability of materials and to student time in the library.
Much can be done to influence assignments if a librarian asks to meet with all teachers in a department to
discuss the matter. This is more satisfying than
criticizing an individual teacher for his approach to
the library's use. We have also used department
meetings in the library as a way of involving teachers
in discarding materials in his subject that are obsolete.
This helps to make him aware of the books we have,
and the need of his suggestions for building a more
adequate collection.

A district of more than one school at each level
could certainly work out an exchange of book lists.

These should be quite complete, including classification number. If paper and mimeograph facilities are available, the making of a list for each student to have for his notebook would certainly aid in his use of the public library as well as the school library.

Why do we not make easily available the high school catalog for students to use – or any other book list that forms a basis of our collections? Students could find annotation reference to the books selected, and the catalog's classified section would indicate where to find it on the shelf.

Traditionally the catalog contains an author, title, and subject entry for all books in the library. A class of forty students plus students sent from other classes every period can scarcely crowd around the catalog file. Maybe we need to experiment with separating the subject entries and establishing a separate subject file for our collections. Do we need to look at many of the things we do with the objective of finding more meaningful ways of doing them? Why does the card catalog remain such an enigma to our students?

School librarians are teachers, too, so we have to teach effectively our library skills. Our district is going to develop a library guide next year. We are planning on starting it by working with each department on "How do you want to use the library?"–and from this we will develop our guide, hoping to correlate it with the subject need. The skills will be taught in relation to actual usage for a subject assignment. We want it to be a practical instrument that will place some of the responsibility on the classroom teacher for implementation.

In our district, we charge book fines only for lost or mutilated books. This has been very successful, and we use that released clerical time for other activities. We are now opening, as an experiment in one of our schools, a special room that we are calling our "college-going room." We plan on having a special collection of advanced books in all areas for our juniors and seniors. The title of this collection, we hope, will

have the psychological effect of having them approach
it with a more mature attitude, and the specially
designated area will furnish them a quiet atmosphere
for the serious perusal of material.

We are considering opening our high school libraries for evening use. Before we do this we will take a
survey of the students to ascertain potential use. We
must remember that part of the evening use of the
public library represents a student-initiated action
as he acts independently in his new role as an adult.
We are also exploring the possibility of opening the
high school libraries during summer school. The
changing nature of our summer school from a remedial
curriculum to one of enrichment is making the use of
the library essential.

As we look at the many current problems of school libraries, we need to sort out the short-range issues from the larger
ones, the trivial from the basic. If libraries are crowded, it
is because students need help. If book collections are inadequate, it is because demand exceeds supply. If the work load
is heavy, it is because we give real service. New emphasis
on the concept that the library is the heart of the schools means
that the energies of many people are being devoted to solving
the library's problems.

5. CORE CURRICULUM AND THE LIBRARY

Fay J. Buttle and June Berry

The core curriculum teacher and the school librarian
should be true professional partners. Both are concerned with
the business of educating children and both accomplish it in a
manner opposed to traditional lecture-textbook methods. Actually, some of the major objectives and characteristics of core

programs are pursued and realized in the library. "Experience curriculum," "individual differences," "fused learning," "common learnings,"—we believe these terms are just as applicable to school libraries as to core curriculum.

The modern school library is intended to be used, not talked about; children learn by doing, not by telling or being told. How does a student learn to use the card catalog? By actual personal experience with catalog drawers. Each individual searches for books indexed in the catalog—books on subjects of interest to him. He locates the books he needs and selects those suited to his reading ability. Corresponding experiences, based on individual differences and integrated with various subjects, could be described of every library resource — whether encyclopedia, Reader's Guide, World Almanac, or Bartlett's Quotations.

We find certain common learnings are taught solely, or at least most effectively, in the library. For example, everyone should learn the purposes of libraries. By using their school library, children recognize its values and realize that all libraries contain similar treasures.

Another common learning which all children need is an understanding of the specific types of library materials — that library resources are tools, and each has its own particular use. We don't use a pair of pliers to mow the lawn; neither do we use the card catalog to find a magazine article.

Core programs are characterized by use of multiple materials, not only multiple textbooks and library books, but also multiple pamphlet, magazine, encyclopedia, and picture materials. And where are multiple materials available and organized for use? In the library. Here, as in no other situation, teacher and librarian may demonstrate the value of many different materials to exhaust the subject being studied. The nature of research, its exactness, its importance, and its unique application to subject matter study, can be fully understood only by actual library use.

As partners, the librarian and teacher must work together when library activities are involved. Both must cooperate to plan the desired objectives; both must understand the process by which these objectives are to be accomplished. If advance planning is neglected—or indeed, if it is inadequate, haphazard,

23

or one-sided–learning will be limited proportionately. The class may arrive and find the librarian unable to supply enough materials on the subject assigned. Or the librarian who does not know the teacher's objective may do or say things which actually prevent its accomplishment.

Let us take an extreme example to illustrate the point. A teacher wishes to introduce the contributions other people have made to our American culture and to integrate the use of biographical tools with this concept. She gives the children an assignment to find the nationalities of outstanding people, instructing them to search in encyclopedias, books of collective biography, Who's Who, etc. The librarian may misunderstand the objective, may actually tell the children the nationalities or find the answers for them and thwart the teacher's intention. To prevent this, or similar "working at cross purposes," cooperative planning is indispensable.

Planning the Library Experiences

Our library activities begin when the classroom teacher is planning to teach a particular unit such as "Our State." Perhaps she wishes to integrate the skill of note-taking with the subject matter about the state. In the initial approach the teacher asks the librarian to reserve the library for the required number of days and describes the materials which are likely to be needed. The librarian's role is considered; perhaps it will be to review library rules and materials, or orient the students to the library.

After this teacher-librarian consultation, the classroom teacher prepares her class for the library visit. She discusses the unit with them and permits each child to choose a specific subject to be explored. One student may select the minerals of the state, one a famous native son, and another a particular historical event. Instruction is given on note-taking–probably in the classroom–possibly with brief practice exercises. The teacher explains the library visit and asks the children to take notes from at least four library sources, including books, encyclopedias, magazines, and pamphlets.

If circumstances permit the librarian to visit during this class discussion, her effectiveness will be increased. Not only will she observe the specific materials needed but also will note other preparations to be made. Perhaps she will borrow books from the public library, make a bibliography of all materials the library has on the subject, or display written materials such as books, maps, and pamphlets on the tables at the designated hour. In some cases she will place books on reserve or on limited circulation. When illustrated notebooks or journals are assigned, scissors, paste, and rulers should be made available as well as magazines to cut out pictures.

Of course, the culmination of all planning is the students' actual experience in the library. After any necessary explanations or library orientation, either by teacher or librarian as previously determined, the integrated learning begins. Each pupil searches in the card catalog, encyclopedias, as other materials; he locates resources pertaining to his subject; and he takes notes on the information.

Both teacher and librarian move around the library helping individual students. Many skills will be integrated with the note-taking; the techniques of paraphrasing, use of quotation marks, dangers of plagiarism, and the correct form for references are related concepts which might be introduced. Note-taking may occupy one day or several days, depending on the wishes of the teacher and the ability of her students.

If the library is needed for other classes, the writing of the final paper or presenting of reports may be completed in the classroom. The teacher usually takes complete charge, checks form, sentences, and content, and corrects spelling, grammar, and punctuation.

However, evaluation is not limited to the students' work. The librarian and teacher will evaluate all aspects of the unit, with particular attention to such criteria as: (1) Were the desired objectives accomplished? (2) Were the children fully prepared for the library visit and activities? (3) Were the necessary materials available and well-organized? (4) Were individual differences served? and (5) How might the experience be made more valuable another time?

Variety of Library-Core Experiences

Although core curriculum courses vary widely in structure as well as content and scope, any program from seventh through twelfth grade can benefit from library cooperation. Many units of study will dove-tail into the library-core pattern described above, and adequate material is in the school library (or can be obtained) to supplement any text or texts in the curriculum. The following library units, for example, have been successful in one core class in our school.

1. Biography. Learning about others' lives is interesting and challenging through the use of biographical dictionaries and other biography books.

2. Critical Thinking. The Reader's Guide, magazines, and newspapers are used to find material on disputable subjects and to search for valid information upon which to base conclusions.

3. World Understanding. The achievements of other peoples and their characteristics and cultures, are studied by using biographical dictionaries as well as atlases, history books, and geography books.

4. Poetry. Enjoyment and appreciation of poetry are approached through poetry indexes and poetry anthologies.

5. Forms of Literature. Library resources prove especially useful for the study of short stories, novels, essays, drama, etc.

Values of Library Activities

The use of the library, with its various materials, and its practical activities, seems to create exceptional understanding of the subject being presented. The students maintain interest in their subject, perhaps because of the change from classroom surroundings, the success they feel as a result of personal interest in the subject, or the variety of resources available to them.

In library learning, students have opportunities to examine all aspects of controversial issues and are taught the danger of believing slanted or propaganda materials. This is an appropriate occasion to teach the fact that being in print does not automatically clothe a statement in truth.

That the variety of library materials benefits individual students – retarded, average, or superior – is obvious. For poor readers, the library offers resources on lower reading levels. Each child is given material on his own level, and consequently achieves some degree of success in his work. Moreover, individual attention is increased because the librarian serves as co-teacher and is available to assist when needed.

Library use seems particularly stimulating to the needs and inclinations of superior students. The materials encountered in the course of their studies challenge their capability and pique their curiosity. Students of superior reading ability are permitted and encouraged to read more extensively than the others, yet they are working on the same assignment or type of project as their classmates. Some may explore all the ramifications of their subjects, often swinging off on a wide tangent to satisfy their avid curiosity.

Frequently, creative and artistic abilities of talented children are developed through library experiences. In their explorations of various materials, these alert people discover charts, maps, pictures, and diagrams – media of communication not only instructive and attractive but also suggestive of ideas to be reproduced on paper. The drawing paper (or poster board or graph paper) is available, as are rulers, colored pencils, paints, or any other materials needed to help children find success and gratification in accomplishing their goals.

Finally, schools restricted by traditional classrooms with no tables are especially benefited by library use and facilities. Library tables furnish ample space for children to spread out their materials and go to work – whether to read and take notes, to draw charts, or to cut pictures and paste them in note-books.

These library-classroom activities are varied and adaptable and can be exciting and challenging. Time and planning invested in library-core curriculum experiences will yield dividends of enriched instruction and genuine learning.

6. THE LIBRARY – A CLASSROOM MUST

Josephine Wortham

"But, when <u>will</u> the library be open? You know that it is a <u>must</u> in the sixth grade!" Larry stood in the library doorway and registered despair. He had been in the new Casis School a <u>whole week</u> and still no library! The librarian might have resented this rebuke when she thought of the long, hard hours she was spending to get the new library ready for use. Instead, she experienced an inward feeling of satisfaction. Larry's words lingered in her mind, causing the big task before her to shrink appreciably. At least she could work with enthusiasm because of this reassurance that the library is so important to children.

Larry's sentiment that "the library is a 'must' in the sixth grade" reflects the way I, his teacher, feel about the library's significant role in the activities of the classroom. It has long been my conviction that in order to provide children with an effective, stimulating program, rich in learning and suited to individual needs, the services and materials of a good library are indispensable. A modern functional library can do much to vitalize, reinforce and implement the classroom curriculum. The teacher who fails to take advantage of its resources and employ its services to the fullest degree is denying herself valuable assistance and depriving her children of many effective learning experiences.

When I consider the role of the library in helping me as a classroom teacher, three things stand out. First, the library is a well-organized source of materials which I consider essential for performing an acceptable job in the classroom. Second, the library is a service center which makes those materials available at the time they are needed. Third, the librarian is my counselor and co-teacher who not only advises me in regard to many aspects of my work, but actually strengthens my instructional program.

I am an ardent advocate of the idea that during the progress

28

of a particular unit of work, the classroom should be literally
<u>alive</u> with all types of instructional materials. The kind of
curriculum that we are trying to carry on today cannot be successful without adequate learning tools. However, I do not feel
that it is possible to assemble all such materials in the classroom, close the door, and do the most effective job of teaching.
Only experience has taught me this! A modern active library
can, as the unit progresses, make substantial contribution
beyond what can be accomplished within the four walls of the
classroom.

In my sixth grade the major portion of language, science
and social studies skills are taught principally through the
realistic context of a unit of work, for which children have a
genuine interest. If we are to teach children to think critically
and to evaluate material, they need to use good reference tools
and to read comparatively in many books under our direction.
If children are to grow in reading skills, books on different
levels of difficulty to fit individual needs and interests must
be available. Improvement in these and other skills, as well
as emotional and social development, require that the teacher
be near by and alert to opportunities for guidance. The classroom is the ideal setting to effect these learnings. However,
it is not possible – or desirable – for each classroom to house
all the instructional materials needed – even for one unit. Expense and the necessity for sharing materials with other classrooms would make this practice prohibitive. But there is
another important consideration. When children participate in
the planning, evaluating, and replanning of activities, the
teacher cannot predict the exact turn a unit will take. The library must be tapped for additional material. Moreover, the
library's orderly arrangement of extensive materials makes
it an essential adjunct to the classroom at all times where
children can develop the ability to locate materials and use
them independently.

My chief reason for considering a classroom collection
inadequate is the important provision for the needs and interests
of the exceptional children in the class – particularly the gifted
learners. These children can delve much more deeply into
certain aspects of the unit than the majority of the class is
expected to do. Logical departures of interest for them would

involve more extensive materials not practical to include in the classroom collection. Their interests are of such unpredictable direction and duration that it is much better to care for them on an individual basis as the need arises. When the rapid learners have fulfilled their obligation to the class project and wish to pursue their study in further areas, related to the unit, the library provides a laboratory where each can work independently.

The library serves as a materials center and study laboratory for all children, and for teachers as well. New materials can be examined and noted, work can be planned in terms of available materials. It is possible to preview slides and filmstrips in the library without loss of time for moving equipment to other parts of the building. A broad and flexible reading program is made possible by a well-stocked library and whole classes can receive library instruction in a realistic setting.

Completely adequate, well-organized materials in a school library will contribute little to the work of the classroom unless they have proper administration. This makes the services of a competent, professional librarian indispensable to acquire materials and to provide their proper and timely interpretation in terms of the unit of work and the users. Teachers have a responsibility in this respect also. Capable and resourceful as the librarian may be, she is not a mind reader, not a performer of magic, and thus can render service only to the extent that we pave the way. There must be a close working relationship between the teacher and the librarian. It is important that we recommend materials, keep her informed on the activities in the classroom, the particular reading interests and abilities of children, and much more if we expect maximum service.

It is my custom to confer with the librarian prior to the selection of a new unit. We discuss the availability of materials, demands for similar material by other classes, methods of implementing intelligent use of materials so that the unit selected can become a worthwhile, interesting and challenging experience for the students. Sometimes they need improvement in certain skills. I seek advice from the librarian on probable topics for study that will do a particular job. Although I do not expect the librarian to assume responsibility for teaching the language skills, I try to make her aware of the ones I am attempting to improve so that she can take advantage of every incidental opportunity to help children during reference periods in the library. We talk frequently about how to improve or extend reading tastes of children. When Jimmy requests books on baseball, football, basketball, she is prepared to guide his interests into other channels which can also challenge him.

During our unit on Machines, I conferred with Mrs. McGuire constantly. When I mentioned the word inventors, she said immediately, "I think it would be wonderful if the children could know more intimately the men behind the machines." Together we planned that she should stimulate an interest in biography by reviewing one for the class. We added to our classroom collection numerous biographies of famous scientists, attractively displayed with the invitation, "How Many Biographies Have You Read?" The children accepted the invitation with enthusiasm. The kind of thing that makes a teacher happy came one afternoon from Andy. "Mrs. Wortham, may I stay awhile after school? I want to read my Einstein." Biography had come alive for these children!

Probably no greater contribution has been made to the enrichment and extension of my class work than the librarian's part in a story-telling project. A class in story-telling from the University happened to perform at Casis and my group was delighted by the excellently told stories. Soon this child, that one, and another, about fifteen in all, were seeking stories to tell from the library. Their pride and pleasure in telling their stories to the receptive primary children quickly overcame their first feelings of insecurity and self-consciousness. We ignored the quality of the story and stressed only the fun of telling until the children acquired poise. It wasn't long, however, until we could concentrate on a more discriminating selection and better presentation. The children outgrew Uncle Wiggly and Nurse Nancy and soon were telling beautifully Andersen's The Steadfast Tin Soldier, Burton's The Little House, and old folk tales in the classrooms, the library, and even to the University class.

I suppose we could have had a moderately successful project without the assistance of the librarian, but with her background in story-telling and its materials, this became an exciting experience in which a group of children achieved a high level of performance. Above all, they gained a love for the art and a richer appreciation for good literature.

The librarian is a key person in whatever success I may have in my classroom. To fulfill her role as counselor and co-teacher, she needs to be a master at the job—and she must be allowed <u>time</u> for the job. She cannot concentrate on the technical aspects of her profession alone. She must be a student of child growth and development—a lover of children— always interested in helping them to strive to the limit of their potential by means of good library service.

7. ARE LIBRARIANS CENSORS?

Donald E. Strout

Daily, in more than 36,000 school and public libraries from one end of the land to the other, librarians go about the slow and often arduous task of building library collections. They are, as one writer has put it, "trustees of the public's right to know," plying their trade in "the market place of ideas." Their public ranges the full span of man's traditional seven ages, with interests and needs as broad and far-reaching as the limits of man's knowledge. Their libraries range from a single room to great, multi-storied structures and the sprawling branch systems of metropolitan areas. Their work is undramatic, unsung, often misunderstood, sometimes pilloried— and, once in a while, praised. But on each of them rests a traditional (and awesome) responsibility which unites them in a common purpose—the preservation, provision and utilization of print for man's information and enjoyment.

The principles by which they work are summed up in the Library Bill of Rights (later expanded somewhat in the "Freedom to Read" statement of the Westchester Conference of Librarians and Publishers): (1) that material presenting all points of view concerning the problems and issues of our time shall be provided to all comers; (2) that in no case shall material be

excluded because of the race, nationality, or political or religious beliefs of an author; (3) that material shall not be removed from libraries because of partisan or doctrinal disapproval.

Thus, willy-nilly, the librarian is right smack in the thick
of controversy. For these principles give rise to problems of
considerable magnitude. It must not be forgotten that, aside
from other factors, the simple act of picking and choosing from
among the 13,000 or more titles published annually in the U.S.
alone involves, in all except the very largest libraries, also
the act of rejecting, either by default or design. And in a climate where fears, pressures and tensions often dominate, and
where the urge to conformity is everywhere evident, the risk
of a librarian's being (to use a somewhat old-fashioned phrase)
"damned if he does and damned if he doesn't" is very real, indeed.

The United States is a pluralist society. Nowhere is this
pluralism more evident than in the pressure groups which seek
to influence the librarian—groups whose motives, however
well-intentioned, often lead them into strange, if not indefen-
sible, ways. There are the "patriotic" groups, like the American Legion, the D.A.R., the V.F.W., the Minute Women of
the U.S.A., with their manifest concern over things (including
books) "anti-American," "pro-Communist," "pro-One World"
et al. There are the "citizen" groups, like the P.T.A., the
Citizens for Decent Literature, Inc., and the variety of local
bodies, which in their concern for the "protection of the young"
set off "anti-obscenity" drives by the score. These, in turn,
are joined at national and local level by the "church" groups:
the Catholic National Office for Decent Literature, the more
recently formed Protestant Churchmen's Committee for Decent
Publications, and the myriad denominationally-oriented organizations, all similarly concerned with the reading habits of the
young. Then there are the quasi-official state groups, like
Rhode Island's Commission to Encourage Morality in Youth,
and Massachusetts' Obscene Literature Control Commission.

Local police, city councils, county attorneys, district
attorneys, state legislatures and their members, the U.S.
Congress and individual Congressmen and, of course, the Post
Office Department and the Postmaster General, serve to round
out the register of the forces whose moves drastically alter,
if they do not indeed shape, the climate wherein librarians

33

move and whereof they are a part.

The frequency with which pressures from these and other sources are brought to bear on libraries can never be fully known. The cautious librarian quietly capitulates; the conscientious, courageous librarian stands firm—and, if the pressures are prolonged, makes headlines. Since 1952 (when the Newsletter on Intellectual Freedom was started), at least twelve libraries have been under severe pressure to remove "subversive," "anti-American," "un-American," "pro-Communist" or "pro-One World" material from their shelves: the Boston Public Library and the Los Angeles school system, along with libraries in Kalamazoo (Mich.), Adams (Mass.), San Antonio (Texas), Mt. Lebanon (Pa.), Akron (Ohio), Punxsutawney (Pa.), Woonsocket (R.I.), Orlando (Fla.), Riverside (Calif.) and North Canton (Ohio). In another four libraries (Illinois State Library; Galion, Ohio, schools; Charleston, W.Va., Public Library; Queens Borough Public Library), outside pressures were directed against "obscene" or "objectionable" books. In recent weeks, libraries in the South are reported under attack for fostering "interracial propaganda," among them the Alabama State Library and the Shreveport, La., Public Library. Demands not to show Chaplin, "pro-Communist" and otherwise "objectionable" films have confronted librarians in Peoria (Ill.), Phoenix (Ariz.), East Orange (N.J.), Glendale (Calif.), and Hicksville (L.I.).

But the number of occasions when libraries directly experience pressures from the outside is far less relevant than the fact that the pressure groups exist, and that they are strong and vocal. Their existence, their strength, their vocalness serve to engender a pervasive and spreading climate of fear. Again, however well-intentioned they may be, they are at cross purposes with the library enterprise, at least as ideally conceived. They are guardians not of the public's right to know, but of the public's right to know only the "right" things. Their main aim, in its simplest terms, is to protect and prevent, rather than to provide.

These outside pressures, however, whether successfully resisted or not (and the record where known shows that librarians do resist and are generally successful), constitute but one of the two major components of the selection-censorship situation. The other major component is the librarians themselves. Luther Evans, former Librarian of Congress, commenting on the demands of pressure groups vis-a-vis librarians, once put it this way:

> [This] is a very real danger and it has caused
> many librarians throughout this land to chisel a bit
> on the doctrines by which they have lived in the past.
> The amount of that chiseling can never be known, because so much of the evidence is locked within the inner
> consciousness of frightened librarians. This book, that
> book, this pamphlet, that pamphlet, this motion picture,
> that motion picture, is excluded from the selection
> process because it is feared some group in the community . . . may be ready to pounce on the librarians
> for choosing it.

A recent study (Book Selection and Censorship; A Study of School and Public Libraries in California, by Marjorie Fiske, University of California Press, 1959, $3.75) has thrown considerable light on "the amount of chiseling" referred to by Mr. Evans by revealing not a little of the evidence which is "locked away in the inner consciousness of frightened librarians." In the course of the study, 204 interviews took place with school librarians and administrators in forty-six senior high schools and with librarians in forty-eight municipal and county library units located in twenty-six communities, representing library service to a majority of California's population.

Put in general terms, the Fiske findings are shocking enough. A surprising proportion of librarians reveal themselves as weak and timid in the act of selection by practicing a kind of ignoble and debased under-the-counter censorship in deliberately avoiding the controversial. Far the most frequent source of objections to controversial books, Miss Fiske found, were not the library patrons, not parents zealously protecting their children, but the librarians themselves. Yet paradoxically, when complaints did originate with patrons or parents, the librarians have often stood their ground and refused to take restrictive measures.

Expressed in more specific terms, the findings are even

more disturbing. Of the librarians interviewed, 18 per cent
<u>habitually</u> avoided, and another 41 per cent <u>sometimes</u> avoided,
any material which, in Miss Fiske's words, "is known to be
controversial or which they believe might become controversial."
Nearly one-third acknowledged that, at one time or another,
they had permanently removed controversial material from
their collection. Miss Fiske found that restrictions of various
sorts had been put upon the use of controversial material in
82 per cent of the circulating library units covered by her study.
Over two-thirds of the restrictions were in response to objections from <u>librarians themselves</u>, or others directly connected
with the institution. When the complaints originated within the
system, the controversial book was removed or restricted in
85 per cent of the cases; again, paradoxically, when the complaints came from <u>outside</u> the book was removed or restricted
in only 44 per cent of the cases.

Miss Fiske's enumeration of the ways whereby a book is
"restricted" is illuminating. Most frequent methods: transfer
the book to the librarian's office; place it on the "reserve"
shelf (so the patron has to ask for it); place it <u>under</u> the front
desk; place it <u>behind</u> the front desk; place it in a locked case.
A other rather popular method, one gathers, was explained by
one librarian: "Oh, I just put the book away for a while"–the
whereabouts of the "away" and the length of the "while" not
being specified.

Some of what Miss Fiske reports verges on the ludicrous.
There was the librarian who had President Eisenhower's free-
dom-to-read statement pasted on the outside of a <u>locked</u> bookcase. There was the librarian who reported, matter-of-factly,
that she found the little "Gift" stamp a most convenient device
for labeling <u>all</u> controversial materials, whether the material
actually was a gift or not. The capper came when the librarian
who "just put a book aside for a while" led Miss Fiske to her
"aside" room. The room contained 2,000 volumes!

The most frequent cause for librarians' locking up, putting
away, or otherwise restricting books was "sex and obscenity"
(46 per cent). Next in order: politics (19 per cent), profanity
(10 per cent), race and religion (9 per cent).

Miss Fiske documents her findings with an impressive
array of summaries, analyses and cross-analyses of data which

are likely to prove of greater interest to the librarian than to the general reader. Of perhaps more than passing interest to both, however, is her treatment of "outside" pressures and their effects on libraries in California. Here her findings take on a brighter hue. She reports only two book-centered "community conflicts" (i.e., wherein major population segments were involved) and only seven "public episodes" (i.e., known to the community, but not involving major population segments) since World War II. In one of the two large-scale conflicts (Mill Valley), a crusade to purge the school library, led by a housewife, was scotched by the librarian, a sympathetic press and an outraged citizenry. The other (Los Angeles) was the scene of a bitter and prolonged struggle over UNESCO in the schools; and the libraries, along with the whole educational system, suffered a jarring defeat. Miss Fiske concludes her account of these conflicts with these words: "A number of both school and public libraries reacted to these conflicts with precautionary or restrictive measures. These actions, with very few exceptions, were initiated within the school or library system, without impetus from the local citizenry." And at this point another paradox (the Fiske study has many of them) emerges: though the Mill Valley conflict was a victory for freedom to read, and the Los Angeles conflict a defeat, it was the Mill Valley incident which was more often cited as justification for restrictive moves in other libraries throughout the state.

One would be grievously remiss in taking leave of Miss Fiske's study without noting what she calls, in a happy phrase, the "semantic conveniences" which librarianship possesses in such bounteous – and dismaying – profusion. A "balanced collection" was explained by her respondents in a half-dozen or more ways; perhaps the most ingenious was, "You provide as much as you can of what anybody wants." A librarian must be sure to read the books which are "too good" (i.e., won't circulate) or "too bad" (i.e., risque or politically dubious) before selecting them. "Controversial" is not only an ugly word; it is at times a useful and convenient one to cloak a multitude of less desirable ones. And in turn, there are endless circumlocutions (or semantic conveniences) for "controversial": "not suited to our collection"; "not in good taste"; "not appropriate";

and (from my own experience applied often to <u>Lolita</u>) "doesn't fit in with community interests." And the school librarian has a couple of well-nigh perfect reasons for rejecting a book: it either "doesn't supplement the curriculum" or it "is at too advanced a reading level." The words "select" and "screen" are, of course, much to be preferred to "censor," which is (in librarianship as elsewhere) a word to be avoided at all costs.

The Fiske Study is a welcome one. More and more of them are needed to produce more and more of the evidence locked up in that inner consciousness of frightened librarians, to uncover the myriad and complex pressures operative inside and outside the individual librarian and to reveal the effects of these pressures on the development of his philosophy of book selection.

Nothing could more strikingly illustrate how individual, and how dramatically contradictory, such philosophies can be than the reactions of two librarians who were pressed to remove a book from their shelves. One did; the other didn't. Said the first, flatly, "You don't jeopardize a whole institution for just one book." Said the other, saltily, "The question is whether we are to be dictated to by every Tom, Dick and Harry who decides he wants a book removed. If we are, there'll be no end to it. We'd just as well shut the doors right now."

8. SOME CHALLENGES WE FACE

Mary L. Tarbox

The public schools today are facing a constant barrage of criticism from all sorts and conditions of people—university professors to whom "life adjustment" is educationist jargon, taxpayers who consider the new cafeteria or music room or library an extravagant "frill," parents who resent the fact that their Susie can't spell "disestablishmentarianism," patriotic groups who discover what they fear are subversive books in school libraries and who worry about undue emphasis on world citizenship, etc. You can think of many more. I should like to discuss three of these criticisms which I think we must accept as challenges, along with all other teachers, school administrators, and citizens who are sincerely interested in the public schools.

The first has to do with reading and is typified by the recent best seller, Why Johnny Can't Read, by Rudolph Flesch. As librarians we might be tempted to sit back indifferently and let the proponents of more phonics battle it out with the believers in reading readiness, the interest factor, learning the natural unit of perception, etc. The trouble is that "why Johnny can't read" is closely connected with another problem, "why Johnny won't read." A recent issue of the New Yorker shows a worried father anxiously scanning the pages of·Mr. Flesch's best seller, while Johnny himself is seen lying on his stomach, heels in the air, completely absorbed in a TV western.

Dr. Paul Witty and other reading specialists have successfully refuted Mr. Flesch by pointing out that stressing phonics to the point of neglecting other methods would lead to mere verbalizing. If we define reading as the process of obtaining meaning from printed materials, Dr. Witty maintains, then the problem becomes more than one of sounding out syllables. It involves wanting to read, having available materials that appeal to the beginning reader; in short it involves, or should involve, a library and teacher-librarian cooperation. If Johnny can't and/or won't read, maybe, then, we have failed to some extent, in spite of the increase in school libraries, and the wealth of beautiful children's books.

Dr. Witty points out in a recent issue of The Nation's Schools that Mr. Flesch exaggerates greatly when he asserts that "our children don't read Andersen's fairy tales or Mark Twain or Louisa May Alcott or the Mary Poppins books or the Dr. Dolittle books or anything interesting or worth while because they can't." On the contrary, Dr. Witty continues, "Chicago school children, for example, read and enjoy with great frequency all the books Mr. Flesch mentions, and many more."

However, there is no evidence as yet to show that children are reading better than they did 20 years ago. "We can and should improve instruction with the knowledge and materials we now have," Dr. Witty states. Part of the answer, you and I know, lies in more and better stocked elementary libraries, with more teachers and librarians who have been prepared in teachers' colleges and library schools to know children's books and to put into practice the principles of school library service.

What happens to Johnny's reading when he goes from elementary school to junior high school, and then on to senior high, and then to college and adult life? Here the studies are more discouraging. According to the report, "Development of Lifetime Reading Habits" by Jean Grambs of the Committee on Reading Development, a distinct drop often occurs in the amount of reading done when the child goes from elementary school to junior high or from eighth grade to senior high. In a recent survey of college graduates conducted by the American Institute of Public Opinion, five out of six had done no reading of a serious nature in the several months prior to the interview. Only 55 per cent could name any recently published book which they would like to read. Out of the total adult population of the United States only 25 per cent read as much as one book per month.

We can all think of many reasons why these conditions are so: the mass media of communication, especially television and the comics; the competition of extracurricular activities and after-school jobs. Newsweek says 49 per cent of the total population reads comics and 60 per cent of the comic-book readers are adults – physically. Miss Gramb's report goes on to say that we seem to be in the midst of a culture in which learning by doing "is often interpreted to mean that anyone who reads will not develop a wholesome personality." Direct personal experience, in other words doing, is essential. To quote Miss Gramb:

> The majority in our society are nonreaders; the result is a low valuation of reading. The nonreader finds it difficult to understand that reading is frequently more intense, more demanding and more rewarding than most of the face-to-face encounters made during a given day.

Recently I came across this statement in a book for teachers on human relations:

SOME CHALLENGES WE FACE

Little Algernon reads well and adds two-place numbers. He is a gentleman and not yet six-years old, and is a most satisfying child because he makes no disturbance and is always clean. He is afraid to try to catch a ball; he wouldn't try to shin up a tree. He retreats into reading and other abnormal activities.

Granted that one can withdraw too completely into the book world. Is it therefore proper to label all reading as an "abnormal activity"? It is indeed a strange paradox that with more libraries, more librarians, and more books, lifetime reading habits are so rarely developed. What can we do about it?

I think, for one thing, that school librarians must accept the fact that public relations, both within the school and in the community, are as important a part of our work as acquiring and organizing materials. We must use television, radio, yes, even some of the appeal of comics, to center attention on books and reading. We must seize every opportunity to talk to boards of education, parents, and teachers. We must see that teachers receive notices of new books, articles in current professional periodicals, pamphlets, and other materials. We must bring teachers and pupils into the library to help us select books for purchase. We must get them to write reviews for the school paper, choose collections for classrooms, make bibliographies for units of study. We must help teachers, who are in many cases overloaded with large classes, to see that a wide reading program is possible even though they themselves may not be able to read every word of every book chosen by each of their pupils.

If we can persuade one teacher that a regular free reading period during school hours is feasible and important, even though it may mean omitting a few of the class unison readings formerly required, we have started something that other teachers may hear about, and decide to try, too. If in addition, that teacher lets go of the old requirement of a set book report for credit, and instead will hold informal class discussions about books, then the result will be so much more enthusiasm among students for reading, that other teachers are bound to follow suit. There are, as you all know, some excellent helps for such

a program: Jean Roos' Patterns for Reading, the recent supplement to the Language Arts Syllabus of the New York State
Education Department, the September 1955 issue of the Bulletin of the National Association of Secondary School Principals,
to mention just a few. We must work on teachers of science,
home making, and industrial arts, as well as on English and
social studies teachers.

Besides interpreting the contribution of the school library,
we must, of course, cooperate with the public library in helping children form lifetime library habits. This is comparatively
easy on the elementary level, where schedules of grade visits
to the library and public librarians' visits to classrooms can
usually be arranged. On the secondary level, departmental
organization and the pressure of final examinations, often make
planned contact between small groups of students and the public
library more difficult. At least an assembly program or a
career-day talk can be arranged. Sometimes a student advisory
council can be formed, to help the young people's librarian select books. Maybe some teachers can even be persuaded to invite the public librarian to their classes to give book talks.

At this point, I know that most of you are thinking, "All
this public relations business would be fine if I had adequate
clerical help!" It is undeniably true that a tremendous amount
of clerical and technical detail must be accomplished if we are
to have our libraries organized well enough to have anything to
urge people to use. But I think we can't wait for the perfect library before we start interpreting it. We can talk about the
need for a bigger book budget and more clerical help, while
we're talking, and we are surely never going to persuade any
board of education of the need for more funds until we demonstrate at the same time that our services are essential to the
program of the school.

Another criticism leveled at the public schools which I
think constitutes a challenge to school librarians, is that we
have failed to teach good citizenship, which must be based on
moral values. We are told that juvenile delinquency is increasing alarmingly. Films like "Blackboard Jungle" have aroused
the public by exaggerating grossly the facts about school discipline, in much the same way as Mr. Flesch's book exaggerates the reading problem. We can answer these critics by

asserting that the home and the church have their responsibilities, too, and that the school has the child for only six or seven hours out of the day, only nine or ten months of the year.

Yet we wonder uneasily about the large numbers of non-readers who come regularly to the library instead of going to the study hall, because they can roam from one shelf to another, thumb through the pages of Life or Saturday Evening Post, and, if the librarian isn't looking, get much needed recognition from their classmates by mutilating a new plastic magazine cover, or expounding monotonously, with their pencil drawings, the facts of life in the margins of the advertisements. Should the school librarian act principally as a policewoman, patrolling the library, silencing defiant groups who have no interest in library materials?

In a recent issue of Clearing House, a high school principal advocates that all study halls be abolished and that longer class periods be scheduled, which would include time for study supervised by the class teacher. His school has tried this plan, and his faculty believe that it makes for better study habits.

We are hearing a great deal recently about the core curriculum especially on the junior high school level. This plan, too, would lengthen class periods and provide for study in the classroom. The secondary school library under this arrangement, would be used almost entirely by classes, scheduled for definite purposes, just as the elementary library is used now. Would this be a satisfactory answer to the problem?

It seems to me that if we want to build informed citizens with lasting habits of library use, then we must make provision for all pupils to have the opportunity to come individually to the library at some time during the day. Five minutes before or after school is not enough, even for the so-called nonreaders.

If we can provide books on all reading levels, arrange or better yet get students to arrange displays and bulletin boards which capitalize on the interests of this group — sports, auto mechanics — yes, even "how to get a man" — and then if somehow we can get it into their heads that it's their library — the battle would be won. On all levels, library clubs and homeroom representatives acting as a library council can help.

Perhaps we need two kinds of student assistants, at least on the secondary level: those who might make recruits for librarianship and those who need recognition and an opportunity for a school activity. Organizing and teaching these groups would tend to add to the work of the librarian and could in no way be called a substitute for regular clerical assistance. For all these student library activities the tone of the school, the support of the administration, and the cooperation of the teaching staff are vital. Now we are back at public relations again.

There are, of course, other ways in which our libraries do contribute to citizenship education. If we put into practice the "School Library Bill of Rights," we are at least making it possible for pupils to gain a basis of fact about all sides of controversial questions, and to form intelligent opinions. The challenge we face in this connection, it seems to me, is the necessity for careful selection of materials to meet the limitations of a budget and the particular needs of each school. In some communities there will also be the question of prevailing opinions, political and otherwise, to consider, and it must be an individual decision, which rests primarily with the librarian, as to what extent she should allow these to color her book selection. The deliberations of the ALA preconference on book selection, held in Philadelphia last June, make us realize that public librarians exercise guidance in their adult book selection. Our main purpose must be, as the "School Library Bill of Rights" so ably states it,

> To place principle above personal opinion and reason above prejudice in the selection of materials of the highest quality in order to assure a comprehensive collection appropriate for the users of the library.

Certainly we can help to meet another aspect of this challenge, too, by providing such books as Ansley's The Good Ways, Fitch's One God, Mable Pyne's Story of Religion and The Tree of Life, which will further the goals expressed by the report of the American Council on Education, "The Function of the Public Schools in Dealing with Religion." This report states that while we cannot, according to the constitution, teach any particular religion in the public schools, we can and should emphasize the importance of all the great religions in formulating moral and spiritual values.

44

SOME CHALLENGES WE FACE

Nor should we forget, in this connection, what folk and fairy tales can do, and great fiction, poetry, and drama. We must provide for the minority that will read and thrill to the great books, and at the same time find some way, through storytelling, book talks, use of abridged versions, television, or assembly programs, of sharing their message with all pupils.

The October 1955 issue of School Review has an interesting account written by a Phoenix, Arizona, educator, on "The Function of Libraries in Newly Integrated Schools." In Phoenix, Negro pupils found it difficult at first because the libraries in their new schools contained no materials written by or about their race. Few of us will be called on to meet this problem, but I think many of us need to build up our collections of material about and by the particular minority groups we find in our schools. By the use of such lists as "Reading Ladders for Human Relations" we can foster better intercultural relationships.

Last and perhaps nearest to our hearts as librarians, is the challenge of individual differences. This enters into every phase of our work and yet some degree of failure to meet this challenge is implied in nearly every criticism leveled at the public schools.

According to Clint Pace, director of the White House Conference on Education, there are 35,000,000 pupils enrolled in our schools now, and by 1959-1960 there will be 42,800,000. By 1965 there will be almost double the number in school that there are today. We shall need 2,000,000 teachers for these pupils, but we are today losing more teachers than we gain each year.

In 1954 the ALA folder "Books and People" stated that 4,000 school librarians are needed at once. The number is probably more now. We can and must help recruit teachers and librarians, but meantime we must also strive to find some way of reaching the individual pupil despite overcrowded classrooms, organizational red tape, and necessary library routines.

Whether heterogeneous or homogeneous grouping is used in the classroom, sooner or later we find nearly all the children in the library, seemingly all around the desk at once, clamoring for the same book assigned by a distracted teacher who had no time to check on library copies. In a large school we can't even learn the children's names, let alone their needs and interests, before they descend upon us in hoards. No wonder some of them become poor library citizens — we have to ignore many of them in order to keep any kind of order and provide even the semblance of a good reading situation!

Yet listen to what Benjamin Smith, superintendent of schools in Greensboro, North Carolina, says:

> No instrumentality available to the school is quite so helpful and effective as the school library in serving these heterogeneous groups and these individual differences.

I surely hope his faith in us is justified. I know we can't do it without an adequate budget for library materials, clerical help to get it organized, an understanding administration, teachers who are enthusiastic library users, and last but not least, close working partnerships with the reading consultant and the guidance department, whose records should be available to us and used constantly by us.

In cooperation with all the staff, we can provide information on vocations, on colleges and special schools, and on personal problems concerned with growing up. With the help of all these people we can do our best to see that this information gets to the right pupil at the right time. All of us can and must often do more. Let me give you an example.

In the current yearbook of the National Elementary Principal, called "Reading for Today's Children," is the story of eleven-year-old Joel, and how he found himself with the help of his own fifth-grade teacher, the kindergarten teacher, and the school librarian. Joel's parents had moved from town to town, and so he had never had the experience of belonging to any group. He read only on a second-grade level. The oculist reported that glasses were not necessary for Joel, but advised that he read books printed in large type to exercise "lazy" eye muscles. The fifth-grade teacher went with him to the library, where the librarian helped them choose an armful of picture books and easy stories. The other children in his grade were told about the oculist's advice, so that Joel was not teased for reading "baby books." He enjoyed reading at home to his five-year-old brother, who suggested that Joel bring some books to the kindergarten and read to the other kindergarteners. The kindergarten teacher invited him to come and made Joel, for the first time in his life, feel really needed. With the librarian's help he became discriminating in his choice of stories, noting the activities going on in the kindergarten and choosing stories to supplement them. His eyes improved. By the end of the year he had read over 100 books, ranging from picture books to books approaching a fifth-grade level. His reading score went up 2.6 degrees. He had learned to read because three people had bothered to help him, and because all sorts of books were available to him in the school library.

In conclusion, I should like to quote from Anne Morrow Lindbergh's last book, Gift from the Sea, a few sentences which I think express the sum and substance of our work as school librarians and teachers.

> The here, the now, and the individual, have always been the special concern of the saint, the artist, the poet, and the woman. In the small circle of the home she has never quite forgotten the particular uniqueness of each member of the family; the spontaneity of now; the vividness of here. This is the basic substance of life. These are the individual elements that form the bigger entities like mass, future, world. We may neglect these elements, but we cannot dispense with them. They are the drops that make up the stream. They are the essence of life itself. It may be our special function to emphasize again these neglected realities, not as a retreat from greater responsibilities, but as a first real step toward a deeper understanding and solution of them. . . .

Aren't these, indeed, the satisfactions — the eager hand reaching out for another book "like the one you told me about"; the return of the former library club member full of enthusiasm for college and grateful for the help you gave him in that senior source theme; the spontaneous catching of an impish eye as a humorous tale is unfolded to a group of second graders. You can all multiply these rewards a thousand times. They are intangible, but they are made of "the here, the now, and the individual — the basic substance of life," and they do come to all of us.

9. SCHOOL LIBRARIAN: COORDINATOR

Benjamin C. Willis

Wherever school systems undertake a cooperative study and evaluation of the reading program in each grade, the library is the one unifying factor which can dramatically demonstrate its contribution at every level. No teacher in the school has a greater obligation than the school librarian to the reading program, nor a greater opportunity to see that reading becomes a delightful experience, meaningful, enriching and satisfying to every child. Thus the librarian is in a unique position to coordinate the total reading program of the school and to make it truly library-centered.

From her vantage point the school librarian sees the curriculum as a whole, and is in a position to observe its strengths and weaknesses, its omissions and duplications. Her special knowledge of materials of all kinds, their sources and availability, their appropriateness in terms of subject treatment, and readability, equip her to make an essential and unique contribution to the development of the school program. To vitalize and implement each unit she is ready to suggest new editions of books to replace old ones, new titles to replace those outdated, easy materials for the slow learner, advanced materials for the gifted student and newer types of instructional media including audio-visual and community resources. This is an important service which must be rendered if the curriculum is to be active and dynamic, and if it is to provide for individual differences, thereby becoming meaningful to every pupil.

In the area of experimental instructional programs the school library functions as a coordinating agency. Two illustrations give eloquent testimony to this fact. First, is the Citizenship Education Project, which is one of the major efforts in the country to improve the practical effectiveness of learning by participation in community activities and projects. The library not only provides the materials which give the necessary knowledge and understanding basic to good citizenship, but it makes possible the sharing of successful practices carried out by other schools throughout the country. The bibliography, including books, magazines, pamphlets, films, filmstrips, etc., prepared by Project Headquarters for use of all cooperating schools, was deemed of such importance that the AASL was invited to participate in its revision. As a result you have an active committee demonstrating that the school library is a coordinating agency in a curriculum experiment at the national level. What an inspiration and incentive this should be to every school librarian, to look for and to make similar opportunities in her own community.

Again, in experimental programs in individualized teaching of reading the school library plays a significant role. Indeed, the school library makes <u>possible</u> such experimentation, for books, many books, are required instead of a basic reader. An abundance of beautiful books on all subjects appealing to the varied interests of children and meeting all levels of reading difficulty, attracts and challenges each child to proceed at his own pace and according to his own needs.

In some schools, with the parents indicating a willingness to cooperate, the library reaches down into the kindergarten to participate in the reading readiness program. The class goes to the library daily, at which time each child, with the help of the librarian or teacher, chooses a picture book to take home to share with his parents.

The school's major obligation is to meet the needs of all the children of all the people, and these children are all different in interests, needs, and ability. Each one, whether he be the average, normal child, the mentally handicapped or the mentally gifted, possesses the inherent right to develop his potentialities to the fullest extent. This can never be accomplished through the use of a single textbook. A wide variety of educational materials of all kinds, on all subjects, and representing all degrees of reading difficulty are needed. The library as the coordinating agency provides these materials and the librarian works with teachers and pupils in utilizing both materials and experiences for the maximum educational growth of each individual. She goes to the classroom or laboratory, the club meeting or the assembly — wherever her services are needed. Class groups, committees and individuals seek help in the library. The librarian, teacher and pupils forge a chain which strengthens and binds together the total learning experience.

The better the teacher, the greater is the demand made by her on the library and on the services of the librarian. The better the teaching, which leads to and develops from the library, the greater the demand made on it by the students. They would say to us, "Put learning tools in our way, then stand aside and gently guide — but do not push. Our feet are small, our steps are slow. There is much to see which you have seen, alas, but see no more."

A variety of learning tools must be put in the way of elementary school pupils who are reading on from 7 to 9 different grade levels in each grade, beginning with the third.[1] The same holds true for the secondary school where from 20 to 30 per cent of students entering junior and senior high school have difficulty keeping up with the class reading assignments. Likewise, the library also has a responsibility to provide for the needs and interests of the particularly gifted child. This area holds one of the greatest challenges, since the schools as a whole are not doing well by the distinctly superior students. In this, as in other aspects of the program, the teacher and the librarian work cooperatively. The aim should be for a wider, more intelligent use of all learning materials.

In schools where interests created in the classroom are extended into the library; where it is difficult to determine the point where the classroom leaves off and the library begins; where teaching is vital, alive, and exciting; where all pupils are challenged to do their best — and do it; in those schools the library truly is functioning as a coordinating agency of the curriculum.

Much has been said about the library as an instructional materials center which it must universally become if it is to fulfill its obligation to the teaching program. The librarian who serves in such a center, as many do now, provides appropriate films, filmstrips, recordings in addition to the usual books, magazines, and pictures. Less frequently found, although of great value in coordinating the work of the classroom with the community, is the resource file of places in the community suitable for field trips, and persons available and qualified to talk to pupils on subjects related to the curriculum. In all that has been said, close working relationships between the teacher and the librarian is understood. The teacher recommends materials for purchase, informs the librarian of classroom activities, confers with her prior to beginning a new unit, checks on the availability of materials, notes any demand for similar materials by other classes, and discusses methods of using the material to greatest advantage. The librarian in turn helps keep teachers informed of all classroom activities, plans, and needs, so that the work of the teachers is coordinated in this manner.

The library also serves the extracurricular activities of the school: the Latin Club in search of Roman costumes, books on parties for the Home Economics Club, material for Scout merit badges. Scarcely an area in the school program remains untouched or influenced in some way by the library when there is a creative dynamic librarian. Let it be said here, however, that the librarian is perhaps the most important factor in the situation if the school is ready for a functional and functioning library.

The goals of education cannot be fully achieved without the resources of a library and the services of an able librarian. One of the crucial problems of today's schools is the maintenance and support of the school library in view of the increased enrollment, larger classes, overcrowded buildings, and teacher shortages. All of these factors, however, make the library and its services even more vital to the school's instructional program, and we must be vigilant to preserve this service center of the school.

More than ever the school library is called upon to justify its existence by continuing to play an active and aggressive role in the teaching and learning of boys and girls. This is a challenge worthy of our best efforts: to provide an abundance of materials and experiences and to see that these are utilized in such a way that the library becomes the wide open range for children's minds, where they gather and sift information, evaluate findings, and form sound judgments. Far more important is this to the preservation of our Democracy and way of life than a mere cumulation of facts. The school library without a doubt is an important coordinating agency of the curriculum in the areas of instructional resources, curriculum improvement, enriched teaching, personalized instruction, and extracurricular activities. This is not a new pronouncement, but it is worth reflecting on in the hope that it may gain wider support from educators generally.

What, then, are the implications for the school library profession and for you? First of all, it means a new kind of education for school librarianship is needed. In order to work effectively with the curriculum and with classroom teachers, and to serve in the dual capacity of librarian and teacher, the school librarian must have a knowledge of the curriculum and curriculum practice, the principles of teaching, and an understanding of children and adolescents — how they grow and develop. Classroom observation and practice teaching are important parts of the preparation in order to give the librarian the teacher's viewpoint and to teach her how to handle groups of varying sizes. Skill in selecting, handling and directing the use of audiovisual materials is also an essential part of the training.

Second, the librarian has an obligation to attend faculty meetings, to participate actively in curriculum work and to volunteer for committees. Third, the library collection should be built in terms of the curriculum and should include all types of learning materials. Fourth, the results of the school's testing program should be available to the librarian and utilized for the improvement of the results. Fifth, time should be made to visit the teachers to determine the work in progress and how the library could implement the work and coordinate similar projects or units underway in the school. Sixth, be on the lookout for pupils who have reading difficulties and endeavor to find ways of helping to overcome these. Seventh, develop an awareness of the study habits of boys and girls and, wherever possible, work on improving these habits. Eighth, consider new and varied ways of working with teachers to improve their use of the library and library materials. One suggestion might be a combined workshop for teachers and librarians. Ninth, look anew at the needs and problems of your school and how you might, through the library, help meet these needs or solve some of the problems and, tenth, be alert to new directions in school library service and the implications these might have for your program.

We must be willing to evaluate our progress and practice and make changes consistent with desirable changes in education. We need to be constantly alert for new materials, new methods of presenting them to teachers and students, new ways of working with pupils, parents, teachers, and administrators. We have come a long way from the concept of the library as a storehouse to its present day concept as a materials center and coordinating agency of the curriculum serving the entire school, but we should not rest until this concept has universal acceptance, until every school has a library and a librarian, and until the existing standards for school library service are brought into line with the demands of our day.

10. CHARACTERISTICS OF EFFECTIVE SCHOOL LIBRARY SERVICE

Robert L. Amsden

A. What the principal expects from the school librarian

1. The principal expects the librarian to have a warm, friendly interest in every boy and girl and in every staff member. People should really feel welcome, feel wanted in the school library. Librarians should know all staff members and most pupils by name. The good librarian must be an outgoing, friendly person in addition to being properly trained and experienced.

2. Librarians must be first of all teachers (at least at heart) and second librarians in the same sense that counselors and principals are first of all teachers. Librarians are expected to know intimately the work and problems of every area and department of the school including guidance and supervision. They must be sensitive to each teacher's strengths and weaknesses and skillful in the use of library resources to help each staff member reach his highest teaching capabilities. It is just as desirable for school librarians to have several years of

classroom teaching in their backgrounds as it is for counselors, supervisors, and principals to have taught prior to accepting specialized responsibility.

3. The principal expects the librarian to organize the library room (or rooms) efficiently and attractively. Books, pamphlets, vertical file materials, periodicals and papers should be so placed that they are easily recognizable and usable. The "right" materials should be available — "right" based on the librarian's careful analysis of the school's program and upon an awareness of the pupils' and teachers' interests. Obsolete and worn-out items should be culled at regular intervals and replaced with appropriate materials to the full extent of the budget.

The charging desk, the stacks, the pupil study areas should be distributed so that "centers" for library service areas are readily apparent. These "centers" (or in many cases separate rooms) should be interesting in appearance and effective in arrangement. They should be developed for such divisions as vocations, education after high school, the armed services, hobbies, current political and economic problems, personal guidance, and many, many more. It is appropriate for a certain amount of money to be spent for library "appearance" apart from the expected visual displays which make a library an eye-catching place. Pupils and teachers should think of the library as the most attractive area in their school, in addition to its being the cultural or materials center. In schools where the audio and visual programs are administered by the library, listening and viewing booths or rooms should be available as well as proper storage.

4. The principal expects strong leadership from the librarian in guiding the administration to make schedule, budget, and space provision to expand and improve library services as needed. The principal expects the librarian to lead the principal to a large extent; not the principal, the librarian! This statement does not relieve the principal of responsibility; it merely points the way to a higher level of supervision.

5. The principal expects the librarian to make suitable arrangements with the faculty so that every pupil in school is trained in the essential knowledge and skills for the use of both school and community libraries. To be useful, this training

must be identified with a real problem or assignment in a major subject field. Lessons or exercises in library usage apart from credit assignments in a subject field are not very effective. In the senior high school, the development and stressing of _investigative_ and _research_ skills follows the learning of basic library skills.

6. The principal expects the librarian to _spend time with each teacher_, and in the case of new teachers, a considerable amount of time helping faculty members learn (and most teachers need to learn on the job) _how to relate their teaching to good library services and materials_. Unhappily, a large percentage of teachers did not have good school libraries available to them as pupils; many have been forced (often without much resistance) into a textbook rut by the example of older teachers or by the lack of good library materials centers in their early teaching experience. One of the librarian's most important and most rewarding duties is the teaching of teachers how to become better teachers through the use of the library.

7. The principal expects the librarian to be an active, although unofficial _guidance counselor_. It is astonishing how helpful a librarian can be to certain pupils. His relationship with pupils does not have the same tensions that the classroom teacher has associated with him; the librarian does not give an assignment or a mark. His awareness of a pupil's problems — either personal or academic — and his skillful suggestions of certain materials, perhaps under the guise of recreational reading, often are better therapy than would appear on the surface.

8. In short, summarizing the incomplete but suggestive items above, the principal expects the library to be the heart of the school. It should be as efficient and attractive as its physical limitations will permit. And most important, the principal expects from the librarian far more than technically competent library work. He expects the librarian to be a superior teacher, a counselor, and a supervisor. The librarian should "make as much desirable difference" to the quality of the school as any member of the teaching or administrative staff.

B. What the librarian expects from his principal
    1. The librarian expects from his principal a _genuine_

interest in and appreciation of the library in the total program of the school. He expects the principal to understand that the library contributes to every area of learning — both in support of formal classes and in the ministering to the personal interests and needs of the members of the school community. He expects the principal to understand that the library is not primarily a "leisure time" area of the school, and is as far from being a "frill" as is the English classroom or the science laboratory!

2. The principal is expected to be willing to be led by his librarian to explore new ways to improve learning and guidance for boys and girls through application of new library skills and insights as these become evident to the profession. It is known to all in education that there is a lag of several decades between promising proved concepts or insights and their general application in schools. The librarian can and should help the administration decrease the extent of the lag.

3. The librarian expects his principal so to set up his master schedule and so to plan personnel and room assignments that the library will not be used as a study hall or as a regular meeting room except for library related activities.

4. The principal is expected to try to make personnel provisions in the budget so that the library may be opened at least a half hour before school begins each morning and remain open until the school office closes each day — usually one and a half to two hours after the termination of the last class.

The library should not be closed at noon time; in addition, sufficient time should be budgeted to permit the librarian to get into certain classes and to attend pertinent curriculum and supervisory meetings. Librarians must get out into the school to observe the life and needs of the various departments in order that they may help determine how the library can best serve the various parts of the total program. This cannot be done properly if the librarian is assigned to the library all day long.

5. The principal must make budget provisions for library clerical help. This clerical assistance is an absolute "must" unless principals are willing to use a quarter to a third of the librarian's time in tasks that a competent clerk can perform equally well. Not to provide clerical help is obviously false economy.

6. The librarian expects the principal in <u>making school enlargement plans</u> (and every principal in the country has been involved in school enlargement!) to be certain that <u>library space</u> (square footage) and equipment both exceed the minimum acceptable standards. The library area and equipment (stacks, files, tables, etc.) must increase as the enrollment increases. The lag presently existing in many schools must be overcome.

7. The principal must give the librarians the same <u>status</u> as the department heads or counselors. Teachers must be encouraged so to plan their work that children and the library are brought into frequent, productive contact.

C. The New "Standards for School Libraries"

New "Standards for School Libraries" [have been] published by the American Library Association. This authoritative revision and upgrading of the former "Standards of the American Association of School Librarians," developed after a three-year study, was made by a highly competent staff aided by an advisory committee representing twenty national associations directly concerned with the contributions school libraries can make to good education. Every high-school principal should secure a complete copy of these "Standards."

Most schools will not be able to meet the "Standards" at once; each year, however, principals should make budget provisions (or encourage their superintendents to do so) so that within a three- or four-year period the improvement in learning that can come through good library work based on the new "Standards" can be realized in each of our schools.

11. AN ADMINISTRATOR LOOKS AT THE LIBRARY

Irving E. Lane

The library program of our high school of 2500 students is a basic and integral part of the curriculum. Not only is it basic in theory, but also in the planning and use by individual departments. This use is not limited to the usual book reports and term papers of the college preparatory English and social studies classes, but reaches out to the many other students in business, vocational, and terminal classes to enrich the curriculum in a variety of ways.

The active school library today is much more accurately described as an instructional materials center and hastens to serve with movies, filmstrips, tapes, records, pictures, maps, and other objects quite as readily as with the traditional books, periodicals, and pamphlets. The instructional materials center provides a diversity of materials and equipment with space to facilitate their use by both students and teachers. Listening areas, preview rooms, and space for the use of the opaque projector are all well used at East Bakersfield High School. There are areas in which equipment is permanently set up, encouraging teachers to preview films and to assign opaque projector enlargements to students. Foreign language, music, and stenography students use the facilities for listening to tapes and records. This expanded program does require added space, and experience has shown that the special usage areas should be centrally located both for ease of access and for supervision.

For a successful library program, the administration must give sympathetic (if not enthusiastic) support. This support should be not only in verbal backing of the librarian and her efforts, but also in choice of quarters — attractive and as spacious as possible. Our reading room of 45 x 100 seats 150 students comfortably. Bookshelves built in around the walls house the book collection so that it is attractive and decorative. More than a dozen original paintings by artists of note add their color and atmosphere to the high ceilinged library. Glass-walled conference rooms, approximately 8 x 12 1/2 feet, open from the reading room and are in constant use by students studying together and doing group work.

A workroom of about 10 x 25 feet with running water, formica counter, cupboards, and bookshelves provides space for processing and mending. The audio-visual equipment room opens into the workroom and is controlled by the library secretary from her desk in the library office. The office is in front of the audio-visual room and separated from the library reading room on the other side by a windowed wall. A preview room, listening room, and storage area extend facilities and use of the library.

The administrator also gives his support to the library by providing a budget large enough to meet the needs of the school and (if possible) well above minimum standards. At this point the administrator frequently finds himself in a dilemma. He can recognize the needs of his school for better library service and greater budget, but he has only a limited amount of money to go a long way. The problem becomes one of getting the best possible service for students and faculty within the means available. His encouragement of optimum use of facilities and materials available often serves to improve library service significantly.

Basically, though, optimum service depends upon adequate personnel. Even with central ordering and processing we feel we are operating on a minimum with one full-time librarian and six hours of teacher help. Two additional hours of teacher time are assigned to the coordination and supervising of audio-visual equipment. One secretary serves all activities of the instructional materials center. In considering personnel, we must not overlook the help of some fifty student library assistants working for class credit who contribute in valuable aid to the library program and to their own knowledge of usage of the library.

In utilizing all personnel to best advantage, it is important to distinguish between professional and clerical jobs and to provide adequate clerical personnel. It is false economy to expect professional personnel to devote their highly skilled and well-paid time to routine chores. The librarian should have time to work with students and teachers directly, encouraging greatest possible use of the library and its resources.

The library program, just as any other part of the school curriculum, should be based on a carefully thought out and clearly written guide including immediate and long-term goals and means of attaining these goals. Using these guides, the library staff should plan and execute a definite library program with frequent evaluation.

The library must give vital, useful service. Facilities must be used! In this day of crowded space and high costs, the library must use the space allotted to it for best results and reach as many students and teachers as possible with its services. However, filling seats in the library does not necessarily mean good library usage — nor do impressive circulation figures alone. Perhaps the most valuable services — reader guidance and reference — are the most difficult to measure.

While the administration can give its blessing and support to the library program, the librarian is the one directly responsible for the spirit of the library, and, as in any service agency, spirit is most important. There should be a friendly, cheerful atmosphere which encourages youth to use the library — not as a social hall but as a haven of quiet in an often too turbulent day — a peaceful retreat where reading can be truly a pleasure and where research and reference work can be done without distraction. This is not a plea for a mausoleum of breathless quiet, but for self-discipline among students eager to reap the benefits of quiet relaxed atmosphere.

The library needless to say should not be used as a dumping ground for discipline problems from the classroom. It should be considered by student and faculty alike as a place of privilege and used accordingly. Students and teachers should feel welcome in the library — welcome to browse, to read, to study and to ask for help if needed, knowing it will be graciously forthcoming. An alert and enthusiastic librarian not only makes everyone welcome who is in the library, but also uses varied devices and services to bring in others not usually using library facilities.

For the library to serve the school well, the librarian must have a thorough knowledge of the courses of study of the various classes and teaching methods and aims of the individual teacher. Not only is this knowledge important in selecting books for the collection, but also in having those materials used after purchase. The successful librarian doesn't wait for the teacher to discover the library, but, with missionary zeal, makes the teacher aware of library services, facilities, and the variety of instructional materials particularly suited to his needs.

Many devices which bring the teacher to the library are useful in extending the awareness of the teacher and thus indirectly extending the student use of facilities. One successfully used method of acquainting teachers with the collection and stimulating interest in library usage is that of having the individual departments evaluate the books in the library which concern that department, making suggestions for discard and for new purchase. This helps too, in doing away with the previously frequent request for a "new" book the teacher had to have which had been on the library shelves unused for some time.

Faculty meetings held in the library; orientation sessions for new teachers; book teas which give teachers an opportunity to share in book selection; book lists for units of study and supplementary reading; sending of materials to the teacher; presentation of materials at department meetings; and personal invitation on frequent occasions are some devices which work well.

Students too must be encouraged to use library services. Interesting and eye-catching displays and exhibits, book talks to individuals or class groups, cleverly designed lists for suggested reading, and books circulating in their bright plastic jackets are just a few techniques used successfully in bringing student and book together. Certainly there is a challenge in reaching the non-academic student. Making him aware of what the library can offer him for his school work, hobbies, and recreational reading is a problem which many of our more academically attuned libraries face. Here again the librarian's enthusiasm comes to the fore; for enthusiasm is contagious even with the most reluctant readers.

It is interesting to consider what an outstanding program can result when an understanding administrator and an enthusiastic librarian set out to build a real library program. Each student and teacher in the school will profit.

12. POLICIES AND PROGRAMS
OF A SMALL COLLEGE LIBRARY

Christopher A. Legge

To be effective a college library must further the educational aims of the institution to which it is attached. At Bradford Junior College it is the librarians' task to maintain and encourage the standards of excellence demanded of the students by the faculty by making an effort to ensure that the collection of books and periodicals, though small, is of the highest standard possible.

Books purchased by the library at Bradford are selected in two ways: the faculty selects books needed by the various teaching departments and a library selection committee chooses all other material. At the beginning of each academic year, a percentage of the library's budget is distributed by the library committee to each of the teaching departments. The use of these funds becomes the sole responsibility of the department chairmen who send requests which the librarian orders. Such purchases are the faculty's responsibility with the library acting in a housekeeping capacity only. All other material, books of general cultural interest, reference works, in fact, any material which does not fall clearly within the province of one of the teaching departments, is bought for the library only after careful scrutiny of the reviews by a selection committee.

This committee, comprised of one faculty member, one faculty wife, and the two librarians, meets once a week to decide which of the many books reviewed in the standard book-review magazines should be added to the Bradford collection. In this manner a variety of tastes is reflected, personal whims are less likely to dominate the purchasing policy, and the considered opinion of four "bookmen" stands behind each book ordered. The criterion used for all purchases made by the committee is excellence of material. Competent mediocrity (many best-sellers fall within this category) is eschewed wherever possible. Experimental, original choices are encouraged.

A SMALL COLLEGE LIBRARY

The young minds of Bradford students want to be stimulated;
they want to have their horizons widened, and through wise
selection, books can play an important part in this process.

A collection of the most carefully selected books is, however, mere window dressing if not used, and one of the major
tasks of a librarian is to promote the reading of good literature
and to encourage good taste in recreational reading. In a special effort to encourage good recreational reading five browsing
corners have been established throughout the campus. In the
largest area, centrally located in a living room of the main
dormitory, a small collection of paperback volumes is available for dormitory reading. Also available in this browsing
corner is a number of periodicals chosen for their excellence
in various fields. Popular magazines, such as Time or Life,
are not included because the aim is to familiarize the girls
with less well-known but equally influential periodicals, such
as the Economist or Harper's, as well as with such culturally
important foreign periodicals as the Illustrated London News,
the Listener, and Réalités. The other browsing corners are
located in a campus lounge and in three of the smaller dorm-
itories.

Under the aegis of the English Department and the library
a further step has been taken to enlarge the students' intellectual horizons. The Pelquin Society has been formed for those
who wish to read, discuss, and add worthwhile but inexpensive
books to their personal libraries. The society circulates among
its members paperback books specially ordered by its members who receive the books at the end of the year as membership dividends.

Displays, reading lists, and individual suggestions by the
librarians are the constant complement to all other devices
used to promote good reading among the students. The library
has over 25,000 volumes and subscriptions to over 150 periodicals, and it houses numerous pamphlets, maps, college catalogs, and a few records.

To make this material readily accessible, restrictions on
its use exist solely to enable all students to have an equal opportunity to use material which is in heavy demand and to prevent loss of college property. Thus, in the circulation of
material, the Bradford library regulations are unusually

liberal; most books (other than reference, reserve, and popular new material) may be borrowed for periods usually over a month in length. In addition, back copies of periodicals and pamphlets may be checked out for out-of-library reading. Restrictions must exist, however, for reserve books — those from which an instructor assigns readings for class work. In order to give every girl in the class access to these books, the librarians put them on a special shelf and permit their use in the library only for a limited period of time. Reference works, such as encyclopedias, almanacs, and the like, by their very nature must remain in the library and should ideally be located close together with ample table and seating space available.

The Bradford library is playing an increasingly important role in the scholastic as well as recreational life of the students. It is open week days from eight o'clock in the morning until ten at night and is used regularly during this time; at night the use is especially heavy. Circulation statistics indicate that an increasing number of books is being read each year (last year's total was over 11,000) and that reserve books are more heavily used.

A questionnaire recently given to each girl entering the library during the course of one week revealed that a large percentage of those answering had done reading outside their class assignments, and many had shown conspicuous discrimination in choice of authors. Results such as these encourage faculty and librarians alike in their endeavor to achieve similar results with every girl attending Bradford.

13. PUT YOUR ELEMENTARY LIBRARY TO WORK

Ben M. Harris

Dan came bursting into the library. He was panting, out
of breath. His eagerness to find a certain word in the large
unabridged dictionary caused him to forget the "no running"
rule. "But, but . . ." he tried to explain as the librarian cau-
tioned him to slow down, ". . . they are waiting for this information!"

Dan was a sixth grader and needed no help in using the
dictionary, so the librarian turned again to the third-grade
class seated in the reading area. She had been reviewing the
location of books in the library with them when Dan burst upon
the scene. Children had been asking questions. As the questioning ended the children were given instructions by their teacher,
Miss Corbett, to browse and select a book to check out.

Just then three little people arrived on the scene from Mrs.
Brown's kindergarten. The librarian walked over, stooping
down to their size to ask, "Well, what can I help you with this
morning?" The two little girls and a boy formed a committee
delegated to select a picture book for their class. Mrs. Brown
was going to read their selection to them tomorrow. The kindergarten class had visited the library before, so this delegation knew where the picture books were shelved, but the librarian went with them to look through, discuss and select the one
large colorful picture book to carry to their teacher.

Had we remained in this small elementary school library
just a little longer many varied activities by many people
might have been observed. The guidance worker might walk
in with a "behavior problem" in hand, a problem growing in
part from the fact that this child had "read all the books in the
room." A fourth-grade teacher might come in before school
to select a record album of folk dances for the physical education activities later in the morning. Fifth and sixth grade boys
and girls might come in periodically all day long to get carts
to take to the classrooms with various kinds of audio-visual

equipment on them. A small group of fourth graders might be found arranging a display of pictures, maps and objects in the glass display case — the results of their recent social studies unit projects. An unhappy group of children of all ages might be found outside the library door on the afternoon it is closed for a faculty meeting. We might see the librarian standing there answering questions — "Why is it closed?", "Can't we come in for just a minute to get a book?', "Why can't the teachers meet someplace else so that we can use the library?"

These and other scenes are commonplace in a modern, well staffed and organized school library. Here is a facility which is in no sense an educational frill. Leaders in curriculum are growing more aware of the essential nature of a library — that of providing a good educational program for little children.

A modern elementary school library is the instructional materials center of the entire school. As such it makes a unique contribution, and is indispensable to the school program.

The library is able to provide something of worth for every child. It is a service center for the teacher, providing on request any of a wide assortment of aids to better teaching. The library well stocked with books, pictures, pamphlets, magazines, recordings, slides, filmstrips and instructional equipment can be the very heart of a good school. It is this heart from which flows the life blood for effective teaching in reading, science, social studies and health into every classroom. The trained librarian who is familiar with the school curriculum is a resource person to the child and teacher alike.

A good reading program and a good library are inseparable. One does not exist without the other. The basic essential for beginning reading is an interest in books, a desire to know what the books contain. Kindergarten and first-grade children make regular visits to a good elementary school library. They browse, select a picture book, gather around and listen to a story.

Children, sensing the first sweet drops of satisfaction from skillful reading instruction, want to turn to a book of their own choice, take it home and demonstrate to all who will listen their new found skills. Is the library at hand to meet this need?

The middle-grade child is gaining independence in reading.

PUT YOUR ELEMENTARY LIBRARY TO WORK

The desire to read is so great that a hundred books may be required in a single year! A skill grows into a joyous habit of life-long duration — if the library is close at hand!

The elementary library is a research center.

As children pursue social studies, science, health, music, language and literature, the library provides a center where real intellectual and cultural growth can come to fruition. Here they can learn the skills of systematic inquiry. The children, under the wise guidance of teacher and librarian, come to recognize that knowledge is not all within the textbook or a single encyclopedia. They learn to use books, magazines, pamphlets, pictures, films, recordings and other material, too, as sources of information and ideas. Skills in using the card catalog, reference books and special files are developed. Children with access to a school library and training in its use need never plead ignorance and know not where to turn for enlightenment.

The elementary school library challenges and stimulates.

Many elaborate programs have been proposed for better meeting the needs of the more able children. The good school library provides unlimited challenge for all children, but especially so, perhaps, for our gifted. Not only can the materials be sufficiently challenging, but their variety and accessibility offer a richness of experience rarely equaled by even the most elaborate special program. Magazines, newspapers, fine literature, the world's great music, science exhibits, special charts and maps, and filmstrips are all part of the modern elementary school library's challenge and stimulation for the more able children.

The elementary school library is an opportunity for the slow child.

In the library, books have no grade levels marked on them. The slow child can browse and select according to his interests and abilities. Pictorial materials will stimulate anew and the slow child can hold his head up high with dignity and pride as he returns to class or home with a newly discovered book.

The elementary school library is a central depository for instructional materials and equipment.

A good elementary school library provides for children and teachers a vast array of materials and equipment. Each classroom may have its own small collection of books supplemented by the unlimited horizons of the main book collection. Many other research materials are available in great variety to all teachers as well. The distribution of all circulating instructional materials is handled from a central location in the school. Maximum service to teachers and children is further provided by having all the necessary equipment — record players, tape recorders and projectors — on hand, immediately adjacent to the library itself.

Whatever the material or equipment needs might be, the teachers refer to one master card catalog to determine what is available and where it is. A search from room to room for the tape recorder, for instance, is unnecessary when the school library serves as a central depository for all circulating materials.

The elementary school library is a quiet operation. But it stands second only to the classroom in its importance to the education of young people, to which our schools are dedicated.

14. HOW WILL THE NEW SCHOOL LIBRARY STANDARDS AFFECT HIGH SCHOOL LIBRARIES?

Eleanor E. Ahlers

For many years school librarians and other educators have been aware of the need to revise the standards for school libraries which were published by the American Library Association in 1945 in School Libraries for Today and Tomorrow. This pamphlet which described the objectives, services and facilities for school libraries has been generally recognized as the statement of national standards for library service in schools of all kinds in the United States. These standards have exerted considerable influence on the development and improvement of school libraries during the last decade.

Revised standards are needed today, however, to provide goals for forward-looking schools, since many schools have gone beyond the standards set in 1945, and to add a further impetus to school library improvement. Centralized libraries are found in most schools at the secondary level, it is true, but how many are adequate for the needs of their schools in regard to physical quarters, size of staff and materials collections? In order to provide excellence in education for children and youth today, it is essential that well-rounded collections of books and other printed and audio-visual materials be available at all levels; that all schools be provided with attractive and functional library quarters, with a professional and clerical staff able and willing to develop a good program of library services.

Standards for School Library Programs will be published by the American Library Association early in 1960, in response to the many requests for a revision of the 1945 standards. These new standards are the work of a committee appointed by the American Association of School Librarians, a division of the American Library Association, several years ago. This committee was composed not only of school librarians but of representatives from twenty other professional and lay organizations interested in quality education for children and youth. Since the principles governing the programs and resources of school libraries are the concern of administrators, school boards, teachers and others, their counsel was sought in the preparation of the new standards.

The qualitative standards for school library programs have evolved from many sources — from the advice, suggestions, and criticism obtained from consultants in special areas, from a two-day work session held at the Kansas City ALA Conference in 1957, from another work session at the ALA San Francisco Conference in 1958 (in which some six hundred school librarians participated), and from information secured from scores of librarians in response to questionnaires, letters and conferences.

The quantitative standards were compiled by means of various procedures — by information obtained from questionnaires sent to schools identified by state and city school library supervisors as having very good library facilities and resources, by the judgment of a panel of experts, including the members of the Standards Committee and advisory consultants, and by the appraisal of the standards by specialists in various fields.

Admittedly the quantitative standards are high and they can be justified only in relation to the type of library program described in the publication. It is pointed out that the most important part of the library program is the work with students and teachers. Quality education is costly, and in order to realize the objectives of the school library program, adequate funds must be provided for staff, quarters and the materials collection. Money alone, however, will not determine the activities and services that make the library an educational force in the school.

What are the necessary intangibles then in the development of a good school library program? The vision of the superintendent and principal planning with a professional librarian who is qualified by training, personality, enthusiasm and ability; the interest of the teachers and the students in the school; the backing of the school board and other citizens of the community. It is a cooperative effort of persons who understand the objectives of the school library in relation to the educational philosophy of the school, who realize that one of the reasons that a school is a good one is because of the quality of its library.

What will be the school library of the future? The emphasis today and in the future is and will be on the services rendered and the program developed. Services must be curtailed if the size of the staff, quarters and collections of materials are inadequate. Size is not the sole criterion; quality looms ever more important. With limited budgets in the past years many school libraries have had small basic collections for average readers, with the addition of easy-reading books to tempt the reluctant ones. Little was provided for the gifted or accelerated readers, for those young people who without stimulation were often lazy readers tending to read far below their level. Today we realize that the library is one place in the school where these students can and should find reading materials and develop methods of research that will serve to challenge them and to carry them on to other larger libraries in the community. In the School Library Bill of Rights it is asserted in part that the responsibility of the school library is "to provide materials that will enrich and support the curriculum, taking into consideration the varied interests, abilities, and maturity levels of the pupils served . . . to provide a background of information which will enable pupils to make intelligent judgments in their daily life."[1]

What kind of library facilities will be needed? Certainly a reading room with an informal and inviting appearance, tastefully decorated, functional as to seating accommodations, shelving, filing cabinets, etc. As the school population grows and the school becomes increasingly larger, however, one or even two reading rooms will not suffice to serve the school. Therefore basic classroom collections will be deemed necessary for many rooms — collections beyond one set of encyclopedias. Portable book shelves, mobile book units and other movable equipment can be utilized to transport materials selected for use with a particular unit of work from the central library to classrooms as needed. One or more conference and listening rooms, an adjoining library classroom, a workroom, storage space for back copies of periodicals and for audiovisual materials and equipment, a librarian's office, areas for teacher use — all are needed to make this a working laboratory and a materials center. A budget will be required that allows for books and magazines for the abilities, interests and needs of students, a budget that also makes provisions for audio-visual as well as printed materials — in fact, for all the instructional materials that may be needed by pupils and teachers in the enrichment of the curriculum, currently defined as all those experiences affecting the child within the school. Sufficient staff so that librarians can both serve in the library and go into classrooms to give book talks and introduce materials will be a necessity, and adequate paid clerical assistants to relieve the librarian of clerical and custodial duties.

What will be the added training and responsibilities of the school librarian? We will expect on the staff professionally trained librarians with at least teacher training if not actual teaching experience, with special training in curriculum, child growth and development, reading, audio-visual materials, and administration; librarians who love children and who have the ability to work well with people. In short the training of the librarian must be as broad as that of the principal if he is to help the library become the learning center of the school.

Working with the school counselors the school librarian will select materials to make of the library a guidance center — reading, vocational, educational, and personal. He will work with teachers and administrators to help foster social responsibility on the part of young people. The school librarian will have made available to him reading and other test scores, as well as individual records, so that he has an understanding of individual pupil abilities and needs. He will serve on curriculum committees and will work with teachers and students in planning units, in selection of materials, in making library facilities available; he will assume responsibility for teaching the use of the library and its tools and resources; he will take the initiative in promoting a love for reading and the use of the public library as a lifetime habit. The librarian will train students to assist capably and profitably in the library routines and services, and will strive to recruit some of these assistants into librarianship as a career.

What about library programs in high schools having fewer than two hundred students? Dr. Conant has indicated in his study of the American high school that the prevalence of high schools with a graduating class of fewer than one hundred students "constitutes one of the serious obstacles to good secondary education throughout most of the United States.[2] Certainly many educators differ with Conant's viewpoint when he states that the instructional program cannot be "sufficiently challenging" in small high schools. Granted that high quality education in small schools is more expensive than in larger ones, it is still possible to have a good instructional program and a good school library. Even in a school under two hundred in size it is practicable with district and regional planning to have library service for all students when a library room and librarian may not be possible in each school. For those concerned with the nearly 50% of American high schools having fewer than two hundred students, the new school library standards provide definite help in a special chapter, where it is pointed out that the services of professionally trained librarians and the materials from a central agency can be made available. In another chapter the supervisory program at the district, county, regional and state level is described, with standards and qualifications for personnel. The library room as a learn-

ing and research laboratory, training in library and study
skills, adequate reading guidance — these aspects of a school
library program may not all be realized for these small schools
without centralized libraries, but the services at least of an
outside library agency can be provided.

The impact of the new school library standards will be felt
as existing high school libraries are improved and as new ones
are planned. Some excellent school libraries today have already
exceeded the recommendations for the expenditure of $4.00-
$6.00 per pupil for books, for the minimum collection of 6,000
volumes in even the smallest schools, for the size of the professional and clerical staff, and the provisions for library
quarters. These goals may not be realized by most schools
immediately; it may take years of careful planning and constant effort for tangible results than can be achieved by the
planning together of librarians, teachers, administrators,
students, and citizens of the community.

15. NEW HORIZONS FOR JUNIOR COLLEGE LIBRARIES

Felix E. Hirsch

Less than a year after the ALA Standards for College Libraries were published, a parallel set of Standards for Junior
College Libraries is ready. The full text of this important
document, prepared by the ACRL Committee on Standards and
approved by the ACRL Board of Directors, appears in the May
issue of College and Research Libraries. This second set
brings to completion the job assigned to the committee, that is
to formulate nation-wide goals for the 1960's both for the libraries in colleges and smaller universities granting Bachelor's
and Master's degrees and for those in two-year institutions.
Only the libraries in the large universities and other major
centers of research were not included in this endeavor, because it is obvious that most of them have reached a level of

attainment which might make any set of general standards less significant, if not almost meaningless.

Just as in the case of standards for the four-year colleges, the committee aimed to draw up a document that would fit all major types of junior colleges. The term covers a great variety of institutions. There is the private small junior college with high educational aspirations and achievements, as it is not infrequently found in the East; there is the junior college, small or medium-sized, serving a particular denomination; the municipal junior college, in its early stages often attached to the high school in town; the junior college which is part of a system revolving around a state university; the technical institute emphasizing vocational aspects in its curriculum; and last, but not least, the community college, serving a variety of purposes by a combination of programs. To find a common denominator for all of them is becoming more and more difficult, because the junior colleges are probably the fastest growing part of higher education today. Rather few people recognize that almost one million students are today enrolled in them and that this figure is likely to increase with undiminished rapidity during the 1960's. This, then, was not the time to delay work on standards by any lengthy investigations of a theoretical nature, especially since the groundwork had been laid long ago.

In a way, the new standards represent the final stage of 30 years of intermittent efforts. In June 1930, the ALA Junior College Round Table had passed a resolution proposing minimum requirements for the then emerging junior college. Among them were demands for a minimum staff of two professional librarians; for a basic book collection of 10,000 volumes for an institution up to 500 students, 15,000 up to 1000 students, and 20,000 above 1000 students; and for a sizeable book budget, expressed in dollar figures. The depression years prevented these standards from becoming reality. After the second World War, a long series of efforts finally resulted in a set of standards adopted by the ACRL Junior College Libraries Section at the ALA meeting in Miami Beach (1956). The ACRL Board of Directors turned this document over to the Committee on Standards a year ago, because it was felt that there was need for new formulations. The Committee was to proceed speedily, because so much valuable time had elapsed. This advice was heeded. After extended consultations with outstanding junior college librarians, the committee which had been enlarged by some of the best experts in the field, held a two-day work session in Chicago. It resulted in a draft which was then submitted to many administrators and librarians of junior colleges, to executive secretaries of accrediting agencies and to leaders of the library profession for their criticisms and suggestions. Out of these comprehensive efforts grew the second draft which the committee examined, word by word, again in Chicago at Midwinter 1960, and which the ACRL Board of Directors then passed unanimously without change.

In their definitive version the standards are meant to give junior college librarians a readable, carefully reasoned document that they can present to their authorities and to community leaders when they want to give them a better understanding of the place the library should occupy in the modern junior college, and to plead with them for more vigorous financial support. The standards should also make useful reading for junior college faculties. It might be mentioned here that the ALA Standards for College Libraries have had a wide distribution; a first printing of 5,000 copies was exhausted in less than three months. The same is hoped for in regard to the new document.

The nation-wide picture of the junior college library field today is far from reassuring. The median figures for 266 junior colleges as published in College and Research Libraries, January 1960, indicate that staffs are too small, budgets too low, and book collections inadequate. Of course, there are some first rate institutions whose administrative officers know what services the library can render to strengthen the effectiveness of instruction and who are willing to pay for them. Last summer, I enjoyed the opportunity to observe informally such a library (that of Colby Junior College in New London, N. H.) in action; I arrived at the conclusion that this well-housed and well-stocked library would be admirable even in a small four-year college. But on my recent journeys in the East, I came also across the library of a junior college occupying only a corner in a high school library room. The contrast between the two could hardly have been more exasperating.

Studying this bewildering evidence with its tremendously

wide range, the committee had to face these alternatives. It
could either formulate standards that would be so low as to fit
the present conditions of the weaker institutions or it could
have the courage to prepare a blueprint for tomorrow that
would reflect the situation in the forward-looking junior colleges of the nation. The committee — in line with the thinking
of many junior college librarians consulted — preferred the
second alternative. Its members knew that in this way they
would not please the "realists," of whom there are only too
many among economy-minded administrators. But there were
three overriding considerations. First of all, only if the sights
are raised systematically with the help of the new standards,
will junior college libraries be able to give that kind of comprehensive service which is essential for a sound instructional
program preparing almost a million young Americans for a
great variety of important occupations. Secondly, only if junior
college libraries are reasonably well equipped will students
cease to be an undue burden on public libraries. The new
standards are very emphatic on this point: "It cannot be stressed
too strongly that the two-year college library must be planned
to give total service, and that other neighboring libraries must
not be used to provide the books essential to the basic junior
college program." Thirdly, among the junior college students
of today are tens of thousands who wish to transfer to good
four-year colleges eventually. They will be stymied if they
must spend their first two years in inferior libraries too poor
to offer enough intellectual enrichment, and which will not
enable them to keep pace with the more fortunate students in
four-year colleges who have access to well-rounded library
collections.

Space limitations do not permit a detailed analysis of the
new standards. But at least a few significant points should be
mentioned here. First of all, the standards envision a staff
of at least two professional librarians, broadly educated combining library school training with a rich subject background.
I would go further, and believe that the Middle States Association of Colleges and Secondary Schools was correct when
stressing in a recent document the value of teaching experience
to the junior college librarian; for, above all, his function is
that of an educator. Professional librarians should have faculty

status and the benefits it entails. The head librarian should occupy a position of leadership, in line, of course, with the policies laid down by the chief administrative officer and the institution's board of control. The junior college library needs courageous and resourceful direction at this juncture of history, and the librarian must be willing and able to stand up for his convictions regarding good service.

What kind of a collection should be found in a junior college library? Of course, the demands of the curriculum must be met first. But there should be also a wealth of standard works representing the heritage of our civilization and interpreting the non-Western world. Many books of high caliber are needed, "which will arouse intellectual curiosity, counteract parochialism, and help to develop critical thinking." A carefully selected collection of at least 20,000 volumes is considered indispensable for up to 1000 students; 5000 volumes should be added for every additional 500 students. These figures may seem somewhat high to the "realists" in view of the meager collections in many junior college libraries, but no instructor can expect his students to read widely, if the library shelves are almost empty. The standards favor also a generous, well-balanced selection of periodicals and newspapers. Finally, audio-visual materials should be administered by the library, if no other department on campus handles them.

It is proposed in the new standards that the junior college allot to the library five per cent of its general and educational budget. This figure is identical with that suggested in the ALA Standards for College Libraries. Experience has shown that this is a reasonable slice of the educational dollar. When a college library falls far below five per cent, there is usually something seriously wrong; the same is likely to hold true for junior college libraries.

Two-year institutions do not always possess separate library buildings. In many cases, the library just occupies part of the administration building or part of a classroom building. The available space is often far too small to permit students to do serious work or to browse leisurely. It is important that the junior college library of the future will be more generous in this respect. Seating accommodations for one-quarter of the student body, as suggested in the standards, may seem costly, but actually they will be a sound investment. They will assure that students can be expected to do some research on their own rather than merely concentrate on textbook assignments.

It would be unreasonable to assume that the new standards will please everybody. They will disturb some intransigent administrators who do not grasp the paramount importance of a well-stocked and well-functioning library for a good junior college. They may not appeal to some conservative librarians either who are absorbed in their special problems, be they regional or local. But the Committee on Standards hopes that its efforts will be appreciated by those educators and librarians who consider strong junior college libraries vital for the progress of American higher education in the 1960's.

16. NEW COLLEGE LIBRARY STANDARDS

Felix E. Hirsch

Expansion of an academic institution is usually a sign of health and progress. But many college librarians across the country look with bewilderment to the enrollment boom predicted for the 1960's. How are they to get ready for it? How are they to face the challenge that this myriad of new readers will present to their concepts of good service. The beginning of a mushrooming process can be observed in many colleges already. Trenton State, for instance, is doubling the number of undergraduate students over the five-year span from 1954/55 to 1959/60; it has also added a large extension division and created several sizeable graduate programs. Hundreds of college and university libraries are forced to cope with similar or worse problems of rapid growth, but these contain only a mild foretaste of the crisis to come in American higher education.

The anticipated needs of the 1960's were uppermost in the thoughts of the ACRL Committee on Standards since it was

assigned the task of drawing up new college library standards
at the ALA Conference in Kansas City two years ago. The assignment was to replace the old ALA Classification and Pay
Plans for Libraries in Institutions of Higher Education, which
had been conceived before World War II and no longer meet the
problems of today. This laborious task has now been completed;
standards have been drawn up for the libraries in colleges and universities granting B.A. and M.A. degrees, but excluding the larger
research institutions and junior colleges. The ACRL Board of Directors, at its last meeting, approved "enthusiastically" (as the
official report states) the new document whose full text will be published in the July issue of College and Research Libraries.

The final version of these standards represents more than
just the thinking of the committee, which includes men and
women with a great variety of professional experiences. It reflects also the opinions of literally hundreds of other librarians
from all parts of the country who were consulted in the course
of the deliberations, among them many outstanding leaders in
the field. More than 30 college and university presidents and
the executive secretaries of the regional accrediting agencies
also advised the committee. Needless to say, not every pertinent suggestion could be incorporated and some compromises
were unavoidable. But the authors of the new standards feel
that they did not sacrifice any fundamental convictions and that
they did much more than merely codify the status quo. They
tried to provide a blueprint for the next decade.

Their aim was to present flexible standards, based on
firm principles. They felt that college libraries are far too
complex and far too different from one another to permit rigid
nation-wide regulation of details. The best to be hoped for
seemed to be a readable basic document embodying the most
modern thinking of the profession. It would provide the college
librarian with a statement of the fundamental tenets that he
could then discuss at some length with his President and perhaps have passed on to Trustees or other officers concerned
with the general welfare of the library. It is cheerful to note
that mimeographed advance copies of the standards have fulfilled exactly this function of classification in a number of
cases, in which the librarians had to explain pressing issues
to their authorities.

What are the most important features of the new standards? First of all, they take a nation-wide view of college library service. Intentionally, they disregard those regional differences in degree of excellence which still exist today, but must be eradicated during the next decade. There should be only one minimum standard, e.g., for the size of library staff and book collection, in all 50 states of the Union.

Second, the standards aim at overcoming traditional variations between certain types of college libraries. They are applicable to institutions both private and public, denominational and non-denominational, liberal arts and pre-professional. In the pursuit of excellence, libraries in institutes of technology and in colleges for teacher education cannot stay behind those in the liberal arts colleges. Of course, there will continue to be certain differences among them because they serve different curricular demands, but the tacit assumption of many administrators that they do not need to be equally rich and strong, must be fought tooth and nail.

Third, the standards are built around the concept of the college librarian as an educator. He cannot be anything less than an equal partner of the teaching faculty. All professional staff members are to enjoy faculty status. But if they are to have the same privileges (and similar opportunities for promotion) as their teaching colleagues possess, they should also be willing to continue their education beyond the first library school degree. The standards envision that many college librarians will wish to add master's degrees in suitable subject areas rather than go on to the Ph.D. in library science. Those with proper academic background may teach courses in their field of subject preparation and thereby help to bridge the gap which so often exists on a college campus between classroom and library. The head librarian is to rank with the chief administrative officers. It seemed wisest to place him directly under the President; for in smaller institutions the power of decision (especially on budgetary matters) rests usually with him. However, the need for close cooperation of the librarian with the academic dean was not overlooked.

The best colleges in America support their libraries generously. But the college library statistics published annually in College and Research Libraries indicate that some otherwise respectable institutions are inclined to skimp as far as the library budget is concerned. For that reason, the standards suggest that normally five percent of the educational and general budget be set aside for the college library; of course, more is needed if the institution is rapidly expanding its student population or its course offerings. Intentionally, no dollar sign is mentioned in the chapter of the standards on the budget, since the purchasing power of our currency has shown such an almost constant decline, making any figures meaningless, if not directly misleading.

Many factors determine the size and character of a book collection. The standards are more concerned with excellence and instructional usefulness of the holdings than with numbers. Figures are mentioned only to indicate the minimum rather than the optimum size; for instance, in a college up to 600 students, 50,000 carefully chosen volumes would seem essential. The collections should aim to present the heritage of Western and Eastern thought in all its richness. Titles needed for class work should be continuously supplemented by a wide variety of books which combine timeliness with enduring value. They should be chosen to arouse the intellectual curiosity of the students and to satisfy their recreational reading needs.

The sad experiences on the issue of censorship of the early 1950's are unforgotten. For this reason, the standards contain an unequivocal pronouncement on intellectual freedom in the college library: "The right of the librarian to select books and other materials representing all sides of controversial issues must be safeguarded by the institution, and any attempts at censorship from whatever sources or for whatever reasons must be resisted."

It could not be the function of the ACRL Committee on Standards to predict coming trends. But its members recognized some fundamental changes that higher learning in America is undergoing and make several references to them, e.g., the impact of independent study on the library. There seems to be more genuine concern in American colleges today with the education of the individual with depth rather than breadth. Such independent study presupposes ample book resources and increased seating capacity. The college library of tomorrow will have to provide reading space for at least one third of the enrolled students; actually some of the best colleges today go considerably beyond this figure in their new or remodeled buildings. The standards are essentially in line with the most advanced project to have come from academic pioneers in our time: The New College Plan: A proposal for a major departure in higher education (Amherst, Mass., 1958). Finally, the standards favor also the most modern ideas about interlibrary cooperation by stating that the college librarian should not lose sight of the important benefits to be derived from pooling the resources of his library with those of other interested libraries in the same community, region, state and in the nation.

No set of standards will last forever. Ideas and conditions change. Every succeeding generation must come to grips with the fundamental issues and redefine the philosophy of librarianship. But the men and women who drafted the new standards for college libraries hope to have rendered the profession a service at least for that era of momentous changes which American higher education is just entering.

17. SCHOOL LIBRARY BILL OF RIGHTS

School libraries are concerned with generating understanding of American freedoms and with the preservation of these freedoms through the development of informed and responsible citizens. To this end the American Association of School Librarians reaffirms the Library Bill of Rights of the American Library Association and asserts that the responsibility of the school library is:

To provide materials that will enrich and support the curriculum, taking into consideration the varied interests, abilities, and maturity levels of the pupils served

To provide materials that will stimulate growth in factual knowledge, literary appreciation, aesthetic values, and ethical standards

SCHOOL LIBRARY BILL OF RIGHTS

To provide a background of information which will enable
pupils to make intelligent judgments in their daily life

To provide materials on opposing sides of controversial issues
so that young citizens may develop under guidance the practice
of critical reading and thinking

To provide materials representative of the many religious,
ethnic, and cultural groups and their contributions to our American heritage

To place principle above personal opinion and reason above
prejudice in the selection of materials of the highest quality
in order to assure a comprehensive collection appropriate for
the users of the library

Part II: IMPROVING LIBRARY ADMINISTRATION

18. BOOK SELECTION PRACTICES
IN THE NATION'S SCHOOLS

Elizabeth Hodges

During the school year 1953-54, over nine million books costing approximately eighteen million dollars were added to the school libraries of the nation. What evidence is there that these books were wisely chosen, what proof that this huge public fund was well spent? What are the leaders in the school library field doing to make sure that the boys and girls of America are getting from this investment the books best suited to their needs?

To find answers to these questions, 61 state and local school library supervisors throughout the country were asked to report on book selection practices in their communities. Forty-one questionnaires from 23 states were returned, along with much supplementary material amplifying the information given on the check sheets. Analysis of the returns showed such a wide variation of opinion and practice that it was difficult to discover a pattern in the procedures reported. By far the most significant information was found in the statements of policy and practice returned with the questionnaires. The following summary of the survey is based on both types of material.

Do Schools Generally Buy Library Books According to a Carefully Developed Plan?

More than half of the supervisors reported that they had no written statement of policy to serve as a guide for the selection of books in their school libraries. Some replies indicated that selection policies had been written out for elementary schools but not for high schools — the implication being that there are few trained librarians in elementary schools to assume responsibility for book selection. Wherever selection policies existed, they had been formulated by groups of teachers, librarians, and administrators, usually with the guidance of the school library supervisor.

The statements of policy submitted had obviously been developed after careful consideration of all aspects of the problem. In general, they gave the purposes of book selection, designated the group responsible for the task, and stated administrative position on such matters as types of books to be purchased, controversial materials, and gift books.

The excellence of the policy statements suggests that they have contributed significantly to the development of well rounded book collections and to the professional growth of those who have served on policy making committees. In addition, they have undoubtedly strengthened the librarians' position in dealing with censorship, pressure groups, and misguided benefactors.

Who Selects the Books Bought for School Libraries?

Three points on which opinion was virtually unanimous were these: (1) Each school should be free to choose its own library books; (2) the widest possible participation in book selection should be encouraged; (3) and the school library supervisor should give assistance in improving and coordinating book selection. Children, parents, and public librarians — as well as school librarians and teachers — were mentioned frequently as participants in the process of selecting school library books.

Evidently, the right people — those who will use the books — are helping to build school library collections. No one subscribed to the idea that book selection should be a one-man job; but all stressed the need for advisory service and coordination from a central source.

What Are School Library Supervisors Doing to Raise the Level of Book Selection?

Many excellent practices are being encouraged by school library supervisors. Mentioned most often were the efforts of supervisors to stimulate the use of approved bibliographies as the basis for book selection. Twenty-one supervisors stated the lists of books approved for purchase by their schools are prepared locally; others expressed the opinion that the many excellent professional lists are preferable, since the latter give a wider choice and are more easily kept up-to-date than lists made for a particular community. A further objection to local lists was that the time and money spent on them could not be justified. However, the supervisors reported two to one that they approved lists of recommended current books, sent from the central office as guides to schools wishing to buy new books not yet included in the standard lists.

Mentioned as being particularly satisfactory selection aids were the Children's Catalog, the Standard Catalog for High School Libraries, the ALA Basic Book Collections, Junior Libraries, the Horn Book, the Booklist, and the Bulletin of the Children's Book Center (Chicago). Also recommended were the appraisals in the bibliographies published by the National Council of Teachers of English, The Association for Childhood Education International, and the Child Study Association of America. The Kirkus service, the Book Review Digest, Junior Reviewers, and current periodicals were also recommended.

Central collections of library books, available to all who wish to use them, are maintained by most of the supervisors reporting; traveling book collections, special exhibits, and book fairs were recommended by many as devices for making books available for examination to those preparing book orders.

The value of book selection committees was stressed in many reports. Such committees, composed usually of librarians and teachers, share with the supervisor the responsibility for formulating selection policies, preparing lists of recommended books, and raising the level of book selection practices. Growth of members in ability to form independent judgments was mentioned as a by-product of committee meetings. It is also interesting to note that in several communities these committees meet on school time, and that in some cities there is close coordination between school and public library groups in the work of book selection.

School library supervisors spend much of their time advising schools on problems of book selection. They study the curriculum, work with teachers, evaluate book collections — all with the purpose of helping each school to develop a book collection suited to its needs.

It is obvious that school library supervisors have accepted the responsibility for helping schools to build good book collections and that they are promoting many practices designed to encourage intelligent book selection.

What Are Some of the Special Problems of Book Selection?
High on the list of special problems mentioned by those
reporting was the failure of librarians to read as widely as
they should. Suggestions for encouraging librarians to read
included formation of selection committees, attendance at book
discussion meetings, and permission to examine central book
collections on school time.

The difficulty of finding books to meet curriculum needs
was frequently mentioned also. In this connection, the importance of selecting books suited to the reading abilities of the
pupils who will use them, and at the same time interesting
enough to be read with enjoyment, was stressed. A thorough
knowledge of the school program and the enlistment of help
from teachers were recommended as partial solutions.

Several replies emphasized the importance of building good
total collections, incorporating the best of the older books with
new materials and maintaining a balance between recreational
and study-type materials. Ways of accomplishing this task
were suggested: comparing the library's holdings with recommended percentages; surveying inventory reports for weak
spots; checking basic lists for omissions; and giving constant
attention to children's interests and school needs.

The matter of censorship appeared less serious than might
have been expected, only 17 replies having noted this as a
problem. Wherever attacks on materials were reported, they
were directed at books on communism, race, sex education,
and religion. A clear statement of policy on the purchase of
books on controversial subjects was recommended as a safe-
guard against such attacks.

"How can librarians know that the physical format of a
book is satisfactory if they have to buy sight unseen?" asked
several supervisors. Attention to notes on format, now included
in Junior Libraries reviews, to some extent in the Children's
Catalog, and in many publishers' catalogs, was recommended;
also, provision for the examination of as many books as possible in advance of purchase. One report mentioned the very helpful articles on bindings carried in the November, 1956 issue of
Junior Libraries. Discussions of such matters as kinds of sewing, publishers' reinforced library bindings, and the pros and
cons of prebinding are clear and informative.

BOOK SELECTION PRACTICES

In some areas, it was reported, publishers and jobbers are allowed to display unsuitable materials at meetings of parents and teachers; in others, mediocre books are actually sold to children at hastily organized book fairs in schools. Constant efforts to gain administrative cooperation in controlling these practices were held to be the responsibility of librarians and library supervisors.

Closely related to the problem of displays was that of publishers' representatives visiting schools. The supervisors reported two to one that they welcomed book men in their offices, but encouraged school visits only by invitation. Some supervisors stated that busy teachers and inexperienced librarians sometimes buy inferior materials because they are represented as "bargains."

Though thoroughly unscientific and far from complete, this study of book selection practices has uncovered many interesting facts and opinions. It is heartening to know that the problems of book selection are being attacked with vigor in so many school communities. The winners in the campaign will be the boys and girls who use their school libraries.

19. AIDS TO BOOK SELECTION

David McAllister

Providing books which will satisfy requirements of number, interests, and reading ability and which, at the same time, are of desirable literary quality, is a responsibility which falls upon librarians, teachers, principals, and superintendents. Librarians and teachers turn to principals and superintendents to find out how much money is available and how that money shall be allocated. Actual selection, however, is usually the province of librarians and classroom teachers.

The selection of library books is more than a matter of filling out an order blank. It is aimed at making the right book available to the child at the time he needs it. Thus, the selector of books must know principles of book selection, titles, and sources. In a school system fortunate enough to have librarians, much of this work is left to them. In less fortunate systems, or those which are more isolated, it is usually the classroom teacher who selects the books for purchase.

The purpose of this article, then, is to mention and discuss some inexpensive sources of help for selectors of library books. This information may be of especial help to teachers who are working under conditions such as the following:

1. Where there is no school library and where there are no public funds for books (In such schools, teachers may have small amounts given by the local PTA for purchase of a few books for specific classrooms.)

2. Where there is no centralized school library (However, small amounts of public money may be available to each teacher to buy books for classroom libraries.)

3. Where there is a small, inadequate centralized collection of books under the responsibility of a teacher or teacher-librarian for a few hours during the school day (There may be small amounts of money available annually for books to be purchased by teachers or teacher-librarians, who need sources of guidance for the job.)

4. Where schools are small, rural, serving Grades I to XII or some part of those grades, with 100 or fewer students. (The library of such a school must serve too wide a range in reading abilities and interests to be efficient.)

Certain professional books come first in this review of aids for selection of books by teachers. These books discuss reading preferences from the standpoints of age, sex, intelligence, maturity, and interests and are concerned with the reading of children as it is affected by their physical, mental, and social development, and by their experience.

In Books, Children, and Men,[1] Hazard wrote a series of delightful essays on the effect of books and reading upon character formation. One of the best sources for principles of book selection is Living with Books.[2] Gateways to Readable Books[3] is another tool for selection of books which should be known to all who have that privilege. Another valuable book for the teacher's background, although intended primarily for librarians, is Munson's An Ample Field.[4] Teachers will find it helpful because it has a discussion of titles which appeal to boys and girls. Arbuthnot's Children and Books,[5] widely used as a text in classes in children's literature, is intended to answer the questions, "What kinds of books do children like?" and "How can we get our children to read more and better books?" Chapters 1, 2, and 19 of that book should be well known to those who choose books for school reading.

The Unreluctant Years[6] gives a background for choosing books for young people. For classes in the junior and senior high school Norvell's The Reading Interests of Young People[7] discusses readers' choices from the standpoints of age and sex. One necessary tool for the librarian and teacher-librarian is the Children's Catalog.[8] Part I contains a list of authors, titles, and subject entries for about 3400 books. The approximate grade level is noted for all books except reference books. Easy books and picture books are designated. Purchase includes annual supplements, and the Catalog is sold on a service basis — smaller libraries pay less than the larger ones.

Many of the books listed in the previous paragraph are intended for the use of librarians. To some extent they are professional tools. They are all books, however, which informed school administrators will wish to make available to teachers so that their choice of books may be wise.

A second source of information about books is publishers' catalogs. A postcard to a publisher will bring his catalog to any teacher. Publishers want to sell their own books, of course, and indiscriminate ordering of books from catalogs is not desirable. Titles should be checked against some of the book-reviewing publications mentioned later. There is a growing tendency for publishers to star titles recommended by such organizations as the National Council of Teachers of English and the American Library Association.

Various associations have issued lists of books recommended for young people and adults. These lists constitute the third source of titles which should be known to book selectors. Among them are Children's Books for Seventy-Five Cents or Less,[9] Inexpensive Books for Boys and Girls,[10] and Reading Ladders for Human Relations.[11] Recommended Children's Books of 1953[12] and Starred Books from the Library Journal[13] are reprints from the Library Journal[14] that list books desirable for school and library purchase "within the limits stated by the reviewers." The books are arranged by grade and subject; an author-title index is also provided. Books "that even the smallest libraries will not want to miss" are starred twice. In addition, twice a year the Library Journal presents a survey of children's books, a checklist of appraised books arranged by grade and subject.

One reliable and easily available source of evaluations of current children's books is the Center for Children's Books, sponsored by the University of Chicago and its Graduate Library School. The Center publishes the Bulletin[15] in which, "all books, whether recommended or not, are listed, with critical annotations indicating the strengths and weaknesses of each book. The annotations also indicate the uses to which the books can best be put in the home, classroom, school, and public library. The grade level of each recommended book is given, and developmental values are indicated."

The Child Study Association of America publishes annually "Books of the Year for Children."[16] This list of books has been selected and arranged to meet a broad range of interests and a variety of individual tastes. "Wherever possible, preference has been given throughout to inexpensive books which offer good value for young readers." The Children's Reading Service puts out annotated lists of supplementary reading materials intended for children from kindergarten to Grade IX. The same company will also arrange exhibits of books for individual schools and for PTA groups.[17] For slower readers, Carpenter has edited Gateways to American History,[18] which is intended for use in junior high schools.

This third category of sources of titles for children includes lists of books issued by city, regional, and state libraries and state departments of education.

Reviews of books published in newspapers and magazines make up a fourth source of aids to book selection. Teachers may find valid estimates of children's books in such periodicals as the Horn Book Magazine,[19] Grade Teacher,[20] and Parents' Magazine.[21] In each issue of the English Journal[22] there are reviews of books for school libraries. Few daily newspapers carry reviews of books, but there are such national periodicals as the New York Times Book Review[23] and the New York Herald-Tribune Book Review[24] which cover children's books with authoritative evaluations.

Magazines for the school library should not be neglected. For their titles and evaluation, Cundiff has compiled 101 Magazines for Schools, Grades 1-12.[25] The pamphlet lists magazines by title and gives publisher and place of publication, frequency of appearance, subscription price, subjects covered in the magazine, and a short annotation. Martin's Magazines for School Libraries[26] gives similar information for a more extensive list of magazines.

Good teaching demands a program of reading for the classroom teacher as well as for the child. For the selection of books on adult levels two good guides are available in the Mentor series of inexpensive paper-bound volumes. Good Reading,[27] "a guide to the world's best books," gives brief descriptions of more than 1250 useful and entertaining volumes in the areas of drama, poetry, essay, history, biography, fiction, religion, reference, and many other classifications. The Wonderful World of Books[28] is dedicated "to those who bend the twigs — the librarians of America, teachers, extension workers, leaders — and to the twigs themselves." The titles of particularly worthwhile chapters from that book are: "It's Time To Read," "The Joy of Reading," "When We Were Very Young," "How To Find Time To Read." Both Good Reading and The Wonderful World of Books are filled with stimulating discussions and usable suggestions.

In summary, a developmental program in reading requires books, and those persons who pick the books determine to a large extent the effectiveness of teaching in all areas. The school's library and its supply of supplementary reading material furnish valid criteria of the quality of instruction and the sensitiveness of teachers to the needs of boys and girls.

20. COST-SAVING IN BOOK CATALOGING

Bertha D. Hellum and Albert J. Biggins

When Mrs. Hellum accepted the appointment of librarian of the Contra Costa County library in the spring of 1954, it was with the realization that this system had always ranked with the best in terms of service and support. Yet, despite the phenomenal growth of the library as measured in book collection and dollars support, population and readers' needs had grown even faster.

Realizing that one person could not cope with this situation, Mrs. Hellum asked the county personnel office to help evaluate the need for a reorganization of staff with particular consideration to clerical and professional duties. The survey indicated the need for such a reorganization and suggested adding a new position, principal librarian of technical services, to effect the reorganization. Specific duties assigned to this position were the co-ordination of all library routines and processes and the study and evaluation of each library operation for the purpose of improving efficiency and cutting costs. In less than three years, several important improvements have been achieved. One of the most dramatic concerns cost-saving in the cataloging of the library's books.

Prior to January, 1955, the catalog department in Contra Costa County Library was operated according to traditional procedure which had been established over the years. A detailed study of the cataloging department was made to determine the step-by-step process, the number of persons working in the department, and their particular duties. This study indicated that time-studies were essential for further planning. A simple 3x5-inch form card was designed to show: 1. Beginning date and time. 2. Number of books (or titles). 3. Operation (process). 4. Ending date and time. 5. Total time. 6. Total time divided by units processed during total time. 7. Initial of person making report.

These cards were made available in quantity with a request

to the staff that a card be turned in for each truck of books as it passed through each step of the routine. This study was made over a period of months. All persons performing the various steps submitted hundreds of cards. No attempt was made to omit unproductive time (coffee break, staff room visits, etc.) from total time, since unproductive time must be paid for and must be charged against unit cost. Additionally, no attempt was made to increase the rate of work on the part of any employee, and when competition developed among different staff members with the result that it influenced time-per-unit figures, these figures were discounted as accurately as possible.

A tabulation of hundreds of cards for each step in the cataloging process produced an average unit-time for each book in each step. A re-examination of each step resulted in several definite time-saving changes in procedure. First, the authority file was discontinued, since each name (except those for discarded items) could be found in the catalog. This eliminated one of the initial searches for a time saving of nearly one minute per book in addition to the time saved in maintaining the file. When the authority file was discontinued, the library bought all available volumes of the Library of Congress Catalog of Printed Cards to provide an authoritative source for items not found in the card catalog.

The purchase of Library of Congress printed cards or Wilson cards for each title was the next time-saving device. Purchase of these cards in each case proved to be less expensive than duplicating them on a typewriter. True, the cards were not inexpensive, but the cost of the cards was more than offset by the saving in staff time. The time saved was fed back into production and the result was more books cataloged per month at no greater salary cost. There was, of course, a substantially greater material cost.

Anyone who has ever tried to improve cataloging efficiency by the purchase and use of printed cards knows the frustration of waiting month after month for the arrival of cards, which, for one reason or another, haven't arrived. The books remain on shelves sorely needed for newly arrived books. Even worse, requests for the books pile up in the request files. Sometimes, in desperation or disgust, the librarian insists that the books be cataloged; the cards typewritten. The new system suffers a small defeat. Weeks later the printed cards arrive and are thrown away. The purchase of printed cards is not necessarily the answer to efficiency in the catalog department.

In August, 1956, the library purchased a Multilith, model 750, capable of reproducing catalog cards of excellent quality. A subscription to the National Union Catalog had already been obtained. In September the library subscribed to Library of Congress proof sheets. Slowly these tools were incorporated into the cataloging procedure.

Books delivered to the catalog department are now checked for authority and for duplicate copies in the card catalog. When a single copy of a title requires five cards or more, a main entry master is typed and revised. After the cards are run on the Multilith, they are delivered to the typist who types the title entry and subject headings on the respective cards. When more than five copies are cataloged, she types separate Multilith masters for the main entry, the title entry, and each subject entry; in addition, she prepares a Multilith master for the production of book cards. This book card master is used to produce the book pockets. All masters are revised by the chief cataloger or her assistant.

Obviously, any system which makes a practice of ordering as many as 20 copies of a novel will save tremendous amounts of time by the Multilith method of reproducing cards. For fiction, only two masters need to be revised (assuming one main entry and one title entry) in contrast to the 40 cards reproduced by typewriter. On multiple orders for nonfiction titles requiring more than two cards, the saving is correspondingly greater.

A most important step in time saving was the re-arrangement of desks to provide for an uncomplicated flow of work from one operation to another. With a smoother flow of work, and with the increase in production, staff morale improved.

What has been the result of all of this study, evaluation, re-organization? In April, 1953, with five and one-half persons engaged in the cataloging process, the department cataloged 1785 books at a salary cost of $1347. The unit cost was 75.4 cents. In April, 1957, with four and three-fourths persons engaged in the cataloging process (including, of course, the Multilith operator) the department cataloged 4678 books at a salary cost of $1642. The unit cost was 35.1 cents. Allowing a saving

in salary cost of 40 cents a book, the savings in the month of
April, 1957, amounted to $1871 (just about the cost of a Multi-
lith machine).

Between 1953 and 1957, the staff realized a 20 per cent increase in salaries. But they produced more than 250 per cent
the number of books cataloged during the previous period!

The next logical step? Several months ago, the county
leased Xerography equipment. The county library has been experimenting with Multilith masters produced by the Xerox method. There is some difficulty in utilizing this equipment, since
it is supervised by a centralized county service agency. The
operators do not, as yet, recognize the specialized nature of a
catalog card. When the county library can arrange to lease and
house a Xerography unit, it is possible that production will take
another dramatic jump.

Meanwhile, the surveys and the cost analyses will continue.

21. COST OF CATALOGING VERSUS PRINTED CARDS
                                    IN THE SCHOOL LIBRARY

Veda Fatka

Recently, as a set of catalog cards was evolving from a
combination of a rented typewriter, a well-thumbed Wilson catalog, plain cards, and moments of despair over errors, I re-
called a statement on page 21 of Books and Readers in the Library, sponsored jointly by the Division of Libraries, State
Department of Education, Tennessee, and the Department of
Library Service, College of Education, University of Tennessee,
for a work conference on library problems, June 3-15, 1946.
It read:

> The actual cost for printed cards is only $2 more
> per 50 books than card stock required for typing cata-
> log cards. In addition, there is no waste of cards or

expenditure of time in making and revising typed cards.

The latter sentence was the one that interested me most, and I decided to keep a diary of time and costs involved in the cataloging for 103 books selected for our school library. The estimate of time and costs in cataloging 103 books without printed cards is based on my experience in cataloging, for it is evident already that I have the printed cards for these books. Also, I am quoting minimum time and money expended. For instance, a typist with the technical knowledge or skill for cataloging would receive more than $1 an hour which I state here. I have based the estimate of time on my own rate of typing which is above average in speed and accuracy.

Plain catalog cards of medium weight are approximately $3.50 per 500. Finding the information for the main entry card varies from 5 to 7 minutes per book. Typing one card requires from 4 to 6 minutes. Each book requires on the average about 5 cards for complete cataloging. If I were typing on the proverbial island with no interruptions and few errors, I could complete a set of cards for a book in a span of 20 to 30 minutes.

Quoting minimum time and costs for cataloging 103 books without printed cards, I have put the results in table form:

CATALOGING WITHOUT PRINTED CARDS

Finding information for the main entry cards —
8 1/2 hours	$ 8.50
Typing 550 cards — 37 1/2.	37.50
Cost of 550 cards.	3.82
Ruined cards (at the rate of 10 per 100).	.70
Wear and tear on the typewriter	?
Wear and tear on the typist	??
TOTAL	$50.52

CATALOGING WITH PRINTED CARDS[1]

Alphabetizing and typing order for cards —
4 hours.	$ 4.00

CATALOGING VERSUS PRINTED CARDS

Airmail letter	$ .06
550 printed cards	11.86
Typing shelf list information and call numbers on cards — 5 hours	5.00
Wear and tear on the typewriter — negligible . . .	0
Wear and tear on the typist — likewise!	0
TOTAL	$20.92

The saving in terms of money is $29.60 not to mention the comfort of relying upon an authoritative source, but the main difference is the saving in time. Notice the tables again: the time consumed without printed cards is 46 hours while the time used with printed cards is 9 hours or a difference of 37 hours. Remember, too, that these are estimates of minimum time.

Consider how these 37 hours may be used:

Reading guidance
Promotion and publicity
Class or individual instruction in the effective use of
    the library
Reference service
Teacher-librarian planning in curriculum development
Reading new books, materials, and professional
    magazines
Creating an atmosphere of beauty, order, and quiet
    in the library.

These and other reasons have convinced me that it is economical to use printed cards.

Bouquets to my instructor, Anna Muller, who told me about printed cards and the estimated 37 hours I will save for every 103 books cataloged in the years to come!

101

22. CUTTING CATALOGING COSTS IN THE SMALL LIBRARY

Edward C. Werner

A method of duplicating catalog cards without a second handling to add headings and tracings has been developed at New Mexico Western College Library. As is usually the case, necessity was the mother of the invention. Ours was the oft-told tale of an increased book budget but no provision for processing the extra books. In our case the book budget was doubled. More student help was made available but no more professional help.

Our first move was to hire more student typists. But doubling the typing staff did not help. Breaking in new typists required too much of the professional cataloger's already limited time. And as the typing staff was increased, turnover of help increased, which meant more new typists to be trained. The situation quickly became desperate.

In searching for a solution to this bottleneck in production we decided that relief was to be found through: (1) Using cataloging and classification crutches wherever possible. (2) Producing sets of cards complete with tracings and headings on a duplicator. (3) Producing these sets of cards in the library without delay and by means of less help, not more.

The purchase of the <u>Library of Congress Catalog of Printed Cards</u>, 1948 and current supplements has materially lightened the load on the professional cataloger. Clerical help now check all new acquisitions against the LC catalog and note the volume and page of each entry on a work slip. The cataloger then examines the LC cataloging and notes any necessary changes on the work slip. The LC entry and the work slip then serve as instructions for the typist.

We have found that over two-thirds of our acquisitions are listed in the LC catalog. For those items not found there, the more laborious method of working out the classification number and subject headings from the Dewey classification scheme and the LC Subject Heading List must be followed.

102

CUTTING CATALOGING COSTS IN THE SMALL LIBRARY

On closer examination of items two and three above, they resolve into one: a fast, flexible method of duplicating catalog cards. We ruled out LC printed cards because of the order work, delay in acquiring cards and the necessity for inserting each card in the typewriter to add call numbers, headings, and corrections. Although the Wilson cards carry classification numbers and headings, these are not always suitable for our library. Furthermore, each card must be inserted in the typewriter to add the work mark. And again the order work and delay in acquiring cards require more typing and professional supervision. Printed sets of cards would not have provided the expediency we sought.

The alternative to printed cards was the production of sets of cards at the library, complete with call numbers and headings added. In searching for a suitable duplicator for this job we soon found that most duplicators are unwieldy in that once the master has been prepared, there is no altering it. There is one notable exception, the direct process duplicator, also known as the Ditto machine. This duplicator makes use of an analine dye carbon master. Rollers convey an alcoholic fluid to the paper which is thereby dampened. Additional rollers press the dampened paper against the master thereby effecting a transfer of some of the dye. The finished copy dries in a matter of seconds and does not require inter-leaving to prevent smudging as is the case with most types of duplicators.

Our method of duplicating cards on the direct process machine is as follows:

A supply of 8 1/2 x 11-inch carbon masters is cut to 5 x 8 1/2-inch dimensions. The typist inserts one of these master sheets in the typewriter so that the typing line will be 5 inches long, the same as the width of a catalog card. From the cataloger's work slip, or the copy of the printed entry in the LC catalog, the typist prepares a master copy of the main entry complete with call number. A triple space below this main entry she types the title entry if one is required. On successive triple spaces she types the subject headings and secondary headings and analytics as required. A triple space below the last heading she types the order information, viz., the accession number, date of acquisition, source, and cost.

The Ditto master is then checked by the cataloger. Proofing

ditto work is easy on the eyes, since the master is made by typing with the usual black ribbon on white paper. Proofing the single master sheet is the only check needed on the typing. Corrections are easily made on direct process masters and entire deletions may be made simply by cutting out the unwanted part with a razor blade or scissors.

After the typing has been checked the sets of cards are run off on the duplicator. The first step in this process is to separate the headings from the main entry. This is done on the paper cutter, the operator cutting off each added entry immediately below the line of typing.

The main entry is then placed on the drum of the duplicator and one main entry or author card is run off. Next the title slip is placed on the drum immediately above the main entry and a second card is run off. The result is the main entry with title immediately above the author line: a title card. The title slip is then moved to the far right end of the drum where it will be used later in tracing the cards on the verso of the shelf-list.

After the title card each subject card, analytic or secondary, is made in the same manner. And after each card has been made, the master slip is moved to the right end of the drum.

After all added cards have been made the order information slip is placed on the drum immediately below the main entry and another card is run off. The result: a shelf-list card. This card is then turned over and hand-fed through the right end of the drum where it picks up the added entries. This serves as a tracing on the set of cards.

If an official card is desired, the main entry with a separate slip bearing the letters "Off." placed immediately above it will give the desired results. A supply of such slips typed "Off." as well as other standard notations such as, "For library's holdings of this set please see main entry," should be prepared in advance and placed near the machine where they will be available when needed.

If for any reason certain information appearing on the main entry is to be omitted on the added cards, this is easily accomplished. The operator has merely to place a blank slip of paper over that part of the master to be deleted. The blind is attached to the drum along with the master. This prevents the carbon deposits of the unwanted part of the typing from transferring onto the catalog card.

CUTTING CATALOGING COSTS IN THE SMALL LIBRARY

The main entry Ditto masters may be saved and later arranged in class-order the length of the drum and run off on half-sheets of typing paper. The result: a list of new acquisitions without any additional typing effort.

This equipment has resulted in a real saving in labor and materials. The direct process of duplicating is a very inexpensive process, the master copy costing less than one cent for most sets of cards.

On the other side of the ledger, direct process work fades when exposed to light. However, in closed files the deterioration is very slow. Upon examining the Ditto work which has been filed into our catalog we could not distinguish between the cards processed this year and those which were processed five years ago. Also, there are those no doubt who will find the purple Ditto work unattractive.

In selecting a duplicator for this work one should choose a machine on which the drum is easily accessible, and the drum should be so constructed that small pieces of work may be placed on it in any position desired. Most machines have fingers which hold the master copy. These are not suitable for handling small slips of master work. We have found the Wolber Copy-rite Liquid Duplicator to be entirely satisfactory.

23. MATERIALS AND METHODS
IN BOOK FINISHING AND REPAIRING

Lawrence R. Huber

Surrounded by the attractively illustrated catalogs from the library supply houses, a fascinated librarian could easily jump on the brightly-colored, ultra-modern, lazy-Susan book truck and swivel off in all directions — stopping only when, like the kitten in the thread advertisement, he had immobilized himself in a cocoon of mending tissues, tapes, transparent adhesives, single-stitched, double-stitched, and not-stitched-at-all binders, electric styluses and electro-pencils. Or he could (perhaps not quite so easily) refuse to look into the promised land and go back to his glue pots and awl.

To buy or not to buy! What are the minimum essentials? From whom shall I make my purchases? . . .

In its attempt to comment on these problems, the following report hopes to be helpful but cannot claim to be complete, authoritative or infallible. It was written at the suggestion of the ALA Equipment Committee to provide brief, easily accessible reference material about the specific properties and uses of some of the products related to book repair and finishing in the library, as listed in this annual buying guide issue of the ALA Bulletin. The information is drawn from the writer's own experience with the products described, or from his knowledge and observation of their use by other libraries. His comments, therefore, should be taken only as one man's opinion of the qualities of the materials, the uses of the products, and the validity of the methods which they attempt to describe.

With these warning signs properly posted, the writer hopes that the following comments may prove of some use to the harassed librarian in his endless search for — Better Buying.

ADHESIVES

Cellulose Acetate Tape. Available in 1/2", 1", and 1 1/2" widths and in varying thicknesses. The half-inch width is used for attaching book jacket covers, the other widths for joining plastic magazine covers or directly reenforcing the backs of magazines. As a temporary measure has been used to reenforce book spines. The thinner qualities are fairly transparent but are not to be confused with transparent mending tape and should not be used for mending torn book pages since even the thinnest quality enterferes with easy readability of page and tends to turn yellow with age. Some varieties of this tape shrink with drying and if used on thin paper will eventually cause surrounding areas to wrinkle and/or tear. Not desirable for tipping in pages since, as the drying process occurs, the adhesive softens and bleeds (oozes out), producing an undesirable sticky substance between the pages.

BOOK FINISHING AND REPAIRING

Cloth Tape

Gummed cloth tape also known as "adhesive cloth." This
tape was originally stocked by libraries in 3/4" or 1" width —
is available in these widths in 12 ft. and 50 yd. rolls, in white
or slate color. This was produced for use where an extra heavy
bond was required, e.g., the reenforcing of book hinges, backs
of map folds, record albums, cardboard files, etc. Many librarians no longer stock this item inasmuch as the advent of
plastic adhesives has obsoleted most of the original uses for
this kind of tape.

Gummed transparent cloth tape, also called "transparent
adhesive cloth." This tape is designed for repair of map faces,
heavy-paper printed pages, and other similar mutilations requiring a mending medium which is both transparent and strong.
Standard rolls are 3/4" by 16 ft. and 1" by 12 ft., but both widths
also available in 50 yd. rolls. Many of the original uses for this
tape have been abandoned because for most purposes the repair
was too strong and too inflexible for efficient use. It is still
however the best thing on the market for repairing the faces of
large cloth-backed maps and posters or for use wherever an
extra heavy transparent bond is required.

Self sticking cloth tape, produced by several firms experimenting with plastic adhesives and sold under such trade names
as Delkote, Mystik Tape, Book-Aid Tape, etc. This newest
of cloth tapes requires no application of adhesive nor even
moistening, yet it adheres tenaciously. It is available in a variety of widths from 1/2" to 4" and needs simply to be pressed
into place. The narrower tapes are used for reenforcing the
backs and edging the covers of magazines, pamphlets, and thin
paper-back books; the wider for rebacking books. This plastic-
on-cloth tape is washable, waterproof, and attractive in several colors. It letters easily with either ink or electric stylus.
In white, the 1" or 1 1/2" widths make excellent hinge material.
Early advertisements for self-stick tape described it as a
temporary or emergency medium for book repair, and it is
that, inasmuch as the tape can be applied temporarily while
the book has emergency use and then peeled off when the book
is taken out of circulation for rebinding; but it has also proved
to be an efficient and completely satisfactory product for use

in making permanent repairs. Apparently the producers and the jobbers did not at first realize the many advantages to be gained from the use of this product, not the least of which is the ease of application and the complete absence of need for a "drying" period.

Glue

Probably the first adhesive known and for years the only thing available for the purposes which it served for the most part satisfactorily. But since glue has an animal base it works best when heated, is sensitive to overheating, and is therefore difficult or at best requires a complicated process to use. And since it tends to crystallize with time it is less durable than some of the newer products which have been originated to replace it. Glue is still used by commercial binderies, by the binding departments of publishing houses, and by large libraries with binding departments in which commercial equipment has been installed. But since glue should be used only in a thermostatically controlled machine its use is more complicated, it is more expensive, no more efficient, and therefore less practical for use in the ordinary library than are any number of its present day substitutes.

Paper Tape

Gummed transparent paper tape. Comes only in 5/8" width and rolls of 225" length. Intended for the mending of torn book pages, magazines, sheet music, light weight paper maps, etc. Although this tape must be moistened, it is comparatively easy to use, and the current product is completely transparent, no longer yellowing with age as it did when first put on the market. Excluding the recently discovered plastic products which need no paper backing, this is the best thing available for page mending.

Masking tape. This is an adhesive paper tape for temporary use. Requires no moistening. Can be used to reenforce outside folds of pamphlets or to strengthen the backs, covers, or edges of paper-bound books. Is not waterproof, does not adhere permanently, and should not be used for other than emergency repairs.

BOOK FINISHING AND REPAIRING

Paste

Any of a variety of adhesives made from water and flour or
other starchy powders. Comes in liquid or semi-solid form and
must be thinned with water to the desirable consistency. Usually
white in color and marketed under such trade names as library
paste or runny paste or gaylo, this adhesive is traditionally
and probably almost universally used for pasting in book pockets, plates, and labels. Since paste is uncolored, it affords
transparency when used with transparent paper for mending
over printed pages, maps, etc. Due to the fact that paste is a
water-based adhesive, all paste-mended articles need to be
dried under pressure. Book covers that have been plated or
pocketed with pastes adhesives will warp or buckle severely
unless they are dried in presses or under heavy weights such
as bricks or building stone. Paste which has dried out may be
thinned and used, but care must be taken not to add too much
water and thus over-thin the paste and over-dampen the book

Plastics

Here we come to the most revolutionary of all adhesive
products. The extensive advertising of plastic adhesives and
the number of "how-to-use" articles appearing in the various
professional journals attest to the fact that these products are
making a place for themselves in the library field and have
rendered obsolete many of the materials used since book mending and repairing began. Plastic adhesives have been developed
in three forms: liquids, tapes, and sheets.

Liquid Plastics. These may be had from nearly all the
supply houses and are marketed under such trade names as
Bind-Art, Delkote, Norbond, Magic Mend, Glue-All, etc.
This product is packaged in 8 oz. and 32 oz. (economy size)
bottles and in an 8 oz. dispenser bottle. It has proved highly
successful when used for tipping in pages, replacing signatures,
or for reinforcing spines where the original glue is no longer
holding. It mends torn pages without the assistance of tape or
other reinforcement, requires almost no drying time and absolutely no mechanical assistance such as weights or presses.
Aside from the fact that this one product will do the work of

several of the older-type adhesives and is thus an economy factor, its greatest value lies in the convenience of its on-the-spot performance.

Plastic Tape. This is the same as the liquid product but thicker and extruded as a tape. Ideal for page-mending. It is pure film, requiring no cloth or paper backing; does not "bleed" or yellow with age. Comes rolled like ribbon with alternating strip of waxed paper which peels off or is stripped off as tape is used. It requires no moistening, is simply applied at desired location and pressed in place. Is not at present supplied by all houses but is available under the following trade names:

Demco-Seal

Two widths only, 1/2" or 3/4"; and in 1500" or 4500" lengths. This is clear, colorless, and almost invisible, providing immediate, inexpensive, and permanent repair for map faces, printed pages, magazine covers, etc. It does not yellow with age, has no glare, and does not obstruct readability because dull finish does not refract the light.

Desk dispensers are available for this product, a "featherweight" dispenser for the 1500" roll and a "heavy-duty" dispenser which will accommodate either size roll. The dispenser provides a certain element of convenience by automatically separating the film ribbon from the waxed paper interlayer.

Plastic-Kleer Tape

An invisible mending film tape designed particularly for page repair. It has a dull finish, is completely transparent, and allows easy reading of covered portions since it has no glare or shine. It does not bleed and will not shrink, grow sticky, or yellow with age.

Sheet Plastics. This is a plastic film available by the yard in a 12" width. It is essentially a foot-wide plastic tape, though it appears to be somewhat thinner and even more transparent than are the narrow tapes. This is used extensively in repairing worn or torn pages of large dictionaries, atlases, and other over-size volumes. One most useful purpose which it serves is preventing the first and last pages of large dictionaries from becoming "dog-eared." By laminating the first several and the last few pages of a new dictionary with this clear plastic film one can prevent for its lifetime those curled up corners that otherwise proceed page by page through any frequently used large volume. Sheet Plastic also prevents deterioration in wall maps, charts, posters, etc., and minimizes fold damage in pocket maps and similar folded papers.

BOOK BINDING AND REPAIRING

Adhesive Mending Tape

Thread-Drawn Tape. A simple form of hinge tape, several threads drawn from the center producing flexibility in bending with no loss of strength. This is a single strip binder and can be used only where a single hinge is required. This tape is carried by practically all supply houses and is available only in white. Stocked by most libraries in 1" by 12' rolls, it may be had also in rolls varying in width from 9/16" to 1 1/2" and up to 50 yards in length.

Perforated Adhesive Tape. Designed to serve precisely the same purpose, this perforated tape is more simply manufactured than the thread-drawn tape, is less flexible, a little less durable, and somewhat less expensive than the original thread-drawn product. It is available in only two widths, 3/4" and 1" and in rolls varying from 18 ft. to 50 yards in length.

Single Stitched Binder. This item may be had from any supply house and is sold under a variety of names: success binder, star binder, center stitched binder, single hinge, etc. It was originated for use in mending a book having one loose section but being in otherwise good condition. It must not, however, be used in a book slated for eventual rebinding, since it becomes too permanently fixed to be removed and is too heavy to permit the book's resewing. It is available in three weights and in a variety of widths and roll lengths, but is less in demand than before the introduction of the tape and liquid plastics. In fact its chief function at present and one it serves most efficiently is the binding or rebinding of single-signature books and pamphlets. For this purpose it is simple and quick to use, may be chosen in the thickness or width most suited to the material being bound or repaired, and will not greatly change the appearance and feel of the materials it is used on. Made in white and gray, but not in bright colors.

111

Double Stitched Binder. This binder has two parallel rows of stitching which run equidistant from the center of the tape, space between the rows graduating from 1/4" to 3" (in multiples of 1/8") and permitting the choice of a tape in very nearly the exact width of the book being worked on. This tape was designed for use in refastening the contents of a book to its covers and it has proved very adequate for this purpose. The lock-stitching prevents any raveling of the thread, the book has an open back when finished, the gray and white color combination can be matched to both end paper and flyleaf, and the over-all result is a strong, durable, and not unattractive repair job.

Cloth

Book cloth is the term applied to certain 36" to 38" materials sold by the yard and designed for use when a book is so badly worn or damaged that it must be completely recovered. It is available in a variety of colors and in rolls ranging from one to 12 yards in length. While this item was originally produced in order to have available a binding material that could be cut to any book-surface area, it may also be cut in strips for replacing spines that have been torn or otherwise damaged or for refinishing spines when books have been repaired with the double-stitched binders. Book cloth is produced in three weights and qualities:

Regular. A medium weight cloth, strong, easily manipulated, and relatively inexpensive, particularly when purchased in 12-yard lengths.

Waterproof. This is a pyroxylin coated cloth which is both verminproof and waterproof. It is easily cleanable but not so sleek as to be greasy to the touch; is pliable enough to be easily applied in spite of its waterproof coating; can be lettered or labeled; has no odor and does not blister or peel. This material is also available in all standard lengths and colors and is priced about 15 per cent higher than the uncoated cloth.

Imitation Leather. A finer quality of waterproofed cloth, artificially grained to simulate leather, and used principally for re-covering book spines. It is produced in the same colors as the regular book cloth, permitting the use of cloth covers and "leather" spine, if such combination is desired. Costs about a fourth more than the ungrained waterproofed product and about 65 per cent more than the waterproof cloths.

Equipment

Minimum essentials for simple hand binding and repairs would probably be:

Stapling Machine. Recommended purchase if library expects to process its magazines or has many thin books to restaple. This is a standardized product, supplied by several companies and under a variety of names, but fairly uniform in quality, style, and function. All makes include two plates which are interchangeable; a flat one for side stapling; and a wedge-shaped plate for saddle stapling. Priced between $25 and $30.

Note: My own experience has been that it is impractical for the ordinary library to attempt such extensive repairs as the entire re-covering of books. Considering as cost the time consumed in doing this work by hand, it is no more expensive to have the book repaired at a commercial bindery; and the bindery will certainly turn out a more tailored-looking and professional job than the most skilled librarian would probably be able to manage. I have also concluded that in many circumstances it might be more practical to use a plastic-backed cloth tape for the covering of book spines. This tape is considerably more expensive in item cost than would be, for instance, a pyroxylin coated cloth and adhesive. But its use involves considerably less time cost, for the book can be repaired immediately and at the point of intake, thus making unnecessary the retiring of the book to a place where space and time will be available for the use of cloth, scissors, adhesives, etc. The choice of methods here would depend a great deal on the library organization, of course. If patron use is so great as to leave no "stand-by" time at the charging desk, then it is less expensive to send damaged books to a repair room where materials and equipment are kept; but in those libraries where several minutes may elapse between the serving of one patron and another, the amount of staff time saved by enabling the charging-in clerk to make on-the-spot repairs will probably much more than cover the additional cost of the plastic products.

Sewing Clamp. This is a device for holding books or periodicals while drilling holes for sewing. Two types are available:

Wing Nut. This is a simple clamp, now available from supply houses but originally "home-made" by boring holes in the ends of two metal strips and inserting wing nuts to obtain pressure. The commercial product consists of two accurately machined pieces of iron with drill holes one inch apart and bolts adjustable up to 1 1/2 inch thickness. It is provided with two flanges for attaching to work table. This clamp may be had in two lengths, 13" and 18", and is priced under $10.00.

Single Crank. This type is somewhat more expensive (around $13.00 to $15.00) but is designed so that the back of the book lies perfectly flat irrespective of the creased hinge. It is a double-threaded, fast operating, single handle clamp made for cleaning, drilling, sewing, buffing, and lettering a book. The two swinging guide bars insure uniformity of drilling. This style clamp is slightly longer than the wing nut, is adjustable to a 2 1/2" thickness which, reversing the back section, may be increased to a capacity of 4".

Press. To insure against the warping and buckling of covers, one must dry under pressure any book which has been plated, pocketed, or repaired with paste or glue. Two types of press are available for this purpose and the choice will depend chiefly on the number of books to be processed each day.

Single Arm Press. The one-armed book-repair press will hold up to five books. It consists of a tripod base, a steel or iron vertical bar from 13 to 15 inches tall, six clamping boards about 7 x 12 inches in area, and an adjustable clamp. Books may be inserted without removal of the bar or handle and several hundred pounds of pressure may be applied simply by turning the wheel. The arm is adjustable, easily operated, and exerts an even pressure. These presses are priced at $10.00 or lower.

Framed Press. This type press will cost about three times as much as the single-arm, but it has double the capacity and will exert about seven times as much pressure (up to 5000 pounds). It is a metal frame 24" high by 15" wide with a rigid clamping bar which locks automatically at any desired position. The press boards are 15" by 7" in area, with slots to keep the boards centered in the uprights.

Paper Cutter. This piece of equipment consists of a straight steel blade or a cutting wheel held in alignment with a square "cutter-bed" of the same size. The surface of the bed is marked into half-inch squares to allow accuracy of measurements. Paper cutters are required by libraries for the cutting of end-papers, cardboards for book spines, mount boards for the reinforcing of magazines, etc. They may be purchased in 8, 10, 12, and 15 inch sizes and at a cost varying from $8.00 to $25.00.

Drill. A drill is needed for preparing magazines for multi-binders and for drilling through the holes in the sewing clamp. It is necessary to have more than one size of drill point, since a different size is required for books than for magazines, and a longer point for the thick book than is necessary for the thin.

Hand Drill. May be purchased from any library-supply house at from $2.00 to $3.00 (not including points which are around 25¢ to 35¢ each). The hand drill does a satisfactory job but not a very fast one, and in spite of sharp points and a specially designed handle, is tiring if used over a sustained period of time.

Electric Drill. Though not yet available from the supply houses, a quarter-inch electric drill is a most useful piece of book-mending equipment and one that will pay for itself in short order by the saving of time cost. It should be purchased with three attachments: wire wheel, grinding wheel, and buffer, and will cost from $10 to $20 for the drill, points, and attachments.

Lacquer and Shellac.

Either lacquer or shellac should be applied to book covers as a protective coating. Book covers so treated will have a hard, smooth, waterproof surface which can resist wear and soil and renders the book immune to water marks and to ink and other stains. Lacquers are somewhat less expensive than are shellacs, and are a little more easily applied. Lacquers will run about $1.25 a pint and shellacs about $1.40. Both are cheaper by the gallon. If both are stocked, care must be taken not to use the brushes interchangeably until they have been cleaned. If thinner must be used, equal caution must be observed; for lacquer has an oil base and must be thinned only with a special solvent designed for the purpose, while shellac has a resin base and is thinned with de-natured alcohol.

Binder's Board

Used only for cover boards when books are to be completely rebound. In my opinion impractical for a library to attempt this extensive repair unless it is fully equipped with commercial machinery.

24. MICROFILM IN THE HIGH SCHOOL LIBRARY

Raymond G. Erbes, Jr.

We at Reavis High School are now in our third year of using microfilm as a substitute for binding back numbers of periodicals and magazines. Because the results have been most gratifying in our situation, other high school libraries, similar to ours, may find the solution to many of their magazine and periodical storage problems answered by purchasing microfilmed copies of the year's issue of magazines.

Cost Factor. While the cost factor is the first item which leaps to the librarian's mind when microfilm is mentioned, a further, complete examination of all factors concerned might point out actual savings in the long run, coupled with many advantages and benefits.

System is Simple. The system used is simple. The library subscribes to the regular paper edition of a periodical which is regularly received. At the same time a subscription is also placed with the microfilm company for a microfilm copy, to be delivered at the end of the volume year. The cost of this microfilm is approximately the same as binding the material would cost.

The original paper copies of the periodical are used in the library unbound, until they wear out or are no longer useful — depending on the type of use, the subject, and space available. At that time the paper copies are disposed of and the microfilm is substituted.

MICROFILM IN THE HIGH SCHOOL LIBRARY

Just as all materials in the library require shelving or housing of some kind, microfilms are kept in a storage cabinet. It will also be necessary to have one or more microreaders to use for viewing the microfilms. These can be purchased from monies budgeted for school equipment. It is also important to point out that a microreader does not wear out and the upkeep is practically nil.

Research Interests Changing. More noticeable than ever in recent years is the heavy use made of the Readers' Guide in completing the junior and senior term papers. Many librarians, English teachers, and social studies teachers no doubt have also been aware of the change in topics selected for these minor dissertations or for speech work, etc. For example, it wasn't many years ago that students were picking such topics as "Medicine during the Civil War," "Witchcraft in Colonial Days," "The Arabian Horse and His Care"—mostly topics gleaned from books, encyclopedias, and other library materials.

Now, however, the trend seems to be toward such live, interesting topics as "Recent Satellite Launchings," "Latest Developments in Mental Care," "Recent Cancer Treatments," "Juvenile Delinquency," etc. —most of which must be gathered from recent periodicals and magazines. Very often we find that most or all of the reference books have very little information on the chosen topic — even though an ample budget provides for many recent book selections.

Since the answer seems to be the Readers' Guide and recent magazines and periodicals, some method of preserving these references must be found. Hence, we are perhaps justified in revising our budget upward for these tools in order to provide sufficient recent material. It is certain that in a world that changes greatly from hour to hour, we cannot depend solely on publications in book form that many times are obsolete by the time they roll off the presses.

Advantages of Microfilm Listed. A few facts concerning our school situation might be pointed out. We have an enrollment of 1,200, hardly any public library facilities, an interested faculty, an enlightened administration, and an ample budget. The advantages listed here are ones that we have found to be helpful at Reavis High School.

1. Microfilm solves the magazine storage problem. We had

previously filled a room with magazines — some bound, most unbound. With continual use, the room resembled something a cyclone had struck. Also, another room would have had to be taken over if we were to continue this method. With microfilm, yearly volumes may be stored in one drawer of a cabinet. However, low-priced cardboard boxes for sale by library supply houses have proven to be just as satisfactory and safe as the more expensive metal microfilm cabinets.

2. Microfilm relieves the librarian from worry regarding current issues which may be lost or damaged in circulation. If one copy is lost or damaged, it will not affect the completed volume which is purchased on microfilm at the end of the year. Current magazines become more expendable.

3. Pictures, articles, etc., may be clipped from the paper issues after the microfilm copy is on file in the library. These are appreciated by various departments in the school. In some instances, we give the entire year of paper issues to a department for its files.

4. By the use of microfilm and microreaders, students are taught another library tool which may prove useful in college or later life. At present we find that five microreaders have proven ample for our student body. Because the original paper copies are kept for a year or two, microreaders are used only for references older than this. Having too few microreaders, however, would be similar to having an excellent reference section which only one or two people could use at one time.

5. Many of our gadget-minded students find use of the Readers' Guide more enjoyable knowing that it involves finding the reference by using a microreader. The use of the microreader is taught along with the use of Readers' Guide, and we have found that even the somewhat retarded students have no trouble in using it correctly. The mechanics of the machine are extremely simple, and to date we have had no film ruined.

6. Malicious clipping of bound volumes or borrowing of volumes without benefit of signing-out procedures has been practically eliminated. And since none of our students possesses a microreader at home, a motive for taking microfilm is non-existent.

There are of course some disadvantages to the use of

microfilms, an obvious one being that materials do not circulate.
However, the current issues are available for circulation up to
a year or two — depending on space available. Many factors
should be considered before a school library decides to purchase microfilms. Among these are the budget, school enrollment, curriculum, use made of the library, bound volumes
available in public library or other nearby agencies, storage
space available, etc. We have found it more than satisfactory
at Reavis. However, depending on many of the factors listed
above, not all schools may wish to or be able to initiate a program such as this. Nevertheless, I believe it is important to
re-emphasize that when considering the purchase of microfilms
a school librarian consider not only the expense of purchase,
but also the long-range saving of money, time, and patience in
using this modern, practical way to house back numbers of
magazines and periodicals.

25. LETTERING WITHOUT PAIN

If you're like many librarians, you weren't trained as an
artist, you can't letter worth a hoot, and you dread exhibit
making because here your most conspicuous work shows you
at your least professional.

If this describes you, take heart. Many of JrL's subscriber-
contributors who sent in suggestions on exhibits faced the same
problem, but one way or another they freed themselves from
the frustration of continually attempting more than they could
do well.

Perhaps one of their solutions will work for you.

If you've always been "all thumbs" then you will probably
favor one of the administrative or mechanical solutions. If you
like to work visually, but wish you did it better, perhaps some
of the "tips from a professional sign writer" will interest you.
All in all, the suggestions range from planning so that you need
no lettering to employing a full-time staff display specialist,

and include using ready-made poster material, using sets of plastic or paper letters, relying on the school print shop or art department, or involving talented parents of pupils.

"Often we use no lettering. . ."

This approach, reported by Eulalie Steinmetz Ross of the Cincinnati Public Library, is worth thinking about. She writes: "We use the books themselves a great deal: jacketed, unjacketed, open to illustrations, open to end papers. We try to group the books imaginatively (sometimes with a few flowers or greens) so that frequently no sign or poster is necessary to indicate what the display is about."

One well-known strip cartoon is wordless, yet gets its m aning across. Often the central idea of a display can be conveyed by an object (autumn leaves, sports equipment, etc.) even better than in words. Books, after all, have attention value in themselves, and where detailed information must supplement the major display elements, it can sometimes simply be merely typed on colorful cards or arrows.

"Try just writing what you want to say. . ."

You chalk an announcement on the blackboard without getting self-conscious. Why not be as simple and direct about headlining your displays? This suggestion comes from Alice B. Cushman of the Fitchburg, Mass., Youth Library. For variety you can try writing with pastel chalks or charcoal sticks or a brush on a variety of surfaces. Handwriting that looks spindly in ordinary chalk often looks quite distinguished when done with a broad charcoal stick. Just take the precaution of ruling in guide lines to keep your lines straight and even — the guide lines can be nearly invisible or can even be left boldly showing as a design element.

Save ready-made materials

You won't need to do so much lettering of your own if you keep a careful lookout for ready-made material. The display material offered by the Children's Book Council, by the New York Times and Herald-Tribune, by Libri-Posters, by Library Products, Inc., by the publishers can be adapted to many uses, especially if you are systematic about filing it away by subject.

120

LETTERING WITHOUT PAIN

A nearby bookseller, even if he doesn't have your business, may be glad to give you the publishers' displays he can't use himself or has already used. In fact, any retailer will gladly give you valuable used or surplus display material you can hoard against future needs.

Ask also in the advertising departments of newspaper or department stores for any clip books and mat services they are through with. These contain timely cartoons, headlines, and layout suggestions for all-purpose use.

Signs of the work-a-day, question-answering kind such as "Information," "Return Desk," "New Books," "Poetry," and printed charts explaining the arrangement of the card catalog and shelves can be purchased from the library suppliers — Demco, Gaylord, Remington Rand, and Bro-Dart.

Where time is money, save both with ready-made letters

A good collection of ready-made letters may require a bit of an investment, but it doesn't have to save much of your time to pay for itself. Saving your own time for more professional work than lettering may be a greater service to the library than trying to stay within a budget that doesn't give you the time saving aids you need.

Roughly in order of cost are the white, three-dimensional Mitten's Display Letters, Graforel cut-out, gummed cork letters (used plain or painted), felt letters, paper letters, and Stenso lettering guides.

Helen S. Henderson of Niagara Falls, N.Y., writes, "Mitten's Letters are the greatest time saver of all, worth any price."

Lucile Hatch of Caspar W. Sharples Junior High in Seattle writes: "The biggest help I have found in preparing bulletin boards is the use of alphabets that my art department has made and that I have made. When I want a sign made, I simply give a student the alphabet I wish her to use, indicate the colors of paper I want used, and she can make the needed letters by tracing them. I have a number of these alphabets and would be happy to share them with others. They are easy to use, permit variety and flexibility, can be any size or design or style, and any color. As the letters are individual, they can be pinned or stapled on the board or can be pasted to a poster. I have some 15 or 20 different sets and hope to add to them each year. Each alphabet is in an envelope which has its own pocket and card. Any student or teacher may check out an alphabet like a book or magazine.

Margaret Griffin, librarian of the University School at Indiana University, recommends a book entitled "Free-hand Letter Cutting," by Cornelia Carter, 1944, available from the author at Lawrenceville, Illinois.

For sheer beauty of letters it is hard to beat Mitten's three-dimensional white Display Letters that can be used in so many ways for permanent or changing signs. If the investment required to get a really good kit of various sizes has stopped you, note that you can, nevertheless, order the letters required for a specific sign without buying entire fonts, and the rates are quite reasonable.

Interesting reverse effects are possible with cut-out letters and spray paint — put down the letters temporarily, spray around them, and peel them off again. While the spray is still wet you can sprinkle on metallic glitter if you like.

Small signs that would not be visible enough if typed can be traced from guide templates with the aid of Leroy and Wrico lettering sets as used by draftsmen, priced from about $7.50 a set. Mimeographed lettering guides can also be pressed into service.

Co-operating on lettering problems

Lettering problems are probably also confronting other departments and organizations. They may be able to help you solve yours and vice versa. Where do they turn when they need lettering? Should you perhaps all join together to make one investment in lettering equipment serve everybody? Or would you be allowed the occasional use of equipment owned by some large local retailer?

Where its purchase can be justified, the Embosograf is a very useful machine. It can turn out neat signs in all color combinations very quickly, yet uses no messy ink. $215 buys one that can make signs up to 4 x 10 inches. Larger models are available at $480 and $670.

One tool that perhaps isn't as well known as it should be outside the display business is the Cut-All. This handles like an electric iron and does the work of a jigsaw. In other words, it is a motorized electric iron with a shallow cutting knife in its nose, and if you turn it on and push it across a piece of cardboard or masonite it will cut through along any line you choose to follow. With proper adjustment of the knife it won't cut through more than you want to cut and won't harm the under surface. With it you can with ease cut out all kinds of useful shapes including outline letters. It's a handy thing to have access to the Cut-All whether lodged in the art department, woodworking shop, or elsewhere.

Or learn to letter . . . it may be easier than you think
    JrL's editors interviewed one professional sign writer to find out what he thought were the usual mistakes of unlettered would-be-letterers. Here is what he said.
    Amateur signs suffer from two main faults. In the first place they lack a sense of proportion as to time values. An amateur may struggle half a day to make a far less attractive sign than a sign writer could dash off in a few minutes. A question for administrators is whether it makes sense for a librarian to put in eight or ten dollars worth of time to make a sign that could be bought in a sign shop for two dollars.
    Let's say, however, that you do want to make your own signs, perhaps because there's no sign writer near you (although don't be too sure about that, there are sign writers in the smallest places because merchants have to get their signs somewhere), or because you like to, or because you can involve students interested in having this practice in a new craft.
    In this case at least do not handicap yourself or your helpers by trying to work with inadequate equipment. Sometimes an amateurish sign is amateurish simply because nothing better could have been done with the materials that were used. If you're going to make signs at all you might as well try to make professional looking ones, and if you're going to make professional looking ones you had best take advantage of every trick and technique of the professional.
    Whatever values are expected from permitting students to make signs, won't these values be enhanced by permitting them to do it with professional lines? There isn't much to be gained by teaching a student to do anything in an amateurish manner.

LETTERING WITHOUT PAIN

What are the tricks of the professional? Well, let's first look at the marks of the amateur. In the first place, the amateur often starts out with black lettering on white cardboard. Your professional will think first of using colored letters perhaps on colored sign board.

The amateur uses capital letters throughout his signs. Not only is this monotonous but capitals are not as legible as upper and lower case. Neither are they as compact. If you've been using all caps, switch most of your words to small letters and note the improvement.

The next thing the amateur does is to start right in on his final sign without a preliminary sketch. If he makes a sketch at all, he will use an ordinary lead pencil which will fail utterly to give him the weight and feel of the letters whose space requirements he is trying to judge.

The professional will always rough in a sign before setting out to finish it, a practice which only takes a minute or two since he makes no attempt to true up each letter. What he does do is use a writing tool that will give him, without extra effort, the width of stroke he is after. He may use a broad crayon, a graphite stick, a pair of pencils held together with an elastic, or (on scrap paper) the same pen or brush he will use for the finished lettering.

Even where your amateur has made a little sketch he will not make it as useful as he should. He will spend too much time on individual letters and too little time on the overall spacing and the squareness of the lines. He will make all his words the same size instead of featuring a key word or phrase. He will fail to notice that his margins are skimpy and his letters spindly. He will laboriously expand a short line until it matches a longer one, little realizing that the sign would gain both grace and freedom if each line is given its due. He spreads his letters too far apart and tends to use larger lettering than the circumstances require.

The professional will use a T-square as a matter of course and automatically get consistently parallel lines without effort, or question. His sketch is aimed at studying the placement of words, not the contours of letters. It has become instinct with him to allow greater margins around the edge of a sign than he is going to use between words or lines.

LETTERING WITHOUT PAIN

When it comes to the actual lettering the amateur is likely to try to construct his lettering in outline and then fill it in. Even if he uses a broad point writing tool of some kind, the chances are he'll make taller letters than look right with a tool of that particular breadth, and he'll either get spindly letters or he'll have to make double strokes to get the heavy lines. The professional selects at the outset a writing tool of the right width for the letters he's going to use and he usually selects one that will give him his choice of thick and thin lines from the same tip to give the characters shape.

The amateur imagines that sans serif letters are the easiest and struggles to keep them from looking too wiggly. The professional has long since learned to make clean looking sans serif letters, but he knows that thick-and-thin letters are far easier and usually more attractive and tends to favor them. They flow more automatically from his pen or brush than do square serif letters. True, you have to know where the thick and thin strokes go, but it is astonishing how quickly you pick this up. A chisel shaped pen or brush properly handled almost forms the letters for you. For quick-and-easy lettering, the professional also favors the powerfully uneven lettering styles used in much advertising.

The amateur makes too much use of the Speedball pen and too little use of charcoal, pastels, or brush. If he uses a brush it's likely to be the wrong one, namely a pointed brush when he should have a chisel point. He tends to think in terms of working with ink, when another medium will better serve his purpose.

The professional prefers show card color as flowing more readily, covering more perfectly and being more colorful. He knows you can put show card color over another color and have no show-through which is far from true with colored inks.

Finally the amateur is always working on the wrong surfaces. He uses paper when he should be using Bristol board. He uses stationery sizes when he should be using show card sizes. He uses white when he should be using tinted stocks, and he uses card board stock when he should be using masonite. He never builds up even a modest supply of the materials he'll need to work with, and he has no facilities for cutting them easily.

His larger displays keep slumping down because it doesn't

occur to him to enlist the aid of the proprietor of the nearest
home workshop to cut out for him on the power saw the simple
structural numbers that give rigidity to a standing display.

26. WHY COUNT THE CIRCULATION?

Sylvia Ziskind

Do you count your circulation every day? I do. And do you
record it on a printed slip made for the purpose by one of the
library supply houses? I do. Do you file it away and keep it
forever? Well — not quite forever. Do you send it to your principal in a monthly or an annual report? I do. Do you compare
it with last year's circulation figures or the year before, or
with other schools' circulation? I do. Do you ever think it's a
waste of time and a pointless routine? I do.

I wonder sometimes why we school librarians are so dili-
gent about counting the circulation, the number of students who
use the library, or the classes that come to the library. Perhaps it is because those are the tangibles and are most easily
counted. The intangible elements in the library, the unmeas-
ureable factors, cannot be tabulated or set down in round numbers but they are no less significant for their seeming obscurity.

A student taking a book out of the library may carry it as
far as his locker and leave it there for two weeks. Or he may
take it home where the book is sometimes read not only by him,
but by other members of his family. Each book gets one count
on the circulation sheet and each count means something entirely different.

We do not count the hundreds of times the young people
pore over the encyclopedias, the dictionaries, the magazines,
or pamphlets. We don't count the students who stay as late in
the afternoons as the library is open because they want to read
or study, nor the boys who are at the door five minutes before
eight waiting to get into the library to read.

WHY COUNT THE CIRCULATION?

We cannot measure the growth and development of the girl who has read girl stories and dog stories and then discovers a book like Sarah by Marguerite Bro or Hawthorne's Scarlet Letter and stretches her mental and emotional capacities to absorb the more mature literary form. Nor can we measure the miracle that takes place in a boy's heart and mind when he discovers that Shakespeare's Midsummer Night's Dream is a rollicking comedy and not just the dull stuff he had always supposed it to be.

Circulation figures are not only inadequate as a means of measuring the qualitative use of the library, but are often misleading as quantitative guides as well.

I visited three school districts in Los Angeles County recently and I found different policies and practices regarding circulation statistics in each district. Indeed, in each instance there were differences among schools in the same district.

In the first district, the school library circulated most books for a period of two weeks and restricted some to overnight use only. Each student was limited to two items at a time, two books, one magazine and one book, or two magazines, or any other combination of two. All materials were renewable. Everything that circulated to students, regardless of the length of loan, type of material — whether book, magazine, or pamphlet — was counted in the grand total of circulation. Materials circulated to teachers, however, were not counted at all.

The second school district did not distinguish between student and teacher borrowers, but counted the circulation of books only and omitted the count of magazines and pamphlets. Omitted also were any overnight books such as encyclopedias or special loan books. This district followed a different policy for its new school libraries, of which there were three in the last few years. Because of an inadequate collection, and because it was desirable to have as many books as possible on the shelves during the school day, all books were circulated for overnight use only and all of these were counted as part of the total circulation. As the first year progressed, the seniors were permitted to keep one book out for one week, and toward the end of the first year, the juniors were also allowed to keep a book out for one week. Because of these restrictions, the circulation figures in one of the new schools had quite a different significance from

127

the figures in one of the old established schools in the same district.

When I visited a school library in a third district, I found that practically everything in the library was permitted to circulate and everything that went out, even for one period, was counted. Students were restricted to one book of fiction at a time but nonfiction books were not limited. In this library, all books, except reference books, were lent for one month and were not renewable. All reference books with the exception of a few very costly or irreplaceable books were allowed to circulate from one school day to the next.

All the variable factors — the length of loan, the possibility of renewal, the type of material that is counted, the number of books permitted at a time to each borrower, teacher or student use of material, the size of the collection, the size and age of the school — all of these must be considered and understood before any appreciation of circulation figures can be realized. Unless an explanation accompanies circulation reports, or all schools adopt the same practices in their libraries, it is of little value to use circulation statistics as a quantitative or qualitative measure of the library's service.

27. STUDENT STAFF ASSISTANTS

Lois E. Wrisley

Organized or unorganized student library assistants will carry with them a basic philosophy or purpose. The primary objective is to improve the library service of the school by undertaking the simple routine duties in order to free the librarian for more professional work. When students are permitted to assist in the operation of a library they soon feel that it belongs to them as well as to the librarian. The feeling of ownership helps to sponsor a greater interest among students in the use of books and library service. This feeling of ownership fortunately spreads to the entire student body, and the keen interest and enthusiasm of the assistants reaches out to stimulate reading interests of others.

By striving to achieve the aims of their philosophy, student library assistants serve as one of the best public relations agencies that the school can have. Not only are they constantly advertising the library to their fellow students, but this advertisement soon reaches the home and then on out into the community until, unknown to us, its influence reaches the public libraries of the community.

No librarian can deny that the average school library would not function as smoothly or as efficiently without student cooperation. Their helping hand lessens the routine load of the librarian and tends to balance her work scales by adding more time to her professional services. The students' strong enthusiasm helps to give life to what might easily become a storehouse of books. They tend to add new ideas and understanding to the library philosophy and principles of operation.

The student assistant may appear to give her all to the library but she in return receives many things of value. Working as an assistant in a library serves as prevocational training for two different fields of work. As exploratory experience for those expecting later to study for the library profession, it is one of the chief objectives of the librarian. It is also a tryout for those showing ability along the clerical lines by developing manual dexterity and accuracy in the routine work.

No individual can work with and handle books, periodicals, and other materials, as the student assistant must, without becoming acquainted with them and their uses. Not only is she learning about the materials available, but also of the services a library has to offer. These may be most valuable for her if she is preparing for advance study in a college or university.

The student assistant is performing a civic duty to her school and community by offering her services. Above all, the library is teaching her responsibility, courtesy, service, and dependability. To be a student librarian is a privilege.

Many librarians feel that an organized club of library assistants is necessary for smooth operation of the program. Our library assistants gave an emphatic "no" to this suggestion. Even though there is no formal organization and all students come to the library on a voluntary basis, some standard for their selection must be had. That the student volunteers his services to the library is evidence of his keen interest in what it has to offer. One of the basic philosophies of the school is scholastic achievement to the best of the students' ability. In compliance with this philosophy, library assistants must maintain a satisfactory scholastic level or they may be asked to discontinue work in the library either temporarily or permanently. It is inconceivable the amount of responsibility which is placed on a student assistant. Therefore high personal qualifications in the line of citizenship are a must. Assistants must be ever willing to take directions and follow them. These directions may come from the librarian or another member of the faculty staff or supervisor. Above all they must be able to receive undue criticism, for when student assistants are attempting a task which is generally performed by a professional, they are naturally not as efficient at it. This often raises criticism from their fellow classmates, who for a brief moment forget the position which the library assistants hold.

After having selected the library assistants with the above qualifications and aims of philosophy, I have found the following method of scheduling work to be the most efficient and one which has received comment from the students themselves:

Each assistant is given a mail box in the workroom. This mailbox consists of a book pocket secured to the workroom bulletin board with the individual's name and work periods typed on it.

The following list of duties is typed on 3"x5" cards, i.e., one duty per card, with page references to the library manual of procedures. For the more common duties such as charging materials, verifying and shelving materials, more than one card has been made.

List of duties performed by the student assistants:

Circulation work:

    Charging materials
    Slipping books
    Verifying and shelving materials
    Reading shelves

STUDENT STAFF ASSISTANTS

Sending daily overdues
Sending second notices
Messenger notices
Clipping
Mending
Special work.

Special Work:

Collating
Pasting in pockets and date-due slips
Stamping new books
Shellacking books.

Each day I drop into the individual mail boxes the card or cards indicating those duties which I wish the student to perform during his scheduled period of work.

When the task has been completed or at the end of his work period the student records on his monthly work calendar beneath the correct date those tasks which he has successfully completed. All cards from his box are then put into a general deposit box to be used again when assigning.

I use the student's individual work calendar as a guide when assigning duties in order to give them a variety.

Having used the above method of scheduling student assistants for a year now, I would not go back to the older paper chart methods. Secondly, I find it very easy to revise the work schedule should I be called from the library for a lengthy period of time, as is often the case.

28. AN ORGANIZED CLUB OF STUDENT LIBRARY ASSISTANTS

Roy D. Baker

While in summer school recently, I had a quiet conversation with the head librarian of the university. I told him how enthusiastic youngsters are to give of themselves in serving others. Specifically I mentioned one freshman girl who comes to the library and asks to work every time she has a few minutes of free time.

Every day after school she will work one or two hours before going home, and one holiday she came to the library and worked seven hours with only a short break for lunch. He looked at me quite seriously, smiled, and in his quiet way said, "Yes, you are taking advantage of her."

Whoa! I was taken aback. Taking advantage of her? I do not recall my hesitant reply but I do know I gave much thought to the sage old gentleman's words of wisdom.

Yes, I must agree, we as school librarians are taking advantage of some of our more promising youth. Our administrators, likewise, are taking advantage of our sympathetic youngsters who are willing and want to serve. They may be doing so by way of condoning the practice of the librarian, but oftentimes it is the librarian who condones the philosophy of the principal who stretches the budget by way of recruiting student labor.

Sometimes, and frequently, it is a matter of needing a "home" for the mischievous boy who has been dropped from a class and needs to be placed. When that happens it is to the library, always in need of help, that he turns for assistance.

An organized library club with established prerequisites for admittance would do much to discourage and control such a practice. In systems where the practice is already imbedded in the minds of the administration, an active library club would do much to abate it; the verdant environment, that for so long has supported it, will no longer exist.

The library club is an organization of student assistants who work in a school library. The movement began as a local

132

project organized, no doubt, as a step toward recognition; recognition for the student assistant and greater recognition for the library as an integral part of the school system.

The movement probably had its beginning during World War II when students were restless and were overly sympathetic and anxious to serve. The harried librarian, short of clerical assistance, might have been equally as anxious to have them assist. Immediately after the war it was well established. As early as 1951, in Florida, where the spark of organization flamed brightly, 69 per cent of all secondary schools had library clubs.[1]

The purpose of the library club is one of many values. Uppermost in importance is an effort through an educative process to better train library assistants for their job and acquaint them with librarianship as a profession while providing a means of bringing the library and its program closer to the student body, the classroom, and the faculty.

Mary Peacock Douglas, in her widely read "Teacher-Librarian's Handbook," lists three purposes of the library club. They are: (1) To sponsor a greater interest among the students in the use of books and library service; (2) To stimulate reading interests; and (3) To improve the library service of the school.[2]

The present practice of enrolling students for practical work in the library is largely just that. It is restrictive. Not restrictive as to who will or will not work in the library but restrictive as to the many benefits and values that are associated with the privilege; and it should be a privilege to be associated with the library and its program.

As an unorganized body, the assistants are unrecognized. They report for work, do their various jobs and hurriedly leave for the next class when the bell rings. Unless a fellow-student or faculty member happens to drop in while a particular student is there they may go through a semester and not realize that Bob or Joanne is helping to operate the library.

And too many times they react with surprise when they do make the discovery for they know Bob as being a model student and wonder why he was "placed" there. They have learned from too many instances of disciplinary action that students are often dropped from other classes and are channeled through the principal's office to the library.

The library should not and must not be manned with

"delinquents." The librarian is not trained in the duties of a truant officer and probably is not too familiar with the penal code. The impression that library assistants are sent there as a corrective measure must not be allowed to permeate the thinking of the school.

Aside from the possible misunderstandings of their motives for working in the library, students miss out on many values that come only from identification with a group.

There are social values, physical and psychological values, and citizenship values that may be lost for lack of opportunities to meet together with their peers and discuss interests they hold in common. Other values such as vocational exploration and personal emulation are limited in that they lack the fertile environment necessary for growth and development.

An organized program for student assistants with prerequisites of scholastic and citizenship standards will do much to correct prevailing beliefs derogatory of the library and remove any stigma that may now be associated with the program of assistance. It need not mean, however, that all "displaced" students are rebuffed by the librarian when they are sincere in asking to be given a chance to defend their honor and prove their worth.

In my particular school the dean of girls — and counselor of boys — cooperates beautifully with the librarian when she proposes assigning a student to the library. She counsels the boy — and nearly always it is a boy — on the honor of being associated with the library. She explains that he will be on probation, that she will be following his progress, and that he may be dropped at the discretion of the librarian. The dean sends him to the librarian for an interview where a common ground of understanding is established and his request is approved or rejected. Nearly always it is accepted. Before the librarian meets the student the dean has contacted him and briefed him on the case and he is ready for the interview with a knowledge of the problem.

Frequently, at the least suspected times, the dean asks, "How is John doing?" Then she may say, "Well, don't put up with any of his nonsense. He knows what is expected of him and I want to know about it if he doesn't cooperate."

Or, as often as not, she follows her inquiry with the com-

ment: "He is a good 'duck'; he just needs a little help in growing up." And she is right. In four years I have dropped two students from the library and they were handicapped in other ways
before they started. It was from the goodness of our hearts
that we let them matriculate at all.

In the preparation of a constitution for a library club I
would propose there be two classifications of standards determining the acceptance or rejection of requests for membership.
One would be full acceptance without reservations; the other
would be limited acceptance with a probationary period of one
quarter. At the end of that "proving" period John would be pro-
moted to full rights or would be dropped completely. There
would be no provisions for an in between or third classification.

Other advantages of an organized program are social,
academic, and guidance. Organized as a recognized group,
with student council sanction, social functions would be scheduled as often as once each month. Early in the first quarter
of the year an informal twenty-minute tea might be given for
the faculty.

The tea would be optional, but the student council might
well be invited. The purpose would be to acquaint the faculty
with the student assistants. Perhaps new faculty members
would want further orientation of the library and its collection
of materials.

The merits of such an informal gathering are obvious. The
groundwork would be laid for a year of good workable relationship between the library and the faculty; the liaison influence
of the student assistants would have begun.

Informal staff meetings conducted as a social hour could
be scheduled monthly or as often as needed. An open discussion
of ideas and suggestions could be held where projects and objectives might be worked out democratically. Group guidance
could be interjected by the librarian without it being obvious.

Individual needs, academically, vocationally, and socially,
could be spotted by the librarian and noted for a private conference at a later date. There are innumerable possibilities
relative to guidance that might spring from these informal
social gatherings.

At least once a year an "outside" activity should be planned.
It may be a "dutch" dinner party, a theatre party to see a play,

or one of several things with educative value. A second and more formal faculty tea might be given at Christmas time or near the end of the year with a few mothers invited to assist as hostesses.

It has been a practice of many school librarians throughout the country to give teas with representative community participation and their value as a means of building good will and library-school-community relations is recognized.

Activities within the school of educative value are assemblies dramatizing library work as carried on by the club and programs advancing the services of the library. Others, extending into the community, are contributions to P.T.A. programs.

One program near the beginning of the year could explain the purpose of the club and outline the year's program. Another near the end of the year, could give a résumé of what had been accomplished with emphasis being placed on the state convention and the benefits derived from it. The parents would welcome such a report and it, too, would contribute to library-community relations.

These are but a few of the possibilities that can be adapted to fit individual situations. One will need to be selective with emphasis being placed on the activities that contribute most to the fulfillment of the club's purpose.

The disadvantages of a library club are so far overshadowed by the many advantages they are negligible. To say that the sponsorship will make demands on the librarian is an understatement. It will, but the improvement in the performance of routines will more than compensate for it.

Supervision will be simplified as the spirit of oneness pervades the group to be reflected in the productivity of each assistant. The librarian will be out of the library for one or two days while attending the state convention but from it he, too, will derive help and benefits of lasting value.

There will be demands on finances required to support the program but that need not be too great an obstacle. There are many programs of service the club can conduct that will earn money throughout the school year.

Some projects are selling book covers, sponsoring automatic vending machines for pens and pencils, and operating a book-ordering service for students and faculty with the discount profits reverting to the club. Many of the expenses for local activities will be borne by the students themselves.

The organization should begin simply and remain simple for the first semester or year. Do not discourage the inexperienced officers and the supporting members with unnecessary parliamentary procedure at the risk of seeing the club bog down in routine that may jeopardize its chances for survival.

The librarian-sponsor will be familiar with the mechanics of organization. With the support of the administration and student council and the cooperation of the deans and counselors a new club — the Library Club — can be launched to become one of the more democratic and popular clubs on a high school campus.

The crowning event of the year will be attendance of the district meetings and state convention. Several states are organized to that extent with stimulating programs provided for the student library assistants.[3]

Conventions are generally held in a college or university town and many times on the campuses themselves. Special speakers are provided, tours of local libraries and other places of educational interest are organized with every effort being made to introduce the aspiring librarians to the many facets of librarianship.

The benefits of stimulation to be obtained from these experiences are in themselves worth all the efforts put forth for organization.

29. TRAINING CIRCULATION ASSISTANTS

I. T. Littleton

The Circulation Department of the University of North Carolina Library has a problem that is common among a number of circulation departments. It must teach part-time assistants, usually students with no previous library training or experience, to page books, shelve, charge out materials to readers, answer routine questions about the Library, and, at the same time, provide prompt and efficient service to Library users.

Five to ten new part-time assistants are employed at the beginning of each fall session, and several at various other times during the year to replace a small number who always resign. These workers must be integrated into the organization rapidly so that efficient service to readers will not be interrupted. Training must be systematic and complete; it must be done in a short period of time; and new assistants, and especially the supervisors who train them, cannot be spared from their jobs during the training period. Possibly the turnover could be lessened if assistants could be hired for full-time work, but some libraries are not located in communities from which they can draw personnel for full-time work of this type.[1] The University of North Carolina happens to be one of them.

Part-time assistants are supervised by two professional librarians and three non-professional, full-time staff members who have had one or more years of library experience. The major part of the training is done by the professional librarians in the department, but some of it must necessarily be done by the sub-professional supervisors.

The best planned training program can fail if the trainers cannot teach effectively. Supervisors must be chosen carefully. The non-professional supervisors are usually students who have served for one or more years as undergraduate, part-time assistants in the department. They are appointed on the basis of their knowledge of the job, their dependability and intelligence,

138

as well as their capacity for leadership. They carefully follow a planned training schedule and observe the principles outlined below.

To insure training that is complete and systematic, a list of all the routines and topics a new assistant must know was prepared. This schedule is really an analysis of the job into its units and consists of forty detailed procedures and topics the trainee must learn.

When a new worker is employed, a supervisor teaches him each of these by showing and explaining to him each step and by letting him perform each routine under supervision. As a step is completed, the instructor writes his initials opposite its description on the Training Schedule, to indicate that that phase has been completed. The supervisors, then, are assured that the steps have been taught in a logical order. Any staff member in the department, by consulting an assistant's schedule, can determine the progress of his training. This enables one instructor to begin where another stopped, if work schedules make this necessary.

The first phase of the program is orientation. Its goals are not to teach routines, but to create attitudes and to impart information about general policies.[2] The major part of the orientation is accomplished by a conference with the Head of the Department. Four topics are discussed.

(1) Purpose of the Department. The Head of the Department stresses the importance of the public relations and service functions of the department, emphasizing that public opinion of the Library rests, to a large degree, upon the efficiency and courtesy of attendants at public service desks. By stressing the importance of the department's function, he tries to make the new employee feel that his job is important.

(2) Relationship of the Job to Other Jobs in the Department. The duties and responsibilities of each staff member, as well as those of the new employee, are outlined. He is told to whom he is responsible and to whom he should direct questions about policies and procedures.

(3) The Relationship of the Department to Other Departments in the Library. The functions of the other departments and reading rooms in the Library, as well as the types of materials and services of each, are explained. The new assistant

must learn when and how to direct readers to every other department.

(4) General Library and Circulation Department Policies. The Department Head explains certain general policies to the new worker. Some of these are: the time and length of breaks or rest periods, the Library's method of payment, the rate of pay, and the conduct and deportment expected of him.

After introducing the new man to all the full-time staff members in the department, the Department Head assigns him to a supervisor, who takes him on a tour of other Library Departments.

The Circulation Assistant does not need to know detailed classification theory, but he should be taught the basic principles of the Library's classification system so that he can shelve correctly and locate books rapidly. This is done in five simple steps:

(1) He reads about the Dewey Decimal Classification in Flexner's Making Books Work, written for the non-librarian; (2) the Supervisor explains the reasons for classifying books by a decimal system; (3) the meaning of each digit and letter in sample Dewey and Cutter numbers are explained so that he will understand the meaning of call numbers; (4) the principles of decimal arrangement are pointed out, with emphasis on the fact that numbers are arranged decimally, and not serially.

The last step is really a test of how well the assistant has learned these principles. He is given a group of cards with sample call numbers typed on them. He arranges them by number. The supervisor then examines the order of the cards and shows the assistant his errors.

Instruction in the use of the Library's catalogs is simple, uncomplicated by theory. It is designed merely to help him locate materials. He is taught four items about them: (1) the types of entries, (2) the filing order, (3) location guides and symbols which appear on the catalog cards, and (4) the procedure the reader follows to secure books.

Learning to shelve[3] follows naturally after the assistant is able to arrange call numbers. The first step is general stack orientation, and such items as bookstack terminology, the use of level and range guides, and directional orientation are included.

TRAINING CIRCULATION ASSISTANTS

Before permitting the new man to shelve alone, the supervisor demonstrates proper shelving techniques. Accuracy, rather than speed, is emphasized. With practice, the average assistant will gradually gain speed, without sacrificing accuracy. Shifting and straightening books are also included in shelf training.

The new worker shelves several truck loads of books under supervision before he does so alone. His accuracy is then tested. He places each book on its fore edge so that an experienced shelver can locate it. His errors are pointed out to him and this procedure is repeated until complete accuracy is assured. Assistants are assigned stack duty for as long as possible before going to the Main Circulation Desk to learn routines. Familiarity with the bookstack prepares him for learning how to locate books for readers.

Training at the desk includes learning the routines for locating, charging, carding, holding, and calling in books, as well as information regarding fines, stack permits, and special materials, such as government publications, newspapers, and periodicals.

In the third section of the Training Schedule, called "Steps in locating and charging books," are listed the various shelves and files where books or records of them may be. The supervisor shows the new man each of these and explains its purpose. If he cannot locate a book or answer a reader's question, he is told to refer the request to a full-time staff member.

Along with each routine, information about library policy is taught. For instance, in addition to teaching the procedure for charging out a book, information about the loan periods for different types of materials is a part of the instruction. The trainee must learn also the reason for each step. It has been observed that if a worker understands why he must do something, he is less likely to forget it. He then performs the routine while the supervisor stands nearby to render assistance if he becomes confused. New assistants must continually review procedures. It is only by practice that the routines become habits; the supervisor must constantly guide the new man for several weeks.

Showing, telling, and doing are the most effective methods for teaching routine jobs, but written instructions must be provided so that they can be reviewed and studied. A staff manual explaining policies and routines in detail has been prepared by the head of the Circulation Department. It is easy to understand, and is illustrated with sample cards and forms. Employees are required to study it before and after their on-the-job training.

At the beginning of the academic year, when the majority of the new assistants are employed, several group meetings are held, at times when they will interfere least with work schedules. At each meeting items in the Training Schedule are reviewed, current policy changes discussed, recurring errors of assistants are pointed out, and suggestions for improvement are offered. Many times group discussions indicate areas needing special attention. Four or five meetings are necessary in order to discuss all the topics in the Training Schedule. Regular meetings are then discontinued.

It is at best difficult to evaluate a training program. However, the Head of the Department, the other full-time staff members, and the part-time assistants have stated that the program has been a tremendous help. The professional librarians spend less time answering haphazard questions of new assistants and they are freed from much routine work. They can devote more time to advising readers, attending to administrative details, and improving service.

Several writers have suggested a training program for libraries organized on a national or regional scale, similar to the Training Within Industry Program for industrial supervisors during World War II.[4] In such a program, cooperating libraries would send their supervisors to a central agency where they would learn proper methods for training assistants on the job. Librarians need to use systematic methods for training both professional and non-professional assistants. However, until a centralized program is put into operation, each library must train its own supervisors and plan its own program of training. Most libraries cannot afford the time or the expense of even library-wide, centralized programs. The job of training, therefore, usually rests with the heads of individual departments. Nevertheless, this training must be systematic and complete, based on sound principles and methods; otherwise, new assistants will not do their jobs well. Where centralized programs do not exist, it is essential that department heads study their individual departmental needs and plan systematic training that will fit them.

30. LIBRARY ASSISTANTS' SELF-EVALUATION

Julie Silagyi

This self-evaluation test is given twice a year to seventh, eighth, and ninth grade library assistants in the Portage, Pennsylvania, Joint schools. It is an excellent incentive for personal self-improvement and for improvement of library service. Perhaps it would be more effective if it could be given more frequently — like scholastic tests — as a periodic check-up.

Directions

(1) On a separate sheet of paper number from 1 to 40 in four columns.
(2) For each question give yourself a number evaluation as follows:

    4 — if your answer is always
    3 — if your answer is frequently
    2 — if your answer is generally
    1 — if your answer is seldom
    0 — if your answer is never

(3) After you have answered every question honestly and to the best of your ability, count up the sum for each column; then total your four columns.
(4) How do you rate? Interpret your score as follows:

    A — 160-130 You're the best — the kind we're proud of!
    B — 129-100 You're good — we can always use your kind!
    C — 99-70 You'll do — but there's a lot of room for improvement!
    D — 69-40 You're no asset to the library — get on the ball or get out!
    F — 39-0 Don't sign up for library again — we can do without you!

A. Can You Sign Out a Book Correctly?

1. Do you check to see that the borrower signs his own name and home-room number legibly on the book card?
2. Do you stamp the date-due on the book card?
3. Do you stamp the date-due on the date slip and the borrower's blue card?
4. Do you check the band dater to see if the correct date is indicated on it?
5. Do you ask the librarian to type a new card for a book card that is filed?
6. If the librarian is not in charge, do you leave the card on her desk with a memo slip to indicate the borrower's name and room number?
7. Do you place the book card behind the proper alphabet-guide according to the author's last name?
8. Do you file a book card for a biography book by author?

B. Can You Place a Book Correctly on the Shelf?

9. Do you check to see if the book card is in the book before you place the latter on the shelf?
10. Do you check to see that the accession number on the card is exactly the same as the accession number on the book pocket? (Remember: the accession number is found in the upper right hand corner of both the card and the pocket.)
11. Are you careful to put the book in its proper location designated for reference, nonfiction, fiction, and short story?
12. Do you place a book without squeezing and jamming it among the others?
13. Do you put a nonfiction book exactly where it belongs according to its Dewey Decimal classification number?
14. Do you clear your table of all book loans before you leave so that the incoming librarians do not have to do <u>your</u> work?

C. Are You a Good Housekeeper?

16. Do you check all the shelves at the end of your period to see if the books are upright and in order?
17. Do you check the magazine rack to see if the magazines are

in their designated places? Do you group the magazines on the shelves neatly?

18. Do you see if the tables are cleared and the chairs pushed back into place at the end of the period?

19. Do you pick the paper off the floor, especially under the tables and near the magazines?

20. Do you check to see that the newspapers are on the rack when you leave?

21. Do you leave in neat order the cut-out-magazine section?

22. Do you shelf-read?

D. How Do You Rate Personally?

23. Are you courteous and patient?

24. Are you quiet and well-mannered rather than noisy and bossy?

25. Do you attend to library duties first and adequately before you start on your homework?

26. Are you helpful both to the pupils and the librarian in every way possible?

27. Do you report to the librarian any irregularities or infractions of the rules and regulations?

28. Do you yourself observe library rules and regulations?

29. Do you refrain from chewing gum and eating candy in the library?

30. Do you ask permission to leave the library?

31. Do you refrain from wandering around the halls or loafing in the girls' room.

32. Do you willingly and unhesitatingly do any task the librarian assigns?

33. Do you volunteer — that is, do you ask the librarian if she wants you to do any special work?

34. Do you like being a library assistant?

35. Do you profit from being a library assistant?

36. Do you cooperate with the other library assistants in your group?

37. Do you get permission from the librarian when you have some special assignment that you must do before you do library assistant's work?

38. Are you neat and clean?

Miscellaneous
<hr>

39. Do you use the card catalog to help pupils locate books they want?
40. Do you listen to, learn, and follow the suggestions presented at the different library assistants meetings?

31. OVERDUES: A POSITIVE APPROACH

Frances Perske

In school libraries overdue books are a perennial problem for which no foolproof solution has as yet been found. A positive step in the right direction is the Library Point System, used by all three libraries of the Eastside Union High School District, San Jose, California. This plan not only eliminates the unsavory business of collecting fines, but also benefits students. It helps to stimulate reading, and it aids teachers and librarians in reading guidance.

Collecting fines is a waste of time. The new system was introduced when the head librarian, Beauel Santa, and I (her assistant), sat down and figured out how much time we were actually spending on the fines. Students did most of the clerical work of making out receipts and fine slips, but considerable supervision and checking were needed. Our filing cabinets were overflowing with filled receipt books. The records for students who paid in part and had to be tracked down to finish payment, or who did not have the money at all and would pay later, were ponderous. Fine notices had to be sent out weekly. Excused absences had to be deducted from overdue time. Student assistants made errors in change. A library assistant needing psychiatric treatment stole money from the cash drawer. We could not use the fine money for library purchases; it went into general district funds.

The attitude of students returning overdue books was, "So

what if it is late, I'm paying for it, aren't I?" The whole thing
was negative.

We felt it basically wrong and extravagant for librarians
to spend so much time and energy on fines, when they could be
doing reading guidance, answering reference questions, and
developing a positive and helpful relationship with students.
Our superintendent gave his whole-hearted agreement when
presented with the facts.

When the new system went into effect, the student attitude
changed. One of our previous worst offenders said, "Now I'll
have to get my books in on time," and he did! Not being fined,
many students apologized for returning books late. And best
of all, there was a slight decrease in the number of overdue
books.

Here is how the system works. A reading record is kept
for each student. For each book he reads and returns on time,
he receives twenty points. An additional twenty points is given
for reading books on three or more subjects during the quarter.
Points are also awarded for library service of various kinds.
The appearance of a student's name on an overdue list costs
him half his points. At the end of each quarter, students having
over a specified minimum number of points and no overdue
books, receive a Library Certificate and their names appear
on the Library Honor Roll. At the end of the year, a perpetual
trophy is awarded to the student who has gained the highest
number of points, and pins to the next three highest. No student qualifies for these awards if his grade average is below
C, or if he fails to pass an examination on knowledge of books
read and of the library in general.

The emphasis of this system is positive instead of negative.
There must be some control and some penalty for offenders,
however. Hence an overdue book may not be renewed, and
severe offenders lose library circulation privileges. Reminder
lists for overdues are sent once a week to counselors, who see
the students daily in class. Failure to respond brings an individual notice to the student. A third reminder means loss of
circulation privileges for four weeks.

This system gives recognition for reading, something
which needs more emphasis these days, and to students who
are not likely to receive it in athletics or student activities.

147

The reading records are valuable to English teachers, counselors, and librarians in guidance. Previous years' records are kept in students' counselling files.

The keeping of reading records might seem unduly onerous, but the work is rotated among student assistants, who usually can type one day's circulation (average 160) from the two smaller schools in a period and a half, or in two periods from the larger school (average 200). Current records are kept at the circulation desk for ready reference by student assistants or the readers themselves.

In many cases the reading record is an invaluable counselling aid. It may give insight into a student's hobbies and interests, or lack thereof. It may show that a student is reading too much, to the detriment of his school work, or that a good reading program correlates with excellent class work.

Of course, the system is by no means foolproof. Students may receive points for books checked out but not read. However, award contenders are asked to indicate such books on their records. Students may check out the smallest book with the least text, merely to add to their total points. A conference with the librarian on the real purpose of the point system can usually correct this situation. In case it does not, the examination for contenders must be difficult enough to prove whether or not the books have been read. Some students may take advantage of the freedom from fines to keep a book long overdue. But not many can afford to lose library circulation privileges because of the extensive use of library assignments by instructors in many departments.

More work needs to be done with teachers and counselors to encourage them to make fuller use of the records. A closer control must be put on students checking out books for friends who have lost their privileges. Further refinements will be made in the system as the need arises.

In five years of use, this system has presented some stumbling blocks, but none insurmountable. The step taken in eliminating fines and substituting library points certainly is headed in the right direction.

32. "BUT I RETURNED THAT BOOK LONG AGO!"

Stanley D. Truelson, Jr.

What does a library do when a borrower says that his over-due book has been returned, yet the book can be found nowhere on the library's premises? Is the customer always right? Should he be given the benefit of every doubt? Is it worth more to the library to write off a few losses each year in the interests of public relations than to recover some of its losses by sterner tactics?

No library can afford to accept at face value every explana-tion made by a delinquent borrower. It is far too easy for a person to forget what he has done with a library book and really believe that he has returned what is even yet lying in his bureau drawer or on the bottom shelf in his study.

But there are ticklish public relations aspects involved in any approach to the problem. In many libraries — may I say, in most? — it is entirely possible for a returned book to get lost in the library while the original borrower is still shown by the records to be responsible for the book. More than one librarian has had to apologize for overdue notices or bills that were unjustified. Borrowers who have received such apologies or who have known of cases where such had to be offered are more than likely to feel that the library is usually wrong.

Examples of situations, on the other hand, where the bor-rower's claims should not be automatically accepted are not hard to find. Consider, for instance, the protective parents who had seen their daughter mount the library steps with two books under arm and were therefore positive that the copy of Balzac et son oeuvre, for which the library was now billing her, had been properly returned. Father felt so strongly as to write the head librarian that he had investigated the library's procedures for handling returned books — that is, he had ques-tioned his daughter as to what she thought the library's pro-cedures were — and he believed that the library did not provide adequate safeguards.

Long thought was given before an answer was phrased to
the effect that in those few cases where the library might be in
error the responsibility for proof must still remain with the
borrower and that about the only evidence which could be accepted as proof was the book, itself.

It was with some sense of vindication that three days later
a staff member unwrapped from a package in the morning mail
Balzac et son oeuvre, accompanied by a note from Mother which
explained that obviously Daughter had not returned the book,
after all, and Mother was terribly sorry that she had carelessly
shelved it in her own bookcase.

One of the problems a circulation librarian faces is the
borrower who refuses to answer overdue notices from the library when he believes they are sent in error. One such borrower was the freshman who wrote hot words to the head librarian — that for some reason of which he was unaware he was
being charged for the replacement of a book "which you must
have mislaid yourselves." Righteously he continued: "I resent
being held responsible for an item of which I took the best of
care and used properly. . . . If I was to pay for this book, I
feel that I would be acting very unfairly to the hundreds of college students who are struggling financially, because if at least
one person protests against an unfair charge, perhaps it will
be easier for others to do the same."

Then came the explanation of months of silence: "I began
receiving your overdue notices some months ago. I never re-
plied, expecting, of course, that you would discover your error
and remedy it. You never did and finally I received a curt notice that my next college bill would include the charge for the
book, which I must say I thought ridiculous, until I now find
that you have actually gone to that poor end in order to cover
your mistake. I would ask that this preposterous charge be
removed immediately, for I will employ every means possible
to avoid its payment. Thank you."

The circulation librarian answered by citing in detail the
library's efforts to find the book and the library's policy of
holding responsible the last person who signed for it. He also
added wearily that in the future it would simplify matters greatly if the borrower were to respond in some way to the library's
communications.

"BUT I RETURNED THAT BOOK LONG AGO!"

The conclusion of this episode came over a month later when the somewhat apologetic freshman brought into the library the book in question. He had found it through some quirk of circumstances in the lost-and-found collection of one of his classroom buildings.

But can a library always enforce the rule that only the book in hand is sufficient evidence that it has been returned? A few cases may occur among the thousands of books circulating each year when a borrower actually does return a book which does not get recorded as returned and which also gets lost either on the wrong shelf or in the hands of an illegal borrower.

One might argue that a library is similar to a business which has to have proof that a questioned account is paid. But a business issues receipts and a library does not, unless it uses borrowers' card and stamps them with dates taken and returned. College and university libraries do not usually stamp such cards, nor do any libraries that use transaction number systems of charging out books.

Who should pay the cost when the book cannot be found? The borrower is positive he has returned the book, and the library cannot, after making every effort to find the book, agree that it is in error. One alleviating procedure is automatically to refund the replacement charge should the book turn up in the future. But the promise of such a contingent refund does not help the borrower who is short of cash and needs his funds now for other purposes.

No completely satisfying answer seems to exist. Some libraries stick by their guns to the very end at the risk of possible injustice and probable hard feelings. But these libraries believe they must take the risk, if the interests of the majority whom they serve are to be protected. Other libraries are more flexible and will, after serious consultation with the borrower, accept his word in lieu of evidence to the contrary. A choice of one of these two positions might well be made in each individual case without necessarily choosing the same position each time.

Rigidity is not a wholly tenable position, but there are times when it is advantageous to be able to resort to it. Probably the only certain conclusion one can reach is that, even though the benefit of the doubt may eventually be given the borrower, he is not <u>always</u> right, any more than he is always wrong, nor in the interests of preserving library materials for further users may he be allowed to think he is.

33. WHY KIDS STEAL BOOKS

Gerald Raftery

"My theft loss is terrible," wailed one librarian. "A constant drain! I worry all the time."

"Oh, yes, I have some minor losses," shrugged another. "Doesn't everyone? It's part of the cost of operation."

When the two compared notes they discovered that both worked in schools of about equal size, and their losses numerically were about the same.

<u>JrL</u> cited this conversation, overheard at a convention, in suggesting an investigation into the reasons why kids steal books today. It appeared, from this incident, that a librarian's attitude toward theft is important and it seemed that an objective look at underlying causes might be helpful.

An unscientific survey of some librarian friends showed pretty quickly that I would not get all the answers that way. Like most questions, the theft problem had two sides — or more. I tossed the ball to some classroom teachers, suggesting that they approach their pupils with: "Of course, I know that none of you ever take any library books, but you may know why others do." Under the cloak of anonymity, I thought we might get some personal disclosures.

I continued to question librarians and to conduct "depth" interviews with especially articulate teenagers. At every chance, I kicked the subject around informally with any adult who was willing to recall his own youthful peccadilloes.

As the reasons piled up, I realized that they didn't give me what I wanted. I was after causes more than reasons, and that called for analysis. These results, therefore, are my personal conclusions and so are open to criticism, but maybe some of them will be helpful.

Resentment is the most puzzling cause. Librarians list it as "lack of respect for law and order" or "vandalism" or "destructiveness," pupils explain it as "hates school," "grudge against librarian," or simply "sore." A psychologist would talk of "hostility" or "aggression" — and we've all got some.

This is the sort of case where a bad boy (Oops, sorry! I mean "an emotionally-disturbed child." We old-timers goof on our terminology now and then.) will steal a book only to throw it away in a locker room down the hall.

Part of the problem is inescapable in the school set-up. Compulsory attendance laws, core curricula, and life-adjustment programs seem to sift out a hard core of malcontents who waste most of their time; if the library is bearing its share of the community burden, they will waste some of that time there. What Isaac Watts said 200 years ago about mischief and idle hands is still true today, and our best defense is friendliness.

This small group has an influence on pupil attitudes far out of proportion to its size, for teenagers see their contemporaries as slightly larger than life-sized, and all their doings as the stuff of saga and legend.

It will pay dividends to greet the loafers cheerily (although you'll often wear your smile as though it were a little too tight). Learn their names and ask them about their interests. Urge them to suggest hot rod or gun magazines that you can subscribe to. For a couple of years, I provided a radio for these troublesome types, but lately I've decided I'd rather risk losing a few books than listen to rock-and-roll all day.

Remember that you're dealing with what the educationists in their quaint patois call "a mass situation"; in English, this is known as a gang. In a gang I've found that the group intelligence is slightly higher than that of the highest individual and the ethical standards slightly lower than the lowest. (This is Raftery's Rule, known more generally as "mob rule.") Fortunately, a gang has a sense of gratitude, but you have to earn it, and not just once but every day. It's worth doing, and not for purely selfish reasons.

Traditionally, a library was a place for reading, study, and research; but so was a school — once. Now it provides custodial care that is often quasi-parental and sometimes quasi-penal, along with at least rudimentary treatment for the mentally and emotionally retarded. The library has to accept a part of the responsibility for these reluctant customers.

"Kicks" is a classification that overlaps a little on the previous one, but usually it is theft merely to show off. This includes a youngster who steals a book for the same reason that some adults climb a mountain — because it's there. One teenager explained it: "A guy steals to show that he has guts, but anybody can steal from a library so it's an easy way to act big."

The underlying cause here is probably the replacement of traditional disciplines with "self-discipline," which educational brass-hats insist is the only really effective form of control. However, the top brass shares with Madison Avenue admen and very small children the belief that if you say something often enough and sincerely enough, it comes true. As a result, no one has ever gotten around to implementing this nebulous hypothesis.

The "kicks" theft is difficult to guard against, because stricter control of charging routines merely poses a greater challenge. Paradoxically the complete relaxation of safeguards may be the best defense, although that would make things easier for the next group.

Greed may be the largest cause of book thefts. This covers a wide range — the boy who steals a book to give to his girl friend who can read, the youngster who takes a volume to sell to some less-daring book lover, and the kid who makes Tom Sawyer's distinction between hooking and stealing (anything non-negotiable which you take from a school is merely "hooked").

Some youngsters collect attractive books, not to read but merely to own. I've heard of kids who took books only to keep a built-in book case presentably filled. At least a few children take books because they want them and actually do not know how to buy them. To defend myself against these, I announce regularly that I will order books at a discount for any pupils and teachers who are interested. One of my former pupils who is now a practising minister told me that in high school he used to "lose" books and then pay for them because that was the easiest way to get them. I count very few prospective ministers among my patrons, so I make my ads for personal book orders frequent and persuasive.

Youngsters in this group, to sum it up, steal books for the same reason that you and I buy them.

Pressure is one cause readily understandable to adults. I note its greatest incidence near the close of a marking period when teachers are pushing for the completion of work. It seems to affect encyclopedias especially. Modern schools have loftily eliminated "busy work" as a teaching device, but some unsung genius has discovered that "research" is a honey of a euphemism for the same thing; many of our assignments involve research, copied either directly from the encyclopedia or via the more imaginative spelling of a classmate's notes.

The best defense against this is to keep a helpful eye on busy youngsters who want to charge out an encyclopedia volume, or who seem too worriedly occupied with one for any great length of time. I usually offer to find them a book they can take home which covers the same material. Most of them, unhappily, prefer the encyclopedia because other books tell them more than they want to know about a subject.

In this case, a librarian is like a reporter. His feet are as important as his head; he must move around regularly to find out what's going on. To mix the metaphor thoroughly — he should, like the commander of an infantry company, maintain constant patrol contact with the enemy.

This seems to be the only type of theft which affects higher education to any great extent (although after World War II, the colleges were the target of some resentment and greed thefts among ex-GI's). But this type goes all the way up; I found one case of a school administrator who filched pictures (administrators don't just steal) for a master's thesis in education, and while I haven't heard of such a case involving a doctoral dissertation, I wouldn't bet against the possibility.

The touching faith of modern educators in pictures is at the root of some of this trouble. They have taken seriously the adage that one picture is worth 10,000 words and characteristically reduced it to absurdity — 10 pictures are worth 100,000 words, 100 pictures are worth a million words, and so on. This has produced college graduates who steal pictures in the belief that they are getting the most out of the library.

Laziness is another cause of thefts. A librarian describes it as "refusal to conform," and a pupil says, "I wanted to enjoy the book undisturbed" — by a return deadline, that is. Longer

loan periods can't do much for this problem, or for the youngster who is too lazy to copy out a wiring diagram or building
plans but ambitious enough to complete a project after he has
stolen the book that tells him how.

The problem is growing, but then so are circulation figures.
Some teachers point out that obeying rules is a habit (and generally a good one) but one which youngsters do not have to form to
get along in school today. This may well be a factor.

No sense of value is probably a separate cause, although
it borders on and overlaps some of the other classifications.
A librarian blames "our economy of waste" and a pupil explains,
"Gee, it's only a book!" The two points of view are far apart.

We librarians formed our sense of monetary values under
an uninflated dollar, in a period when a book was a book, and
usually valuable. Youngsters have somewhat less respect for
a forty-cent dollar, and in their scale of values the paperbacks
have blurred the distinction between magazines which are expendable and books which aren't. This is piled on top of the
traditionally careless handling of school texts, which carries
over to tinge the attitude toward all books. This, of course, is
not an excuse but a partial explanation.

In conclusion, I'd like to qualify my pontifications a bit.
These random observations were made in urban centers and
are probably valid only for such areas. My very spotty check
turned up two small New England towns where the problem apparently does not exist. The teenagers there are not immune
to the standard difficulties of their age involving sex, alcohol,
and fast cars, but they do not steal library books. Geography
may have something to do with it, but I suspect that size is the
significant factor. I have not touched on private schools at all,
but I would guess that the problem there would also vary with
the size of the student body. This unfinished business, I dump
happily in the lap of anyone seeking a subject for a master's
thesis — without pictures.

A final word on attitude! There are days, after I've missed
some sleep and forgotten my vitamin B, when the discovery of
some new book losses sends me into a fury. But the next day
when things may look a little brighter, I smile sadly and consider that the loss is really a form of non-recurring circulation,
and a heavy-handed compliment to my skill in book selection, so
I reorder the missing titles in an unending effort to fill the demand.

34. THE UNCONSCIOUS MOTIVATION OF LIBRARY FINES

Bernard Poll

After many a day at the circulation desk accepting overdue books and their fines it occurred to me: is this doing any good?

I'm enforcing a fine system designed to get books back on time. In the pedagogical spirit, I hope this punishment, taking money away from borrowers with overdue books, will change them a little and for the better. But I wonder . . . Do fines help, either by getting books back when they are due, or by teaching book delinquents to change their habits?

Perhaps I've got the whole idea wrong. Fines could be necessary, not to cure, but to keep delinquent patrons of the library from erring further. Fines may keep a kind of status quo between borrower tendency never to bring the book back at all and librarian tendency never to let the book go out. Certainly there is evidence for both these tendencies. Some people take books out and never return them; every librarian has some books that are not allowed out of the library. Fines would then tend to keep a bad situation from getting worse.

Without evidence I don't know what is true. Would these habitual book delinquents continue as before without fines? If so, then I could cut out all of this time-consuming bookkeeping. Or would they even improve without fines? In which case, I ought to drop fines fast!

We do not know what causes people to keep books overdue, or what causes them to bring books back. I do know, by seeing the same faces over and over again, that it is the same borrowers who are late most of the time.

Keeping books overdue may be a reflection of a basic personality trait which is out of the reach of the effect of little or big fines. My experience of these habitual late borrowers is at least one indication of the ineffectiveness of fines. But we never test or question the fine system. Why? It is not an insignificant routine, it costs money, takes time, and has very doubtful public relations values.

Is there a reason why we don't explore the effectiveness of

157

fines? Does the fine system satisfy more functions than its alleged use as a book-returner?

Individuals who administer the library, a public organization to manage the sharing of books, are caught in a conflict. Librarians have values opposed to common ownership as has the general community, and they don't like handing out books as common property. They don't realize this, but the over-the-counter situation is filled with feelings of tension and righteousness. And lo, we have the fine system to alleviate this distress. It allows librarians to get this uneasiness and anger out in a fairly acceptable manner. Fines then punish patrons and relieve librarians of their anxiety.

Happily, this view requires no special assumptions about the nature of librarians — good or bad. Given the public library, part of whose function conflicts with the values of its environment, and given ordinary persons as librarians, this is what we should expect: a conflict. We then have a natural solution to a natural conflict: an unproductive ritual. ("Unproductive" in the sense that it doesn't end overdues; it certainly is a productive solution to the psychological problem — think what we might do to the public if we didn't have fines to level at them!)

Far from advocating the abolition of fines, I think we must not question their function or look into their effectiveness further. The possibilities are frightening.

Part III: THE LIBRARY AND READER SERVICE

35. DEVELOPING INTEREST IN THE SCHOOL LIBRARY

Joseph F. Shubert

School library service has been slowed in its development
because large numbers of teachers and administrators do not
know what the library can contribute to the total school program.
This fact has been acknowledged by school librarians for many
years, and the struggle to have the library emphasized in the
professional education of teachers and administrators has been
going on nearly as long. Advances have been made in this field
but there is still much to be done.

No less important as a means to our goal is what the librarian can do in an individual school toward giving what we might
call "in-service training." No librarian need fold his hands and
be a martyr to a disinterested administration and faculty. There
are many things he can do to change their attitude about the library. How much can be done, and what methods can be used,
depends largely upon what spark of interest may exist. Some
librarians may have fairly adequate funds with which to work
merely because state or accrediting agencies require them.
These have a preliminary advantage, but no librarian will be
without some means in his campaign.

Consultation with teachers is a basic part of the book selection process, but if teachers are not interested, the librarian,
using his taken-for-granted knowledge of the school's curriculum, can select books and call them to the attention of the teachers later. Perhaps it is difficult to get teachers to look ahead
to spring when they are preparing the October book order, but
there is no reason why the librarian cannot.

Books can be called to the attention of teachers in many
ways. Lists are the most frequent way, but many librarians
use conversational tactics in introducing the subject. Broaching
the introduction in this way and following it up with the book and
a note is one of the most effective methods.

Access to a teacher's interest has even been gained through
students. Frequent, well edited articles in the school newspaper

161

can draw the attention of teachers, as well as of pupils, to library services and materials. Attractive displays and exhibits, particularly outside the library, are most effective. Displays of books on current topics may bring home to teachers the fact that the library does have material for papers and speech assignments — and may even provide teachers with a somewhat superficial check on completeness of bibliographies.

Booklists need not be limited to the monotonous "new books in the library." They can be dressed up in many ways. Real selectivity and short, provocative annotations should be used in making up subject lists. The librarian need not depend exclusively upon his own lists. Permission to reproduce those of other librarians often is readily granted. Do not be afraid to ask for it.

The principal and every member of the faculty should receive a copy of every list prepared or distributed by the school library. Limiting distribution to "interested" teachers is a poor economy. Let everyone see them, particularly your administrator.

By this time someone will have objected that "teachers in this school just aren't interested — they don't care about library books, and they don't read anything, particularly mimeographed materials from the school library." Is there no one, just one, teacher who might be capable of developing an interest? Work on him! Buy books for his subject areas, develop good library service to that part of the school, if nowhere else. After all, successful demonstration is a large part of selling.

Problems in getting teachers to make full use of the library vary from school to school, and, interestingly, stem from different combinations in training and experience of individual teachers and administrators. Problems can range from converting the new social studies teacher who plans to use nothing but his college sociology texts, through winning over a few teachers who know that the library is good for all subject areas other than their own, to securing adequate funds from an administrator who never used a school library in his own teaching.

A librarian who needed the interest of the faculty, but already had the support of her principal, worked out a library introduction as a part of teacher orientation before the start of the school year. She provided a mimeographed work packet which all teachers were expected to complete. Illustrated with

clever line drawings, it called attention to library procedures
and rules; had space for teachers to note books they "discovered," located filmstrips, reference books, pamphlets, and
other library materials; and even left space for teachers to
record the things they didn't find in the library. A special section on the new professional shelf informally called for an appraisal of the subject representation in the collection, and even
diplomatically solicited contributions for the shelf with "I will
place my professional magazines here for others to browse
through," and "I would be willing to kick in a dollar toward a
new title that would be of use to all of us."

Such a program would be impossible without the approval
and backing of the administration, but is something which could
prove worth while in many schools. A more modest attempt
might be made in schools where this cannot be done. The librarian in these schools might be included on the agenda or program
of a faculty meeting. At any rate, he should be alive to the opportunities to inject the library into discussion at such meetings
even if he cannot secure an actual place on the agenda.

Use of the faculty bulletin board may prove helpful. A small
poster with a few book titles interestingly presented, or even
something clipped from a jacket will attract the interest of
people who would never bother to read a long list of titles or
a wordy memorandum. In making up any bulletin board notice
or mimeographed bulletin be sure to break up large masses of
type with good margins, spacing, and interesting sub-heads.

The librarian who once succeeds in making the resources
of the library available to a teacher should not fail to make use
of an appropriate follow-up. The class which used library materials in building a noteworthy project or in producing an outstanding assembly program can be complimented by a note or
word from the librarian. Personal relations are an important
part of building the confidence and interest of the school and
this might be one good starting point.

The "walled up" librarian will not attract new patrons. Being at assemblies, joining the crowd at coffee break or in the
lounge for the last few minutes of the lunch hour can be as important as all the booklists an electric mimeograph can turn
out in a semester. Sometimes more can be learned about the
needs of the teachers by being a part of these groups than by

hurried or strained consultations over the standard catalogs. That can (and will) come later. Finding the time to do this doubtless is a real problem. Here is where well trained student assistants can free you from routine work for an important part of your job.

Developing a community consciousness of the importance of the school library may be an indirect but useful device. Enlist that source of never-ending aid — the PTA. Make sure your unit has its reading and library services chairman, but don't let yourself be named to this post. Make sure you have at least one other interested person. Parents need to know more about reading materials for children and young adults. Here is a forum for one of the most important aspects of your school library work.

Parents' night is a good time to emphasize the role of the library in the school's program. In a school which uses the "back to school night" in which parents observe the schedules of their children, one librarian used study periods to introduce parents to the library. Displays outside the library, and even outside the school, if policy permits, can contribute much to a school's observance of education week.

That many administrators and teachers have little understanding of real school library service and the work of the librarian is patent. Not long ago an administrator who had been toying with the idea of establishing a central library in an elementary school of nearly 900 children listened to a discussion of all the things we expect a good librarian to do in a school. Amazed, he came up with the question, "How can we find anyone who will be able to do all those things and still work for a salary we can pay?"

The answer, of course, is twofold — he needs professionally trained school librarians, and he needs more than one. But doesn't the question raise a challenge to the librarian who will begin library service in that school?

36. THE LIBRARIAN AS PERSUADER

Jean Parriss

Vance Packard's The Hidden Persuaders has received a considerable amount of publicity and has doubtless been on the request lists of many libraries. The implications of the book for the librarian are also of interest.

In today's world, where museums advertise on street cars and churches employ high powered organizations to raise funds, the librarian can perhaps learn something from a survey of advertising methods such as those described by Mr. Packard.

He considers the new advertising approach known as "motivation research,"[1] which is a "depth approach" to the factors influencing behavior. Advertisers survey the "whys" of our behavior so that they can more effectively manipulate our habits and choices in their favor.

Many of the findings of advertisers can be corroborated by librarians. It is found, for example, that it cannot be assumed that people know what they want. They may ask for a nice story set on Cape Cod and go out with a travel book on Spain which has an appealing jacket.

Advertisers also find that consumers rarely tell the truth about their likes and dislikes even if they know them, like the woman who likes to read "really worthwhile books only" and after rejecting the best of the new non-fiction is seen slipping out with Homing.

Having agreed with the conclusions of Madison Avenue in these two respects, we can move on to examine some typical selling techniques. It is highly desirable to create wants in people of which they were not previously aware. "Fancy not having a floor polisher — however do you manage?" (How extraordinary you've never read War and Peace — even if you've seen the movie. I can't understand it.)

Another factor beloved by advertisers is the desirability of creating psychological obsolescence. This is not so desirable from the librarian's point of view, as the desire for the newest books can rarely be satisfied by the copies available.

Against this, the loyalty to brands without being able to recognize them, is a finding with distinct possibilities for the librarian. Mrs. Jones wholly devoted to F. P. Keyes might perhaps with time, tact, and sleight of hand be transformed to Taylor Caldwell and others.

In learning to sell to the subconscious, secret miseries, and doubts, guilt feelings were exposed; for example, the woman who uses instant coffee is regarded as a poor housewife. This unanimous disapproval of shortcuts does not appear to extend to reading digested versions of current books. Perhaps the librarian can do something here!

The importance of the eye-catching package is a strong argument for the use of plastic coverings for book jackets. Women are perhaps less likely to forget their glasses than when going to the supermarket, but the number of times that assistance is required because "I left my glasses at home" makes it a factor in the library too!

Marketers find that "splurge" items should be at eye-level. This is a finding which could be of interest in our arrangement of library shelves, though we already know that unless lower shelves are tilted people wearing bifocals find them impossible. On the other hand, the dictum that people like to see a lot of an item does not extend to library books. Three or four copies of a particular title seems to arouse suspicion rather than desire. "It doesn't go out much, does it?"

Impulse shopping, however, can be paralleled in selection of books; the number of books which will go out when plucked from the dull recesses of 300s and 500s and placed in a prominently placed WE SUGGEST is amazing.

Equally amazing and horrifying is the "psycho seduction" of children — "the future occupation of all moppets is to be skilled consumers." The possibility of an endless series of comic books exploiting the successor to Davy Crockett (complete outfits from $5.95) is a tremendous challenge to the children's librarian who alone can reveal the joys of the Mad Hatter's tea party or the river picnic of Mole and Rat.

As far as adults are concerned, marketing now finds an appeal to such hidden needs as the following:

emotional security — if you have a home freezer, you
will never be without food (If you study some specialized subject in your spare time, you will have a valuable asset.)

ego-gratification — the steam shovel may move the
load but it could not do so without the man operating
it (books on many subjects will give a man the necessary "know-how")

This leads on to creative outlets which are a fruitful source
of income from cake mixes to tool sets. While we may regard
with doubt the statement that every time a woman bakes a cake
or grows a petunia she relives the act of creation, we can at
least appeal to and help satisfy the creative urge in many. The
sense of power appealed to particularly in the sale of larger
and more powerful autos, we can try to capture under the aegis
of Bacon's Scientia potestas est.

The sense of roots, the appeal of times past has proved a
satisfactory background for many advertisements and is one
with which the librarian can have a field day. Most obviously
there comes to mind, under a poster entitled THE GOOD OLD
DAYS with horse and buggy, those biographies and autobiographies with such evocative titles as Peace and Dripping Toast
or Period Piece. There is also the pleasing progression of
ideas recorded in different ways, e.g., Men and Gardens by
Nan Fairbrother, or the recollection of an epoch as in Ursula
Bloom's Victorian Vinaigrette.

Yet another desire to which advertising is slanted, particularly in the insurance field, is man's longing for immortality.
While the acquisition of a library card does not assist a borrower to this end, we librarians are in a superb position to
point out the enduring quality of the written word, against which
so many monuments are but "the irregularities of vain glory,
and wild enormities of ancient magnanimity."

These are apparently all basic impulses discovered and
subsequently exploited by advertisers. We can follow their lead
to some extent in these particulars and also make a very great
appeal to the imagination, open magic casements on time and
space, beguile the reader with earlier centuries and distant

lands. Today there is a whole industry at work promoting the "care and feeding of positive thinkers" — "I must have this or that," and looking forward to an expanding market when automation increases leisure time.

As far as libraries are concerned, it may be objected there is nothing new in all this. Maybe not, but are we offering our wares in the most effective way? Few libraries could afford the expense of motivation research, but they need not be too proud to note the findings of the MR experts and avail themselves of any suggestions to be found.

Gone are the days when a Carnegie Library offered "realms of gold" eagerly explored by those who had never dreamt of such munificence; now the librarian has to sell a belief and a product. Two centuries ago Samuel Johnson noted that "People in general do not willingly read if they can have anything else to move them." Today the variety and accessibility of rival amusements must exceed the Doctor's wildest imaginings.

As librarians we march with the times, aided by photocharging, punched cards, and the like, but our chief job is still to get the right book to the right reader; to persuade people that they should be readers. To do that in 1958 we must organize all our resources to become truly persuasive persuaders.

37. WHAT LIBRARIANS HAVE TO SELL

James H. Cherry

The school librarian has a mission. This mission is to bring together the vast storehouse of human knowledge, the teacher, and the pupil.

The knowledge stored in the library covers every field of human thought and accomplishment. Your clients are from the whole range of human personalities. The scope of your professional responsibilities is so comprehensive that it can provide a dozen lifetimes of study, growth, and experience for each member of the profession.

WHAT LIBRARIANS HAVE TO SELL

Like most jobs of salesmanship, selling the library to the school involves knowledge of the thing to be sold, understanding of the people who buy it, and a deep appreciation of both. Particularly, and in an over-simplified way, you "sell" information and services.

The school administrator expects to find evidence that the school library is organized to accomplish its mission and to perform its functions. Facilities and personnel, within limits determined by the governing body, compare favorably with those provided for other segments of the school program. Staff members are well-trained, interested, personable, and competent to inspire the confidence of professional associates and students. Alertness to developing trends and to opportunities for rendering services are in evidence.

In assessing what the librarian has to sell to the school, the administrator is prone to think objectively and subjectively, critically and through value-judgments, of some of the following:

1. Information and services that demonstrate an appreciation of the changing role of the library as it relates to teaching and learning.

The school library is a storehouse of knowledge so arranged and a service center so organized that it is capable of providing information, instructional aids and materials, and resources for teaching and learning to whoever needs them, whenever and wherever they are needed.

Operating within this point of view, the library should be on the way to assuming responsibility for the instructional materials and equipment of the school except those that are needed in the classrooms either daily or in a frequently recurring cycle that is programmed. Further thought along this line seems to justify a rapidly expanding notion of the nature of the library.

Education is basically a process by which knowledge, skills, attitudes, appreciations, and behaviors, past and present, are communicated to the learner. Prior to the invention of other means of transmitting ideas, the teacher was the primary means through which this body of knowledge was conveyed to the pupil. The inventions of writing, printing, photography, recording machines, radio, television, and other recent devices, particularly through the development of electronics, have successively affected the relationships of the teacher and the pupil.

The school library has too long been thought of as a center

for the collection, care, and distribution of books and other printed matter. Perhaps this is because of the long span of time between the invention of the printing press and the invention of other means of recording human thought. In order for the educational program to keep pace with a rapidly developing culture, the library must move rapidly toward the concept of being a storehouse of knowledge. Such a center will feature books, periodicals, pictures, recordings, films, radios, television, and the various other recording and transmitting devices and machines so organized that they can be located quickly, assembled swiftly for the learning experience being planned, and made available for individual and classroom use.

2. Effectiveness as an Administrative Agency.

The librarian and library staff must have a delegation of authority and a budget of power to coordinate the entire school program in library services and use, to carry on in-service training programs for its own and the entire teaching staff, and to supervise library staff members in the effective performance of library functions. This presumes sufficient authority to make and enforce needed controls, including the assessment of penalties. As an administrative agency the library staff must have enough clerical help to perform purely clerical tasks of the library, including the maintenance of adequate systems of records for accounting and library use. The staff must include technical knowledge and personnel to operate and maintain the increasingly complex equipment and devices that the library houses, and the ability to train other people in the proper use and operation of these machines.

The library staff must have adequate time and space in which to work, time to exercise leadership in acquainting others in the school with teaching and learning resources in the library, and to make plans and recommendations for effective maintenance, development, and growth of the library.

3. Effectiveness as a Consultant Service.

This includes the development of programs to make the entire school staff and student body aware of the growing importance of the library and its responsibilities, resources, duties, techniques, and services as these are seen to be of value in teaching and learning. It involves assistance in interpreting the materials which the library houses and the services which the library can perform in developing school curriculums and activities programs. It involves working with members of the teaching staff and students, individually and in groups, concerning the resources that are available in the library or that can be procured.

4. <u>Effectiveness as a Service Agency to Teachers.</u>

The effective school library studies the teaching staff for clues to both group and individual needs and seeks to render services that make the work of the teacher in getting and using library resources less burdensome. This involves the location of pertinent printed matter, recordings, films, and information concerning community resources. In the case of recordings, films, and other similar teaching aids, service consists of the delivery of necessary machinery and devices to the classroom and their return to the library. Library staff and students are organized and trained to perform these services with efficiency. To encourage the use of field trips, the library should keep information concerning what may be seen, when it may be seen and who should be contacted for arrangements. Files containing information about persons who are willing to come to the school to tell about special topics or programs are an important evidence of the alertness of the library to community resources. If a public library is located in the community, the school librarian is well-informed of its resources and works closely with the public librarian in all areas in which coordination can promote teaching and learning.

5. <u>An Effective Service Agency to Students.</u>

The library staff stands ready to counsel with and to give information to students concerning the library, its facilities, resources, and use. It services requests for help promptly and courteously so that students may get or learn how to get what they need. There is adequate organization, resources, and help to avoid waiting lines and lists as a regularly recurring feature. The library is easy and pleasant to use because the people in charge are anxious and proud to have it used.

6. <u>An Effective School-Community Coordinating Agency.</u>

The effective school library will work toward making it possible for teachers and pupils to make dynamic use of all school and community resources for educational purposes. This involves working with other libraries, and with other groups and agencies in the community which have anything of value to contribute to teaching and learning. The library staff, of course, is not over-possessive in these efforts, but it is alert and active. Its records and counseling reflect knowledge and competence as a result of labor in this area of responsibilities.

With demonstrated effectiveness in these six dimensions, missions are accomplished, and selling is a satisfying by-product of a job well done.

38. THE SMALL AND MEDIUM SIZED COLLEGE LIBRARY

Johnnie Givens

Dr. Kuhlman asked me if I would bemoan the problems or dream into the future of "Teaching with Books" in the small and medium-sized college library. I want to do both. Am I not in an enviable position? You have no argument with me. We are all in agreement — we believe in teaching with books or materials or anything that will be helpful in teaching. And we are a closed group. There are no master professors of English, or Mathematics, or Geology, or Russian among you to refute any of my complaints. So here we sit, safe from all college presidents, in whom rests the final responsibility, says Branscomb,[1] and like maiden aunts we can talk about how the teachers are partially teaching our students.

Since it is so obvious that no one can make use of a book which he does not have, I suppose it is logical to term the circulation department of the library as the port of final responsibility for students using books. Reasoning along this line, I assume it is safe to blame the circulation department if students are not receiving, getting or asking for the books to be taught by and with. And Dr. Kuhlman has quoted us figures to show that students are not taking home as many books now as they formerly did. I wonder why . . . .

When I stopped to think, it seemed to me there are at least

172

five reasons why a student might not give a book a chance to further his education. Not necessarily in order of occurrence or importance but just as they came to me, I will give them to you for your consideration. (1) The student doesn't know what he wants, so how can he use the library? (2) Even when he knows what he wants, he does not know how to find the material. (3) The book he wants is not easily accessible to him. (4) The resources are limited on the subject with which he is working. (5) He does not even come for the material because he has not felt the need or has no interest in satisfying the need. Any one or combination of more than one of these reasons can play havoc with circulation statistics.

Before we go into more detail as to the responsibility of the circulation department for each of these situations, let me define our terms, if we may become educationists ourselves for a moment. This is the picture of the small or medium-sized college library. The collection numbers less than 75,000 volumes and is staffed by from one to five librarians. The library is housed in a centrally located wing or building on the campus, because the campus is small enough to be reached in every corner. There are few if any separate collections, the bulk of the volumes being housed in one place. The stacks are open and the collection is built primarily by the requests and selections of the instructional faculty. The budget is small, but in most instances to satisfy the requirements of regional and local accrediting agencies. The librarians are professionally trained and filled with hopes and aspirations and ideals for the service to the campus and community at large. Then why are we failing?

I may be just a little prejudiced, but I am not at all sure that the entire blame for students not utilizing the library to its fullest extent in their educative process rests entirely with the librarians, and even more pertinent to the point of discussion this minute, certainly not entirely with the circulation librarians. So, unless you have settled yourself for, perhaps, a delayed convention nap, let us think in turn about each of the reasons I have listed and establish a line of defense. Do we have one?

I think we do when the student does not use the library because he does not know what he wants in the way of service or material from the library. For an instant let us forget about

173

the free reading or interest satisfying reference he may do.
Certainly every librarian should and does meet each request
with the enthusiasm such a request deserves. But what about
those needs which are a part of every course in the curriculum?
Must we take the blame for not answering the questions resulting from a misunderstood or incompletely made or poorly conceived assignment? Certainly, it is not totally ours! Just as we
all know faculty who would lose their voices in the classroom
as readily as they would have to do without library resources,
so do we know others who either view the library and its staff
as a convenient substitute for an unprepared hour or seem to
flatter us by thinking we, unwarned, can take an unlimited number of freshmen with an unlimited number of topics, or each
with the same topic, and satisfy the request no matter how ob-
scure the subject may be. And the only classroom direction
given has been to point in the direction of the library. It is true,
we may be lacking in background information or even subject
information. But for the student to know what he is looking for
helps. And when administrators, both college and library,
realize that on the small college staff little time for professional research and study and preparation can be taken in an eight
to five schedule, then perhaps we will enjoy a schedule which
allows for these within the working day in the same ratio as
our classroom associates. For as my song on our campus goes,
"They must keep abreast of only one field, and we must teach
in all."

We must accept responsibility for the second reason I mentioned for students remaining uneducated. For years the library
staff has initiated, cooperated with, and successfully executed
instruction in library practices and procedures for the entering
and often returning college student. We are all familiar with
the various plans and degree of success which may be expected
from each. We have read, or written, or spoken about them before. Just to go on record in expressing thanks for the faculty
assistance we have received and to urge that we seek more, I
leave you to evaluate how these plans may deter or increase
the use of library books outside the library. We certainly are
making the attempt to eliminate any blame because the student
does not know how to find the material.

The third and fourth reasons why the student may fail to

use the library seem to reflect little blame in the direction of the circulation librarian. It is hard today to find a librarian who is a keeper of books instead of a believer in using books, so if a title is not easily accessible to the student who calls for it, the reasons may be entirely out of the hands of the profession. Open stacks with its advantage of browsing also brings the disadvantage of a mis-shelved book; a small campus with its centrally located collection also may bring a centrally used single copy because there is not money for additional copies; or the growing size of the Music or Science or Social Science faculty may emphasize the static size of the library staff with the delay in service this may cause. Each of these problems can be handled differently at different times and there is no mail order solution nor is there professional departmental blame. Likewise, if I asked each of you to raise your hand if you have holdings other than books in your collections, I have no doubt that every hand in the room would go up. So, while the resources on a student's topic may be limited because the faculty has been lax in building the collection in that area, certainly we are facing the problem on the college level of supplying materials for instruction instead of books. And since this is a problem which has been a topic for discussion in both professional literature and meetings, suffice it for us today to say that we are extending our resources to meet the advances in educational psychology and theory and practice, and our blame here is not that of negligence.

Thus far I seem to have built up quite a case for the circulation librarians. Maybe we have no blame, for certainly it is the responsibility of the faculty to challenge the student to feel the need of the library in his education and to hold the "big stick" over him until he is interested in meeting this need. So perhaps the case rests. But just as I have tried to point to a joint responsibility in the other areas, so here, too, do we fulfill a need. Too often, I believe, we have been at fault in allowing the library to be considered as a tool which can be adapted to any subject area instead of making it a resource division within each subject area. Let me be more specific. My ideas are not new. They have been tried in part on some of the campuses Dr. Kuhlman mentioned, and they come in part from ideas found in the literature last year, last month, or even the next issues of professional journals. But they have not been tried on any wide scale nor on the small, relatively poor campus. Here, too, I think it would prove its worth.

First, let us cease to make a speech-worn cliché of "The library is the center of the curriculum" and initiate it as a fact. Instead of requiring courses in library instruction with assignments correlated to the subject courses being studied by the students, let us reverse the situation. Would it not be worth the solving of whatever problems arise, to offer with each subject course a seminar, weekly, bi-weekly, monthly — in which a professional librarian helps the student to use the library resources in solving the projects or problems or assignments he meets in the subject area? Of course, this cannot be done if it is an added assignment to an already-busy staff member. So I go even farther in projection and suggest a staff member who might be called a "circulating" librarian. He or she would be a subject matter consultant, well schooled in library practices and deep rooted in a philosophy of library usage in education. He or she would work in the classroom, conference room, stacks, or wherever there was need for planning and making known the value of the library in supplementing the lecture and the textbook, both to the student and to the faculty. He or she would become in a very real way a teacher-librarian. It is neither an easy position nor is it an inexpensive one. But it does offer a challenge.

Certainly a staff member such as this is not meant to take away from the individual contact now established by both circulation and reference librarians. Nor is it assured of startling, immediate success. It is something any staff member today could and would initiate, given the freedom from technical and janitorial duties, and the opportunity to follow an experimental plan. Let us awake from our dream and say aloud, "Today we will offer the same services while we are small which we dream of offering when we grow big."

39. WHAT MOTIVATES
SECONDARY SCHOOL VOLUNTARY READING?

Virginia Tozier

The majority of pupils in a secondary school are enslaved by the collective opinion of the group, which powerfully affects all personal activities including voluntary reading. Since this is so, the school librarian who would increase the reading of books for pleasure and enrichment would do well to give first attention to what "the gang" thinks of the library and the librarian. If she can be objective enough to face the truth, and brave enough to tackle public opinion should it seem to be negative or worse, a great deal can be done to promote reading in that school.

If, as in most cases, the school library has been imposed upon the school by state law or regulation, and not set up to fill an expressed need by the students and teachers, her task is to create interest in and identification with the library through participation. A library board should be set up to function under the chairmanship of the librarian, meeting from time to time at her request. The principal, teachers representing each department, and students representing each grade, should be the members. They should be appointed by the principal for terms of one school year, to serve in an advisory capacity to the librarian with special attention to the following areas:

To develop a program of library service to the school.

To assist in making library policy for selecting, evaluating, and discarding books.

If board members are capable and popular leaders of the student body and the faculty, and if they can be made to take responsibility for identifying the library needs of the school and advising the librarian as to ways in which they may be met, the library will begin to be a vital part of the school. If the

177

librarian will graciously guide, inform, and carry out the decisions of the board, she too will soon enjoy a closer and more meaningful relationship with her patrons, and take on a new dimension in the life of the school.

Equally important in effective public relations is bringing student library assistants actively into the management of library operations. A central committee of three library assistants can be set up to supervise the weekly work schedule, suggest improvements in routines, and plan special projects and displays. By appointing each member for three weeks, and staggering the terms so that one is added and one dropped each week, continuity and participation by all student library workers is assured.

Other influences on any student's attitude toward reading for pleasure and enrichment come from teachers, librarians, and parents, and such mass media as the moving pictures, radio, and television. Parents who set a good example in the quality and quantity of their reading, and then take the time to discuss books and share ideas with their children can promote voluntary reading. Teachers and librarians who know young people individually, and the books they like through having read them, can recommend appropriate selections and increase enjoyment. If the teacher uses good group techniques in reading projects such as letting friends work together, and good readers helping poor ones, she can increase her effectiveness. The school librarian should demonstrate her friendly cooperation with all teachers, and especially with the public library if the library good will, and voluntary reading are to continue outside of school. Instead of replacing reading, popular entertainment nowadays can promote it if skillfully used.

When the many and not the few look upon the library as a friendly and interesting place to spend time regularly, it is necessary to consider the quality and the quantity of reading materials in relation to the needs of the students, and the practical matter of accessibility. Because of the rapid growth of interests and abilities from grades seven through twelve, a six-year school has what amounts to two libraries. Books which are right and appealing to children in grades seven, eight, and nine are of little use to those in ten, eleven, and twelve and vice versa. Of course, there is some overlapping, but far more

books are needed than in a three- or four-year school serving
the same number of pupils because of the two different publics.

Supplying books and other materials to meet the basic needs
of the curriculum is of first importance, and this includes reference materials, core materials, and enrichment reading as
well as books suitable for the various maturity levels and interests and abilities of all the pupils. To build the reading habit
and a lifelong enjoyment of books, and to replace the trashy
books often picked up by students outside of school, the library
should provide pleasure books of all types. In selecting these
books, it should be guided by the natural interests of the students so as to stimulate the greatest amount of voluntary
reading.

Magazines and newspapers have great appeal to students,
and also provide pleasure and relaxation. The books in a school
library should be attractive, and using plastic covers to protect
the colorful book jackets is worth while. Constantly changing
displays of books and book covers create interest. Including
student news items, jokes, etc., on bulletin boards in the library make it an information center. Using such themes as
"Reading is fun!" and organizing reading clubs publicize the
entertainment to be found in reading. Although library publicity
planned around student ideas may not be as professional as that
initiated by the librarian, it is more apt to strike a spark with
the student body, and so should have priority.

In almost every instance, books in a school should be under
the administration of the school library, and be in the library
when not in use. Classroom libraries should be borrowed from
the central library for the period needed, and then returned so
that all the children in the school and not just one class may
read them. The fact that the librarian is responsible for the
care and the circulation of all the books means better service
for the whole school. Of course the school library must be freely accessible to every student before and after school, or for
one or more periods during the day. If it is not, those who come
on late buses or leave early for work and have no free periods
can never use the library.

When a study hall is held in the library it ceases to be a
library. Space is wasted by students doing nonlibrary homework, and time is wasted by the librarian doing nonprofessional

monitoring. Necessary study hall discipline can destroy the most carefully built-up library atmosphere and good student-librarian relationships, by substituting policing for relaxed informality.

Individual differences powerfully affect voluntary reading because they complicate the problem of book selection to meet varying needs. The student should be helped to find a book he can read with ease, no matter how much below or above his age group it may be. He should be encouraged to enjoy reading books at a level where he is, and then led from there by the librarian as his growth in reading ability and maturation make improvement in taste possible. The good reader should be complimented for his success, and the superior student should be constantly challenged so that his vital powers are not dissipated or wasted but stimulated and developed. All students should be exposed to new interests through the books they read, in order that they may grow in insight and broaden their horizons.

Curiosity is a built-in mechanism in every child from the brightest to the slowest, which is an invaluable aid to teachers and librarians. It is especially strong in the junior high school when childish interests begin to give way to adolescent awareness of the world outside the self. These are the years when imaginations are most active, and young people are not quite so busy with school and social affairs as they will be later. Although individual interests are as evident at this age as at any other, the background of experience during these years is more uniform than in older students, so that in general the interests of these years tend to be somewhat stereotyped. The interests of boys of all ages are more alike than those of boys and girls in any age group, so sex is the most important factor in interest. Such themes as adventure, animal life, nature, child life, excitement, humor, mischief, thrills, mystery, realism, and suspense have great popularity in books.

In grades ten, eleven, and twelve books which introduce all kinds of adult problems are of general interest. Current events, problems of national life, vocations students may later follow, sports, personal development, and such questions as the meaning of life, true values, right and wrong become important. Since interests become more unique and individualized in these years, through varying experiences which enrich background and develop personality, the librarian must constantly be alert to the growth and changes in each student to keep his reading appropriate to his development. As competition for his time becomes more intense, more stimulation should be given to his interest in reading through books of more immediately practical or pleasurable value to him. Up-to-date, timely books will be read, and provide vicarious experience to youth. Through films, trips, radio and television programs curiosity can be guided into a will to learn by means of the enrichment reading in books, or it can be killed by dull and repetitious or inappropriate material.

Travel books are popular with both girls and boys in these years. Girls become interested in romantic literature at about thirteen, while boys only become interested in this type of novel during late adolescence. Magazines about mechanics, sports, athletics, and G-men appeal to boys, while sentimental adult fiction, "true life" stories, and stories of movie stars are read by girls. Once they have acquired the taste for adult fiction, both boys and girls read no more juvenile material.

J. M. Ross says that "Children read because of three fundamental characteristics of their nature — curiosity, desire for wish fulfillment, and the tendency to imitate," and the librarian would do well to use all three in the promotion of reading. Consider the comics which are among the favorite reading matter of all children, even those who read good literature. Luella Cole says:

> Their vocabulary is relatively easy. Each book of comics contains about 10,000 words, of which 9,000 are among the commonest in the language. There is some slang, but such words do not exceed five per cent of the reading matter. The chief appeal of the comics to children rests upon love of excitement, adventure, mystery, sport, and humor — but they act also as wish fulfillment of all things children would like to do or be.

To find out what wishes children may have, ask them to write the answer to the following three wishes.

I wish I were —
I wish I could —
I wish I might —

If teachers and librarians can find such clues to children's dreams through the above method, or by talking with parents, books might be suggested which would provide excellent voluntary reading.

How many young people today are surrounded by older people they can imitate who read, enjoy, and discuss books as a normal and regular part of the daily routine? In the school library the student who never sees his parents, brothers, or sisters read can watch teachers and classmates browsing, taking out books, enjoying reading and discussing books. Since a very large per cent of secondary school books are of adult level, teachers can do nothing which is more influential in promoting voluntary reading than to frequently and publicly take out books from the library and then to share the pleasure they find in them with their classes. The best school library is the one used regularly by everyone from the principal to the youngest pupil.

A librarian in a small or medium-size school who is closely associated with the pupils from the day they march through the library as a class making the seventh-grade orientation tour of the school to the triumphant recessional march on graduation day, can work wonders in developing taste in reading through guidance. Knowing the reading level of the child and his current interests, and winning his confidence to the point that he goes to her for help and advice, she can lead him from wherever he is, to broader and deeper interests in keeping with his mental and physical growth and experience. This, of course, takes time and patience, as nothing is gained by cramming books down students' throats.

Such an old but effective trick as telling the most exciting or appealing bit of a book and then leaving the listener "cliff hanging," full of interest and anxiety to know what comes next, is indirect guidance which has motivated the reading of many a library book. Teachers who make their own curiosity clear and contagious, and sometimes start an assignment with "The other day I was reading . . ." rather than "Read this chapter and hand in a report tomorrow" are guiding and motivating good reading. However, honesty should be basic in giving such advice. When you do not like a book some student asks you about, tell him so; and if you add that many other people have liked it, he may still read the book, but will respect your truthfulness

Literature courses are included in the secondary school curriculum to enrich the students' background of ideas and to foster interest in good books and fine writing so that reading may be a lifelong pleasure. In practice required reading, which is inappropriate to the maturity level and reading ability of many pupils, has caused a great number to hate not only the required classics which they read, but all reading. Book reports which are often copied from some book digest, without reading the book at all, turn the attention of the reader from what suspense there is in the book to the conventional details required by the teacher. Both of these common practices are an enormous handicap to voluntary reading. It is reasonable that a minimum of quality be required in school reading, but a list is never as satisfactory as individual help by the teacher or librarian, and when a required list is made, it should be long enough so as to give suitable books for all levels of readers. If the pupil is below his mental age in reading ability, the teacher should take the responsibility for helping him to improve. Book reports which stress helping others to know about the book, through suggestions as to who would like it and why, shift the emphasis from cross examination to points the reader liked in the book. Allowing some freedom of selection is most necessary as young people do not expect to enjoy required reading.

Dr. Samuel Johnson once said:

A man ought to read just as inclination leads him; for what he reads as a task will do him little good. A young man should read five hours a day, and so may acquire a great deal of knowledge.

Since involuntary task reading is all too often approached with apathy and antagonism nowadays, and inclination leads to television, a school librarian who agrees with Dr. Johnson needs to understand the psychological factors underlying adolescent motivation in order to encourage more and better voluntary reading.

40. PROMOTION AIDS FOR THE HIGH SCHOOL LIBRARIAN

Alma N. Stanlis

To various groups within the high school, the title of "Librarian" holds many meanings. To the school administration, the librarian has to shine as an efficient, economical "keeper of the books," and as an artistic designer of displays. To teachers, she has to be a source of quick information and inspiration, and an eager lender of materials. To the students she must reflect friendliness and helpfulness. If she doesn't disintegrate from the strain, the librarian's ability in all these directions will show in the worthwhile use made of the library by the total school population. How else can she measure her work?

Two obvious tangible devices for attracting students and faculty to the library are displays and newspaper publicity.

The school newspaper offers more than an opportunity to publish book reviews. Try using students' and teachers' preferences and library habits for a good article. As Mark Twain said, "A good compliment will last me two months," and students love the compliment of seeing their names in print.

A successful publicity stunt at our school employed a technique used in the automobile industry. Instead of publicizing the twenty-millionth automobile, we made a celebrity out of the student who checked out the 6,000th book in the circulation count. We took his picture, gave him a prize, and put an article in the school paper. This dramatized the circulation figures in a unique way, and provided good publicity material.

Another minor but well-used device is a group of annotated booklists, divided by reader interests. Carefully chosen book jackets are used on the folder covers, and they are given such titles as "Especially for Girls," "Animal Adventures," and "Into the Future." These annotated lists are more interesting to the average reader than the card catalog, and give him a starting point when he needs inspiration. They must be kept up-to-date by adding notations as books are processed. It is also a good idea to issue to all teachers and administrators a

184

complete list of new books added each month, and have those lists in an accessible folder.

One big special event such as a book fair can do wonders to arouse interest in reading and in the library. If the fair is to be a success, the sponsors need to enlist the enthusiasm and aid of the total school staff, both in selection and selling. The Senior Scholastic Magazine has an excellent kit of ideas for such fairs; paperbound books seem to be the best choice because they are inexpensive and offer a wide variety of titles. A unifying theme for the displays, advertising, and arrangement of books is helpful, as is a tie-in with either a total school project to raise money, for example, or with Book Week or National Library Week.

There is good publicity and prestige value in having a specialty of some kind in your school library. Many public and college libraries are able to develop special collections, and by careful buying, school libraries can do the same on a smaller scale. Make a point of ordering a few books for that specialty each year. You may choose to emphasize history and biography related to your own state, to build an outstanding vocational collection, to secure autographed books, or to specialize in materials on one or more foreign countries.

Some intangible ideas for promoting use of the library depend solely upon the librarian for fulfillment. She may have wonderful displays, and fine publicity, but may still be falling short in her personal attitudes which directly influence the climate in the library. It is very important for her to be careful of her answers to students and faculty, especially when she is harrassed and hurried. If she isn't careful, she may discourage friends by negative or half-hearted responses. Replying with many "ifs, ands, and buts" to a teacher who asks if she can bring her class in during the last hour that same day will not encourage her to try again. Telling a student to "look in the card catalog" when he asks for help is not the right answer. A positive reply will soften the blow, even if you must tell the teacher she is very welcome to come tomorrow, and if there is not much material available for the student's term paper problems. Flexibility in scheduling and in rules should be the librarian's byword. I don't mean a whimsical disregard for rules one day, and an iron hand the next, depending upon mood;

I mean a <u>prudent regard</u> for the individual student and his difficulties, and for the primary purposes of the library.

Another intangible attitude concerns book selection policies. Not only is it essential to order and process new books all year long to maintain the interest of the omnivorous readers, but also to select widely as well as wisely, for the gifted as well as the poor students. Even if only two persons read Plato and Homer, for example, the classics in world literature must still be available to those two. It is easy to provide for the reluctant reader, and perhaps harder to justify purchases for the few gifted ones. But the librarian has an obligation to emphasize quality, to show leadership in the choice of good materials. Don't sell the best students short just because they are outnumbered; they are the saving remnant of American education.

Through personal experience, I have found that the standard lists do not provide enough scholarly or mature materials even for a basic collection. For College English 11 and 12, a carefully selected but wide range of novels of all <u>genres</u> and nationalities is vital, along with good critical histories of the various literatures. The Modern Library editions offer a very satisfactory selection. In the field of science, an excellent buying list is furnished by the American Association for the Advancement of Science, in Washington, D.C., called "Books in the Traveling Science Library." Up-to-date, challenging books are essential in the pure and applied sciences if the collection is to be well used.

One last suggestion: don't be afraid to try something new. Rearrange the furniture; try a reader interest grouping; buy some of the drugstore booklets on cars, guns, etc., out of fine money; subscribe to a new magazine or two. Most important of all however, let's never forget that the <u>best</u> publicity device is the librarian's own reading and enthusiasm for books. Get one good student to read a favorite book, and you will start a chain reaction among other students and possibly in their lives. This sort of influence is certainly intangible, but is of inestimable value.

41. SYMPOSIUM: WHAT MAKES A BOOK TALK GOOD?

There are as many systems for giving book talks as there are libraries which sponsor them — so a look at the policies of some of the larger young adult departments would indicate. Each system, however, is based on a clearly thought out philosophy of the hows and whys of the book talk and is adapted to the particular needs of its youth and size of the Y staff.

As a sample of how one program is conceived and executed, here is librarian Helen Mekeel's description of her program in the Kern County, Calif., Free Library.

"Book talks for us are primarily means whereby we hope to inveigle boys and girls of high school age into using the branch nearest them; we cover a wide range of interests in the 40 to 45 minutes usually allotted to us, hoping to find something for everyone. Our talks, therefore, usually consist of a series of thumbnail sketches, lightly held together by a theme which may be only "What's New," or as abstract as "Courage," as concrete as "Travel" (any one of which can include fiction, biography, books of self-help, hobbies, personal narrative, general information.)

"Because we're trying to catch the interest of a great many young people of varied backgrounds and abilities, our criteria for the selection of book talk material are:

"(1) Suitability to the age and cultural group. Is the book too sophisticated? Immature? Because there are completely dissimilar cultural groups in different areas of the county, this applies to fiction and to developmental nonfiction (books on manners, grooming, speech, college, vocations, etc.)

"(2) Does the title have fairly wide appeal? Is it of interest to both boys and girls? To young people with a limited reading background?

"(3) If fiction, is it a good story? There is no point in working up enthusiasm if it tends to bog down under the weight of "authentic background material." Does it have some developmental values for this particular age group? (Developmental values sometimes offset literary mediocrity especially if the

187

group is of lower than average reading level.) If the book is selected for the discriminating reader, can you transmit something of value from it to those who will not be able to read it for themselves?

"(4) General readability. No matter how authentic, no matter how much research went into it, if a book is dull reading, we reserve it for its informational value. We don't try to use it as reading bait.

"(5) Does the book tie in with the school curriculum in any way? Good public relations! We try to include at least one such title.

"(6) Is the book new? If we choose titles that have been in the collection a year or so, chances are that the top students will already have found those books in their interest field. For this reason we hold back new books about which we plan to talk, putting them into the local branch at book talk time.

"(7) Does the reviewer like the book? If you like it well enough, your enthusiasm can sell even a difficult or unusual book.

"Since all three staff members browse through all new titles as they are received at headquarters, this is the moment for selection of a book for review. Where or when it will be used is immaterial; if she knows she can make a particular book go, and if it fits into the above criteria, the librarian works up her preliminary notes there and then. How full these notes are depends upon the individual. Except for occasional phrases or for some specific effect, none of us memorizes his talk lest he lose spontaneity. None of us uses another's notes, lest the result sound canned. The spark which comes from the librarian's own remembered enthusiasm for a book is, I feel, most likely to ignite a kindred spark in the listener. As beginners, staff members are urged to practice in front of a full length mirror.

"The book talk program is planned more or less to a pattern. It always begins and ends with a sure-fire title, with the first book aimed directly at the boys, the last one directed to the boys and girls. For the young teen-agers, freshmen and pre-freshmen (high eighth graders), a 45 minute period would include 11 or 12 books, some of which receive only the briefest comments — just enough to captivate the listener — others a

fuller coverage. We try to include: a sports story (this is a
good, sure-fire sendoff for boys); a girl's story (contemporary);
a biography; a developmental nonfiction title; a hobby book; two
fiction, one past and one future, i.e. historical and science fiction; another contemporary girls' story; a contemporary boys'
story; one or two more nonfiction titles, one travel or personal
narrative if possible; and, to finish, an animal story.

"For upper classmen, the pattern is not so apparent, but
the first and last titles are foolproof; fiction is outweighed by
non-fiction by the introduction of more self-help books and by
personal narratives.

"How do we start a book talk? Well, we don't start a book
talk by telling about the library's services — we've learned the
hard way that the TV technique is more effective: capture your
audience first, and work in your commercials along the way.
We always hope we'll be introduced, though some of our intro-
ductions would run close second to Emily Kimbrough's.

"Actually we don't start the book talk with the introduction;
we start it as the first youngster comes through the library
door, or when we walk into the classroom or sit waiting to be
introduced. We start a book talk by catching the eye of every
student, if possible. They're looking at you, they don't know
just what to expect of you, what kind of person you are, and
they're curious. It's an easy thing to establish rapport. If a
girl looks as if she'd like to smile at us, we smile at her first;
if two or three boys and girls are looking at us, giggling, talking behind their hands, we don't wonder if our slip is showing
or our lipstick is crooked, we smile at them instead. And I
don't mean a grin . . . only the slightest suggestion of a smile,
a sort of just-between-you-and-me smile is enough. I find it
helps to say (mentally, of course) 'Hi!' Even the sullen boy in
the front row will respond!

"Having established a friendly feeling with practically
every person in the room, it's time to speak. Introductory
words are of the briefest; they vary according to the circumstances, but informality and, if the library is the meeting
place, hospitality are the keynotes.

"Since time is of the essence, we don't encourage discussion during the book talk period. Response can get out of hand:
even controlled response tends to keep one book, of interest

to a limited group, in the limelight. We'd rather cover more
territory, reach the interests of more young people. If the talk
is in the library, instead of a classroom, we try to leave time
for browsing, and we find that discussion comes informally at
that time.

"It is a little difficult to determine the exact amount of
time given to book talks. Since the area of Kern County is more
than that of Connecticut, Delaware, and Rhode Island combined,
it isn't unusual to travel 150 miles for two or three talks; we're
apt to start out at seven in the morning and return close to six
in the evening. Counting travel time, actual preparation time,
and the talks themselves, about two-fifths of the staff hours
are devoted to book talks.

"We try, when possible, to have classes brought to the library, for when we talk at the schools, we feel we're still in
a school-centered atmosphere of discipline instead of a library-
centered atmosphere of informality. If we do talk at schools,
we try to talk to individual classes — time consuming, but we
can establish rapport with a small group more effectively. Out-
side-of-school-groups, such as YWCA, church groups, social
clubs connected with school activities, we contact at their own
place of meeting."

Selecting the Books

Though the methods of selecting and presenting the books
vary, most would agree with Grace Slocum of the Brooklyn,
N.Y., Public Library that the aim of the program is "to encourage independent reading and use of books by young people
above and beyond the requirements of a school curriculum. The
correlation between school and books is so fixed in so many
people's minds that the use of books after formal school days
are over drops off to a high degree. The book talk, we think,
is one way of making books so exciting and necessary that reading continues as a lifelong habit."

All agree that the first book should be a sure-fire title.
Elaine Simpson of The New York Public Library begins with
two titles on the reading level of all the group and with appeal
to all the group, going on to books which challenge the reader's
ability and open new fields of interest.

Madeline Margo of the Public Library of Youngstown and

WHAT MAKES A BOOK TALK GOOD?

Mahoning County in Ohio writes, "I usually begin with two or three new books dealing with national and international affairs, trying to tie them in with newspaper headlines and magazine articles. I feel this is not only timely but lets the student know that you know what is going on."

Learned Bulman of the East Orange, N.J., Public Library begins with a class-catcher like Roy Chapman Andrew's Heart of Asia or Cousteau's The Silent World, then alternates a book of interest to boys with one of interest to girls, with dual interest as often as possible.

Mrs. Simpson advocates using a carefully planned presentation of three or four books, though the experienced librarian may vary this. "Although other titles are displayed or lists are provided, the use of more than three or four books in the talk itself has been found to result in a confusion to the listener similar to that felt by a person surveying the wares in a ten-cent store window."

Eleanor Kidder of the Seattle, Wash., Public Library writes, "I generally take 30 to 40 jackets with me and am prepared to speak briefly or at length on any of them. These run from the easy to the difficult and are used accordingly as I gauge reaction and response in the class. I generally use one or two lead books sure to seize attention and tell an incident from it, giving a brief preliminary setting and the conclusion . . . Most of the books which I treat this way are nonfiction, not because I urge the reading of nonfiction, but because they lend themselves to talks much better than fiction. Then, according to the amount of time I have, I give a brief characterization of other books, with a wide range of appeal."

Ray Fry of the Dallas, Tex., Public Library introduces his main talks with teasers on about five or ten other books in the same category, moving into the main talk sooner if the audience is restless.

Librarians working under Margaret Edwards in the Enoch Pratt Free Library in Baltimore, Maryland, give out lists and lead up to the main talk by calling attention to related books on the list.

"It is impossible to prepare a set program in advance," writes Mr. Bulman. "There is no truly homogeneous class. Whether slow or fast it still contains a variety of interests all

191

of which should be catered to in the course of a session of book reviews. . . . Have at least 15 or 20 titles for a single class and 30 to 40 for several classes in one day. . . . At least a dozen titles can be discussed in 25 minutes. Even showing the book, starting to tell one of the exciting bits and stopping with 'Sound interesting? Wondering how it ends? Why not read . . . ?' is often sufficient.

"By checking with the school librarian on arrival the reviewer is able to tell the students which titles are available in the school library."

Preparing the Talk

Ray Fry: Choose a situation or incident that will serve as an appetizer. Cut the talk, including as much introductory information as necessary, outlining the plot, introducing the main characters, and setting the scene. Incidents from some books need little introduction. If the author is a good one, use his own words. (Most librarians would have difficulty improving on Michener, Richter, Buck, Benet.) The finished talk should run four to five pages double-spaced. It can be shorter, but if it runs the full five pages, interest must be sustained all the way. Memorize the talk until it does not sound memorized. This may hurt in the beginning but as your repertoire builds it will prove worthwhile. A talk memorized in '46 comes back rapidly if needed in '56 and they are usually needed.

Grace Slocum: The type of talk we use is related in a way to storytelling. An incident from a book that is fairly complete in itself and that gives the flavor of the book is lifted and told pretty much in the words of the author, with some cutting and summarizing. These talks are typed out and may or may not be learned word for word. By writing the talk out you know what you are going to say and will not fumble for words. There is also the advantage of having the talk on file for future use and for exchanging with other staff members. Such a talk would be from six to nine minutes long.

Eleanor Kidder: After selecting the incident to be used in detail, jot down an outline to give setting and conclusion to the part to be used. Develop the incident mentally so that you never hesitate. Make cards, to be filed but never used in public, with introduction, development of the incident giving key words, page and paragraph references to save time when you need to refresh your memory to use it again in the future.

Elaine Simpson: The mechanics of preparation are left up to the individual librarian. He selects one incident or one section of each book to relate as a story. He lets the book speak for itself through this incident. He does not tell the entire story nor give a synopsis of the plot, he does not talk all around the book without telling any of the story. He does not give a critical analysis of the book. He does not memorize. He uses the author's words occasionally if they come naturally. He may write out the talk; he may make guiding notes (but never uses them while talking to a group); or he may just re-read the incident and think about it until he knows what he wants to say and how he wants to say it.

Jane McClure, co-ordinator of work with young adults in Philadelphia: Staff members draft their talks and give a dry run before the co-ordinator or assistant co-ordinator.

Margaret Edwards: Occasionally we choose a subject using five or six titles, gradually building up to stronger and stronger incidents until we end with a clincher. We use the subject "Decisions" which introduces three or four titles very briefly, Call It Treason in more detail, and ends with the terrific scene in The Cruel Sea where the captain of the "Compass Rose" must decide whether or not to send the depth bomb after the submarine below the swimming men.

Introducing the Talk

"Because we think identification with the branch is important, the branch librarian and I make the class visits together when possible," Miss Kidder writes.

Mrs. Simpson suggests that the talk may be started by mentioning a well-known news item, a TV program, a seasonal event, the weather — anything to tie books naturally into the group's interest or experience.

Response During Talk

Here again practices differ. Some solicit response, while others discourage it.

"We rarely get response during a talk but talk with any student who wishes to speak," writes Mrs. Edwards. "Our emphasis is on introducing 20 or 25 titles to the students during the period rather than leading a discussion — not that the latter is not valuable, but our primary aim is to get students to use their school libraries and to come to the public library, and we center all our fire on this one purpose."

Some like Mr. Fry and Miss McClure make time available at the end of the talk for questions.

"Always be prepared to take advantage of a question or unexpected remark and use it to bring another title to the front. There is no damage and considerable gain in referring to other books not with one," writes Mr. Bulman.

Miss Slocum finds that group response or participation is not too satisfactory with the "story" type of talk because the spell tends to be broken.

Mrs. Simpson writes: "An informal give and take between the librarian and teenagers is encouraged as long as it is pertinent to the subject of the book being used, or reading in general, or the library. Sometimes the librarian will throw out questions, ask the young people for titles read and enjoyed, or if one of the group has already read a book the librarian had planned to use, he may let that student tell the story. The degree — and success — of the response depends largely upon the experience and self-confidence of the librarian. A new librarian rarely tries to initiate comment or discussion until he has read widely in teen-age books and feels completely at ease.

Time Allotted to Book Talks

Staff time allotted to book talks varies, too. In Dallas where the Y program is only a year old, book talks are just getting underway, while Enoch Pratt has three women and seven men in its speakers pool and they spend 250 to 300 periods a year in the city high schools. Three librarians work as a trio with each speaking for 15 minutes of a period.

In Seattle, Miss Kidder gives most of the book talks. The preparation consumes so much time that the branch assistants seldom have the time to devote to it.

In New York in 1955-56, 1,763 talks and seven assemblies were given by approximately 40 librarians, more than 35 per cent of whom were inexperienced. Individual time spent varies from the inexperienced Y librarian in a branch with perhaps

six classes a year to the field worker with more than 300 classes a year.

Mr. Bulman spends approximately 10 per cent of his time
on book talks.

Book talks are most effective with small groups, and the
position taken by Miss McClure is the most generally accepted
one: "We prefer to talk to smaller groups, individual classrooms, small club groups, or groups at a recreation center.
But we never turn down any invitations."

42. LIBRARY ACTIVITIES FOR AN ELEMENTARY SCHOOL

Helen B. Baldwin

Children's reading is everybody's business. Since the
school library is the hub of reading activities, the librarian
must plan activities that will reach the children from several
directions. The principal in his office, the teacher in her classroom, the librarian at the nearest branch library, and the parents at home have a mutual interest in the progressive development of the reading habit in the elementary school child. With
their cooperation, at some time during the year library activities should touch every child from kindergarten to the eighth
grade through his classroom or his interests.

The old saying "Well begun is half done" applies to the
librarian's contact with the primary children. Frequent visits
to the classroom with new books for the reading corner provide
a natural way to win the confidence and friendship of the younger child. If the librarian makes some special contribution to
the group each time, then the air of expectancy that attends
these visits will carry over to regular library periods at a
later date.

A good story always finds a receptive audience. One time
a story may be told; another time one may be read. Children
also respond with enthusiasm to stories or poems requiring

group participation in word or action.

Storytelling can be more than entertainment, for it is also an open sesame to shared reading experiences. Favorite stories take on new meaning when they are dramatized. Stick puppets provide the younger group, especially the shy ones, with a wonderful opportunity to be heard but not seen as they retell a story. The exhibitionists may prefer to pantomime a story. It is the impromptu dramatization of a story that has been enjoyed that is its greatest recommendation. An entire class reacted enthusiastically to the suggestion that they dramatize Millions of Cats by Wanda Gag. The children took turns playing the old man and the old woman while the rest of the class willingly fought and meowed as millions of cats would.

The first visit to the library should be a memorable occasion. If the children have made any drawings illustrating stories the librarian has told in their class, these drawings should be prominently displayed. After the group has become acquainted with the library and feels at home, the relaxed atmosphere should promote a spontaneous and informal discussion of books.

Picture books were especially popular with a combination class of second- and third-grade children. One day during a library visit a little girl confided to the librarian that she had made a "book." Thus a pupil-initiated activity was born. All the children wanted to make "books." The librarian showed them numerous picture books, noting especially the cover, title page, and dedication. The children discussed their stories, the layout of their books, and the dedication. Since it was near Christmas time, the dedication was obvious. Each child wrote his own story and drew appropriate illustrations, copying the format of picture books. The stories showed keen imagination plus a good sense of artistry and balance. The books were proudly displayed and later wrapped as Christmas gifts for parents.

After hearing the story Stone Soup by Marcia Brown, a third grader seized the suggestion that they write a play based on the story. Little rewriting was needed. The adaptation provided for a narrator and twelve speaking parts. A play requires an audience. So it was that a classroom book program for parents was planned. Those who did not have a part in the play displayed a wide variety of books they had enjoyed. Their own unrehearsed comments provided proof that there was a book for every interest.

LIBRARY ACTIVITIES FOR AN ELEMENTARY SCHOOL

If it is desirable to win the confidence and friendship of the child entering school for the first time, it is equally desirable to enlist the understanding support of the parents. Any principal should see the "ounce of prevention" technique behind the plan to invite parents of first graders to a tea in the library. The principal, first-grade teachers, and the branch librarian should also be invited. In the atmosphere of books the librarians and teachers can help the parents understand the place of books and reading in their children's lives. But more important, they can help parents understand the great part they can play in helping their children discover that books can be fun. If possible, give each parent a copy of the pamphlet Family Reading and Story-telling, by Margaret E. Martignoni, or purchase several copies to be circulated among the parents of each class. The branch librarian can suggest that the family come to the library as a group; that each member of the family have his own card; that the parents read regularly to the child; and that they keep an ever-changing variety of library books in the home even if the child seems disinterested. Eventually he'll become curious.

Before parent or teacher knows whether Johnny can or can't read, help these parents to understand that some children will listen to anything or read anything; others are more selective; still others show no interest in books or reading. Urge parents not to worry and especially not to nag the child who is apathetic towards books; suggest that they work with teachers and librarians to discover the child's interests and lead him to books through them. A copy of Growing Up with Books or a suggested booklist covering all possible interests for first graders could be given to parents. With a wide variety of books on display, the purpose of the tea should be accomplished.

Regardless of grade level, parents need to keep posted on reading materials for children. A harrassed PTA program committee should be open to the suggestion that one program each year be library-centered. Let the students themselves appear at a meeting to show and tell about the variety of books at their disposal. A forum offers a good opportunity to inform parents of material available for their children. A library play presented for a school assembly could be repeated for parents, while Parents' Night at school also provides an opportunity to emphasize the role of the library in the school program.

Those who love poetry have often wondered how they could

197

instill a love of poetry in children. In Baltimore County, Maryland, a highly successful poetry project was carried out by a school librarian. She began by arranging an ingenious display outside the library door. The glass doors of her display case were covered with colored construction paper, leaving only a small round opening through which children could look. The only caption on the outside was the one word, "Peek!" Children were so intrigued that there were several around the display case most of the time. Inside the lighted cabinet was a poster announcing a "Silver Pennies" contest and suggesting that children come to the library for details. Several books of poems were a part of the display which took as its theme: YOU MUST HAVE A SILVER PENNY TO GET INTO FAIRYLAND. Blanche Jennings Thompson's delightful collection of poems, Silver Pennies, was placed in a prominent spot.

At the first meeting of the interest group, the librarian talked about the pleasures of reading poetry and read several poems aloud. The point of the contest — to have one's name added to a poster showing fairyland — was explained and the simple rules announced. Admission to fairyland was gained with a silver penny (a foil-covered slug, or a candy "penny"), awarded for learning a stated number of poems. Pupils were encouraged to borrow books of poetry and to write original poems. Emphasis was placed on enjoyment of poetry, sharing, and voluntary memorization. The result was that children discovered the delights of poetry, enthusiasm ran high, everybody had a wonderful time — and the poetry shelves were stripped for weeks after the contest was over.

Hobbies play an important part in the life of many children. Since there are books for every hobby, many school libraries sponsor an annual HOBBY DAY. Others prefer to focus attention on one hobby at a time. Whether the aim is to promote an interest in hobbies or to publicize the achievements of hobbyists alongside books they used, such displays stress better than words the importance of books. A very reluctant reader suddenly showed an interest in encyclopedias. Later he was noted thumbing through other books with unprecedented concentration. A short time afterward he came to school with a windmill he had made from an Erector set. His interest had been aroused when his teacher explained the use of windmills. His working model was a composite of several pictures found in books. It became the focal point of a display that featured fiction and non-fiction books on the Netherlands as well as wooden shoes, native dolls, pictures, and other art objects.

In the intermediate and upper grades as the interests broaden and reading ability increases, the library can and should be a paradise for the insatiable curiosity of children. To stimulate an interest in research one elementary school librarian capitalized on children's curiosity. Nature objects were displayed on several tables for identification. Everything from seashells to wasp nests was included. The fourth, fifth, and sixth grades vied with each other to see which group could name the most objects. Each child was given a piece of paper containing numbers corresponding with the objects on display. At the end of the contest individual scores were compiled, divided by the number of the class enrollment, and the score for the grade thus determined. However, each child knew his own record as a researcher, and was so sure he could do better next time that similar contests had to be held.[1]

Convinced that reference materials are understood when they are voluntarily used, another librarian gave the workshop plan a new twist. Each seventh- and eighth-grade class was given the same list of questions to be answered within a limited time. The source of information as well as the answer was to be given. Accuracy was stressed. In event of a tie the classes understood that the most complete answer would be given preference. Although each student worked on at least one question, it was evident that they double-checked on one another and so shared the benefits of others' research. The primary purpose of the contest was to familiarize students with the use of reference materials, but it also created a genuine interest in hitherto unexplored areas of the library.

Many teachers and librarians agree that little is gained in reading contests that place a premium on an impressive list of books read by pupils. With the feeling that it would be better for children to keep their lists private, the librarian in a small community school gave folders entitled BOOKS I HAVE READ to seventh and eighth graders. The folders were kept on file in the library, but were available to the students at all times. A simple system of starring books according to their appeal was suggested. No annotations were required. Neither librarian nor teacher checked on the folders. However, students referred to each other's lists. "What's it about?" they could be heard asking as they noted some two-star listing. As a result, many of the students began to write brief comments after each listing in the folder. Later in the year when the librarian asked these classes to suggest books for purchase which they had read, but which were not owned by the school library, the lists were eagerly shared. The classes also compiled a bibliography on BOOKS WE LIKED BEST for the use of classes the following year.

Formal book reviews, be they oral or written, dampen a child's natural delight in reading. Most students regard such reports as a check-up on their reading. The reviews are stereotyped and dull. Yet teachers and librarians know that many of these same students talk enthusiastically about their books in private. A regular feature in the Wilson Library Bulletin suggests a good heading for a bulletin board, and incidentally a good way to get enthusiastic book reviews voluntarily. SEASONED TO TASTE could be the headline, with salt and pepper shakers used to carry out the idea. One week the subtitle could be I LIKE HUMOROUS BOOKS. Book jackets of such books could be displayed with a short signed "sales talk" about each book. Another subtitle could be I LIKE ADVENTURE, or, I LIKE FAMILY STORIES. The students could suggest categories. A schedule could be posted so students would have time to prepare a "sales talk" (book review) for their choice. All reviews should be submitted voluntarily. Circulation and requests for books thus reviewed could be checked to gauge the effectiveness of each "sales talk," or students could vote on the best one.

Many class activities terminate in an assembly program. It is a good idea to tie in with that program by having an exhibit in the library of books used in planning the program, alongside murals, shadow boxes, or other handicraft produced in connection with it. Such exhibits have usually served their purpose in the classroom and will have a greater audience when displayed in the library.

The teachers of music, art, physical education, home economics, and industrial arts deserve the unsolicited cooperation of the school librarian at all times even though they do not avail themselves of the library's services as frequently as others may. Events of interest to those departments — such as Health Week, an art convention, or a special children's concert — should be featured on library bulletin boards and in special exhibits. Home economics classes may be invited to display their canning or sewing projects. The work of industrial arts classes may be highlighted in the library, along with related books. An appreciation of good music could be fostered by the playing of records in the library occasionally, followed by a story of the composer or background details which would be of interest.

A local florist set in motion a new activity in an elementary school when he offered to send cut flowers to the home economics class in order that the girls could be taught flower arrangement. The future possibilities of flower activities are without number. The most ambitious suggestion to date is a flower show. In the meantime, books and magazines featuring flower arrangement are in constant demand.

Most of the activities described so far terminate outside the library. It is when the children come to the library as a class that the librarian has her opportunity to show that the library is truly a happy hunting ground. Towards that end she will give the children freedom to browse, to handle new books, to read — in short, to get the feel of the library. Because not all children will have that instinctive desire to browse, the librarian must encourage the use of the library without seeming to interfere with individual freedom. The reading of a brief incident in some book followed by the display of the volume in its colorful jacket may arouse the curiosity of a reluctant reader. A film or the playing of a record of a Newbery award winner may encourage students to look for those books on the shelves. The desire to know what others are talking about has led many a student to read. To vary library routine the librarian could suggest an impromptu class debate as a means of stimulating a discussion of books. OLD BOOKS ARE BEST could be the subject with half the class taking sides in the debate and the other half acting as judges. Each team member would be expected to support his argument by referring to a book he had personally read.

Miscellaneous activities in the library may well include a faculty tea early in the school year as a means of establishing

SOLOMON

rapport, while also giving faculty members an opportunity to see new book acquisitions.

New libraries especially, and old ones as well, may need help in building up a picture file. The detailed description of how pictures were acquired and how they were handled at the J. P. Dudley Branch Library in Buffalo, New York, would prove a helpful guide for school librarians.[2] Children and teachers could be encouraged to bring back issues of such magazines as National Geographic, Life, Holiday, Time, and others that contain pictures of interest to classes. The library club could have as its project preparing the pictures for use. Duplicates are desirable since several classes frequently study the same unit simultaneously

Since no one knows when a child will suddenly discover that reading is fun, the school librarian must always be on the alert, ready and eager to help kindle that spark of interest, further an appreciation of good reading, broaden horizons, and make the library a welcome part of the child's recreational and educational life.

43. ANYONE CAN TELL STORIES . . .
. . . INCLUDING STUDENT ASSISTANTS

Lynn L. Solomon

While shelving the easy books, my thirty young library assistants became interested in the pictures and stories and asked to take the books home to read to younger brothers and sisters. After checking out books for several nights and reading them at home, they felt that some of them could read to one of the primary classes in school.

We decided first to study what makes a good "oral" reader and through a workshop where each one read his favorite book aloud, and after many criticisms and suggestions, we developed the following set of rules:

ANYONE CAN TELL STORIES

1. Be familiar with the story. Read it through at least twice before reading it to a class.
2. Wait until you have everyone's attention before beginning to read. If there is any talking while reading — stop and wait.
3. Hold the book so that everyone can see the pictures.
4. Modulate your voice. Pronounce well. Each word should be clear and distinct.
5. Read with feeling — be dramatic and emphasize special words.
6. Follow up the reading with a planned activity such as drawing pictures of the story, a quiz, acting the story out, telling of similar experiences, etc.

After the aides became proficient in reading aloud, we set up a schedule for each one to come to the library when there was a primary grade and read two books to the class. I was present at all times to encourage, suggest improvements and maintain discipline if necessary.

At first the library assistants were nervous, and lacking in self assurance; but as they began to read and saw how attentive the classes were, they began to develop their own style of reading and gain confidence in themselves. All, by the time the project was ended, had gained poise, skill in reading aloud, and much self-reliance and ingenuity in how to "hold" a class, plus many techniques in handling younger children. This project also helped develop a greater appreciation for children's books, an interest in the authors and illustrators, and at the same time gave the younger children a chance to have a change and hear someone else read a story.

Together, we worked out a bibliography of books the primary grades most enjoy hearing read aloud. This would, of course, vary from school to school, depending on the collection, and interests of the pupils.

This reading project need not be limited to library assistants; it might very well serve as motivation for more reading in a regular classroom (the teacher could make arrangements with the primary department to have her pupils read to the others in their classrooms), as a special service the student council members perform for the younger grades, or as an extra activity for the gifted.

44. THE LIBRARY: KEY TO CURRICULUM COOPERATION

Walter R. Lund and John C. Roman

Cooperation within and among the various departments of a school is a condition much to be desired. It tends to break down misconceived ideas such as, "My course or subject is the most important course or subject in the school." The subjects that a teacher teaches are not altogether the important thing — it's the students; for no matter how gifted a teacher may be in his subjects, he will get nowhere if he cannot become gifted in the handling of his human subjects. Cooperation leads to actual achievement because everyone is working together to get a job done. In short, a school where cooperation exists is characterized by friendliness and a good psychological atmosphere where teaching and learning can take place.

Since the librarian is a cooperative worker, his work is made infinitely easier in a school where unwholesome competition is eschewed and cooperation exists. This cooperative spirit breaks down the feeling of "ownership" of materials on the part of individual teachers and replaces it with a spirit of "our materials center." Working in this kind of atmosphere a librarian and library can provide service of the highest and most extensive type and be an integral part of the school's curriculum.

A practical example of how cooperation can be encouraged in a school and of the part the library can play is our experience at Central High School.

As is true in many high schools throughout the country, Central High School has a display case in the main lobby of the school. This display case, as usual, was filled with dusty, drab athletic trophies dating far back into the school's history. Something had to be done to enliven this case, so a paragraph was inserted in the manual of instructions for teachers:

> The . . . lobby display case is used by the teaching staff of the various subject fields for publicity relative to the achievements of and information for

various subject fields of the school. The librarian with the subject field chairmen cooperatively plan a calendar for these displays. In preparing these displays they may solicit the help of the teachers of the art and distributive education departments.[1]

The attention-getting qualities of the several displays which have been thus far created have generated interest and enthusiasm on the part of our students, teachers, and visitors. But probably of more importance is the sense of pride from cooperative accomplishment which has come to the students and faculty who created the displays.

By cooperating in the creation of curriculum displays of this kind the librarian and the library has much to offer and in turn has much to gain. Among the things which the librarian has to offer are his knowledge of materials available. This saves much misdirected effort in the planning of the displays. The librarian knows publishers who specialize in the production of materials for schools. This saves time in acquiring the raw materials from which the displays are created. And since the library is a materials center, much of the display material is on hand there. By working on curriculum displays the librarian is assisted in developing a better library program. He acquires more intimate knowledge of the subjects of the curriculum by working with teachers on the displays than he can glean from reading and digesting ideal, formal courses of study and can thus acquire materials that meet the needs of the curriculum. He also becomes acquainted with teachers on an informal basis which breaks down the formal barriers to library service.

By providing display materials and courses of these materials, by becoming acquainted with the subjects of the curriculum and the teachers of these subjects, and by helping to knit subjects, teachers, and students together in a common purpose, the library becomes the key to curriculum cooperation. The door that this key unlocks opens onto two vistas: a cooperative friendly school pervaded by a good psychological atmosphere where learning and teaching can take place and a well developed school library program.

45. "CATCHY" CAPTIONS

Amy Fenner

The purpose of this list is to present the sort of caption that not everyone can think of when he needs it, the one that gets away from the straightforward ones all librarians use anyway and which certainly have their place. These were collected with the help of Margaret Scoggin, co-ordinator of young people's services, New York Public Library; Jane S. McClure, co-ordinator of work with young adults, Free Library of Philadelphia; Othella Denman, librarian at Waco, Tex., High School; Anne W. Handley, of the circulation department, Providence, R.I., Public Library; Margaret A. Edwards, co-ordinator of work with young people, Enoch Pratt Free Library, Baltimore.

January
Turn over a new leaf
Resolved: to read more
Take-off (to tomorrow)
New arrivals
Present perfect, past perfect, future perfect
Cast your weather eye
To meet the test
Accent on you
Stop — Look — and Learn
It's a small world
Open fire!

February
It started with Washington
How to tie a beau
Cross your heart
Heart campaign
Amo-amas-amat!
Sugar and spice — that's what!

Hearts are trumps
Heroes and heroines
Who's who-whooing?
Toujours l'amour

March
To be or not to be
Lucky you
Look ahead
Make your future bright
They started out young
Among friends
People of note (musicians)
It's your concern
Blasting off! (space)
Footlights and spotlights

April
Hook line and sinker
Bait
Bait for your line (etiquette for

206

"CATCHY" CAPTIONS

boys
Stories to crow about (rooster)
Teen trifles (cooking —
  romance
Whistle stops (beauty guides)
Dutch treat
A "hit" for the baseball fan
Going to bat

May
Colorful reading (books with
  color in title)
Our neck o' the woods
For the love of Mike (radio)
The eye listens (art)
It's all in the angle (photog-
  raphy)
It did happen
Globetrotters
It pays — to be smart — to
  look
Short but sterling
May we suggest?

June
Love's old sweet song
Moonlight and magnolias
In your own back yard
Plus fours (golf)
Memo: take along books
The language of the baton
For report card "blues"
Art for your sake
Off again (travel)

July
Dive into these
Americans by choice
Ring for liberty
The America we defend

Swing around America
United through books
Mmm! 28 varieties!
For your funny bone
Out of this world!
Hats off!

August
Cool, calm, and collected
  (story collections)
Dillies but chilly (mystery)
Keep cool with a thriller
Rhyme with reason
Space on my hands
Nonsense!
Portraits in print
Jest for fun
It's all in the family
Tip top
Try the large economy size
  (long stories)

September
Best on the slate
Slated for reading
Headlines for September
You can bank on these
It's a myth
Cheer up (cartoons)
Prescriptions for pleasure
  reading filled here
Getting more out of life
Calling all cars
Music hath charms

October
A "haunting" we will go
Tales with a grave end
  (mystery)
A wise choice (owl)

Trick or treat (party)
Hand picked (apples and books)
Tales with a kick
Pigskin vs. sheepskin
"Kick off" to good reading
A fall of favorites

November
Drumstick days
Thoughts for thanks giving
No time like the pleasant
It takes courage
Punch (boxing)
Caught on the rebound (re-
  bound books)

I'd stalk a mile for a good book
Here's looking at you (groom-
  ing)
For the shutterbug

December
Mistletoe and sleighbells
Hearthside tales
Evergreen tales
They too believed (religions)
Let's sing
By candle glow
It's party time
Men of the moment

46. LIBRARY ORIENTATION

Philip S. Ogilvie

The primary objective of any program for orienting children to proper use of a library should be the developing in them
of a sense of security in the library, and successful realization
of that objective is dependent on an orientation program designed
to satisfy curiosity and provide some understanding of the multi-
farious functions of the library. Basic to this program is the
recognition that lack of consideration for others is not normal
behavior in children, but that curiosity and insecurity in unfamiliar surroundings are and often manifest themselves in incon-
siderate actions. Disciplinary measures are necessary only in
proportion to the causes of disciplinary problems. The satisfying of curiosity tends to relieve insecurity. Logically, then, the
first step to be taken by the librarian should be the analysis of
his thinking toward the end of fitting the library into the lives
of children rather than toward fitting children into the static
routine of a library.

LIBRARY ORIENTATION

A child cannot be expected to fully comprehend the intrica-
cies of library routines, but to feel secure in the library he
must be "in the know" to the extent of his capabilities. Admittedly to give a small child some understanding of the why's and
wherefore's of a busy library is no simple task, but neither is
it impossible. Actually, besides patience and warmheartedness
(both standard equipment in a successful librarian), few tools
are needed. Furthermore, the tools are readily available. They
are the building itself, the specific area set aside for the shelving of children's books and children's services, a local telephone book, and a half dozen sheets of stiff cardboard approxi-
mating enlarged catalog cards. In general the program procedure
is to lead the children from the familiar to the unfamiliar by
using the method of association.

The initial step in the inauguration of the program is made
by the librarian at a meeting of elementary school teachers.
There she outlines her proposed program of child orientation
in the library and requests teacher co-operation in scheduling
individual class visits to the library. The librarian also asks
the teachers to prepare their pupils for the visit with a talk
about what they might expect to see and an explanation that the
library is a tax supported institution provided by their own parents and other citizens of the community to give service to all.
He asks the teachers to attempt to inspire in their pupils a
sense of personal pride in the library as an accomplishment of
their own parents and relatives who are taxpayers; this sense
of pride will go far in guaranteeing a salutary respect for the
library and its resources both during the class visit and thereafter.

The librarian's pre-planning should include the preparation
of (1) blown-up facsimiles of catalog cards (at least one author
and one title card for a fiction title and one nonfiction subject
card) (2) a cardboard presenting in bold figures the annual library budget for the children's department, and (3) a cardboard
depicting a rural mail box.

When a class arrives for a visit, the librarian meets them
at the children's entrance or the main entrance of the library
with a few words of welcome and a genuine smile, and conducts
them at once to the children's section (where enough seats have
been provided in advance). Realizing that children, particularly

in unfamiliar surroundings, tend to resent frequent queries about their own names and interests by people who never think to introduce themselves, the librarian introduces himself by name and gives a brief explanation of his duties. He repeats his words of welcome, and explains that he has led them to the section of the library especially set aside for their use and containing all of the books ordinarily required for their reading interests and school work. He may also at this time point out a special display of books relating to a field being emphasized currently in their curriculum. Before he goes far in his explanations of the children's department, however, remembering that in our day evaluation and respect for things is often based on cost, he will mention in round numbers the annual expenditure for children's books and services, and to emphasize this factor he will hold up for all to see the card upon which the amount, with dollar sign, has been printed. This information will be found to engender childish respect for the materials assembled and will enhance their view of their own importance as library users.

Mention is also made at this time of the regulations regarding registration. The time for launching into a full explanation of the proper use of the library is not yet, however. Until childish curiosity has been satisfied and a sense of security in the library attained, an engrossed, undistracted audience cannot be expected. The youthful audience is consumed with curiosity about what goes on in the rest of your building, and the wise librarian will interrupt his instruction to lead the guests on a complete tour. Preparatory to leaving their seats the children are told briefly what they might expect to see and are asked for respectful quiet in deference to other patrons and busy staff members they will encounter on the tour.

The tour, even for primer pupils, begins with the preparations department. The librarian explains in as much detail as necessary the workings of the department, always permitting questions. He shows them publishers' catalogs from which books are selected and the order forms, points out the freight door through which they arrive and indicates books being unpacked, lets them watch busy typists and peek into supply cabinets, shows them the various kinds of cards used, the book pockets, paste and brushes, sinks, white-inking tools, and sprays. Even the dullest parts of library routine are of interest to curious children. New books destined for the children's shelves should be pointed out; and the librarian should not forget to introduce all the staff members encountered to their visitors.

In concluding the visit to this department the librarian explains that their visit to it is a special privilege in that the nature of the work there requires quiet and concentration and is ordinarly out of bounds for visitors. A brief comment on the quiet required by their own parents when making out reports and tax forms will suffice to impress them, and there will be small likelihood of their ever interrupting the routines there.

The visitors should also be given the privilege of a brief look into the librarian's office, and the tour should continue with a walk through the stacks (on all levels if they are tiered). A running commentary on the restrictions observed in the use of the stacks accompanies this portion of the tour although these things will have to be repeated later when the group is reassembled in the children's section. Also, while in the stacks first mention should be made of the fact that each book has its place on the shelves and that a carelessly misplaced book is about the same as a lost book since it is not readily available to someone who might need it.

The tour continues through the reference, periodical, special collections, and special services rooms or areas, the importance of each book being in its rightful place repeated all along the way. Meanwhile, the locations and designations of rest rooms and water fountains should be pointed out with care, for familiarity with the locations of these facilities are vitally important to making children secure in their library surroundings. The tour might profitably include the heating plant and a peek into locked storage rooms. Despite its thoroughness the tour should be brief as possible but not so brief as to fail to satisfy curiosity. Each visit to out-of-bounds areas should be specified as such and given the aura of a special privilege.

This thorough concession to the normal curiosity of young library patrons will decrease their meanderings into adult areas or those ordinarily closed to the general public. The wandering about and prying of curious children is one of the most disconcerting of all disciplinary problems. Understaffed libraries must cope with the problems of games in the stacks and raids on the adult periodicals unless the initial orientation has satisfied their normal curiosity about the building and provided them with understandable reasons why some areas are closed to them.

Their natural inquisitiveness satisfied, the children may be expected to listen to orientation instructions with receptive minds. The librarian begins by pointing out the same general pattern of arrangement in their section as was observed in the other sections of the library. He mentions again the fact that each book has its proper place and should never be deliberately misplaced on the shelves.

Now, the card catalog. With local telephone book in hand, the librarian takes a position beside the card catalog. He asks a pupil to explain the use of the familiar telephone book, and, expanding on the pupil's answer, points out the relationship between a telephone directory and the card catalog.

"Children, let's suppose that I am new in our town. I want to build a house here. That will require lumber, but I do not know the location of a lumber company. I can take a telephone book and look in the yellow pages. These pages are known as the classified section of the telephone book. They are arranged alphabetically, so I will turn to the L's and look for the word lumber. Here it is, and under lumber I find the names and addresses of three lumber yards. I will jot these names and addresses down, ask directions to the lumber yard of my choice, and proceed to go there without any difficulty.

"You of course are no longer strangers in your library after your visit and tour today. You know more about the library than lots of grownups in our town, but you do not know and would not want to have to remember where every book on every subject is located on your shelves here. You will remember the location of some that you might want to use often, but for others you will need a classified directory. Let's suppose you would like a book about dogs. You would come to this card catalog, arranged alphabetically like the telephone book, pull out the drawer for the letter D, and look along the cards until you come to the word DOGS in capital letters. Here."

He points out the location of the classification number using his prepared facsimile, and he walks to the shelves and locates one of the titles. He also points out the consecutive numbering

of books on the shelves. Finally, to impress this knowledge
upon the young patrons he repeats the performance with one
or two other subjects, locating them first in the card catalog
and then on the shelves. It goes without saying that the subjects
should be of general interest to most children or related to
their curriculum. Questions might be asked at the end of this
demonstration in order to ascertain its effectiveness.

The task of teaching the location of fiction titles is also
relatively simple. The librarian begins by holding up a poster
depicting a rural mailbox with name clearly printed on it and
explains that if he were looking for a family out where streets
and house numbers are not used, he would look for the name
of the family on the rural mailbox. He then points out that fiction titles are not given classification numbers but are shelved
together alphabetically by the name of the author. The works
of an individual author might be thought of as the children of
that author, and the librarian can use this thought to explain
that they would naturally live together on the shelves under the
name of the author just as members of a family would be expected to be living together in the house identified by a rural
mailbox bearing the family name. Here the librarian should
choose a familiar author whose works are visible on the shelves
to demonstrate the point. Here, too, he shows the facsimile of
an author card for a fiction title, finds an author card in the
card catalog, and locates a fiction title by author on the shelves.
The same procedure can be followed in demonstrating title
cards. The librarian will carefully point out the author's name
on a title card and show how to locate the title or volume itself
by looking for it on the shelves under author's name.

After a verbal recounting of all that the young visitors
have seen and learned, the procedures for registration as borrowers and for borrowing and returning books should be explained. All regulations pertaining to these procedures should
be adequately explained and demonstrated. Special mention
should be made of the necessity of returning books to the desk
to be checked off, and it should be explained that books not so
returned will be as good as lost, still checked out to the person
who had borrowed it, and that the borrower will be expected
to pay for the book unless it is located. Fines can be explained
along with an explanation of the loan period and renewal

procedure. The method of checking out books should be demonstrated thoroughly whether the process is handled manually or by machine.

Registration cards should be distributed at the end of the orientation program. This finished, the librarian should thank the teacher and the children for their visit and should accompany them to the door.

In all this program should not require more than 90 minutes. Naturally it must be adapted for the various grade levels. A story, read or told, replaces the detailed instructions on the use of the card catalog when the children are of primary age. It has been found, however, that some third graders and most fourth graders can understand the use of the catalog and acquire some proficiency in its use in a very short time. Unquestionably the annual repetition of classroom visits to the library will make the vast majority of children able users of the library over a period of three to four years.

47. LIBRARY INSTRUCTION IN HIGH SCHOOL

Violet E. Peterson

There has been much discussion, pro and con, on the merits of scheduled classes for instruction in the use of library materials. One theory is that no classes should be held, but that all instruction should be integrated with regular classroom work.

Trying out the latter theory at Montclair Academy (grades seven through twelve) for one year, we found that is was impossible to reach every boy in the school, so we returned to scheduled classes which have proved most successful in our case. This is "our story."

In September 1949, when I took over as librarian at the academy, the head of the English department asked if it would be agreeable to me to hold regular sessions to teach the use of the library. We started with the seniors — and I found that I had a job on my hands. "What is there to learn about a library? Everybody knows how to get a book from a library! What else is there to know?" And so on. Library class was considered to be nothing more than a swell free period in which one could "have fun." Even at the end of that first hard year, however, I was rewarded with the "thank you" of three boys who had already discovered that they had learned something that would prove very helpful the following September when they entered college.

Now, six years later, we give instruction to the entire school starting with the seventh grade. A graded course that carries through the senior year has been developed. This course has been an evolution, more or less. It grew and developed as the boys became more efficient in the use of the library; also, much has been added because of some difficulty encountered by one boy after entering college. His problem and its solution were incorporated in the course with the result that we now feel that the way should be fairly smooth for our students when they find themselves standing on their own feet in a college library.

One very fine reward for the struggle to "put across" library instruction has been the letters received from the boys expressing their gratitude for their library training. Several have written that they have obtained coveted jobs in their college libraries because of their knowledge of library tools and procedure. Some day we may even find that a few have chosen librarianship as a profession.

In the latter respect I wish to mention the splendid system of monitorship that we have in the academy. Seven seniors are appointed as monitors of the reading room and there are several senior assistants to the librarian; these boys help to train the younger boys along with their library tasks. The requirements for monitorship are: passing grade in all subjects, high citizenship rating, recommendation by the faculty, interest in the library, an attitude of helpfulness, willingness to do any task assigned, neatness, a love of books. Ability to type is considered not essential, but desirable.

Below is a copy of the course of instruction that has been developed at the academy. As to the question "Should scheduled classes be held for instruction in library usage?": all we can say is that in the case of the academy the right answer is "Yes."

COURSE OF STUDY IN LIBRARY SCIENCE

7th Grade: alphabetizing and introduction to catalog cards; film strips on library procedure; learn to designate rooms and material by proper names.

8th grade: introduction to Dewey Decimal Classification System; learn locations in library by making a floor plan; parts of a book, types of cards in catalog, call numbers, call slips.

9th grade: introduction to indexes; interpretation of entries; encyclopedia and dictionary exercises; card catalog work-out with call slips.

10th grade: introduction to bibliography: working and finished, with exercises in indexes, encyclopedias and dictionary.

11th grade: looking up answers to specific questions in available reference material — calls for use of all types of reference works; reading cards in the catalog, making call slips and finding books; making bibliography on assigned subject, without assistance, finding own material, with work to be finished in not more than 2 periods; final senior exam try-out.

12th grade: work-out in handling all reference material to be found in library; trip to public library for further work-out in reference material (magnificent cooperation from the Public Library — a public librarian takes over this period and gives the lecture); become acquainted with Library of Congress classification system and compare it with Dewey Decimal; card catalog work-out; final test.

48. TEACHING LIBRARY SKILLS IN ELEMENTARY SCHOOL

Bess Gray

Library instruction can and should be a pleasant experience for all concerned — pupils, teachers, and librarians. Librarians are inherently blessed with the atmosphere of the happy learning situation for which educators are constantly striving. Even the self confessed non-readers welcome a visit to the library as a break in school routine. It then devolves upon the librarian to maintain this happy, cheerful attitude. One should be quite serious about <u>what</u> she teaches — but not necessarily in her method of approach.

If one can face the fact realistically that the average elementary student can absorb just so much library instruction and no more, the battle is half won. The librarian can then settle back and enjoy what she does, teach without feeling frustrated by all of the finer points of library usage which are being left out and which no one — with the possible exception of another librarian — would feel the need of, particularly at this level. The acquiring of library skills is a continuing process. If an elementary school librarian can help pupils to use the library independently for pleasure and research, she has laid the ground work for more intensive instruction at the junior high level.

Children in all grades should be acquainted with the arrangement of the library, library procedure and practice, and the care and appreciation of books. The use of the card catalog and special reference tools, research and organization of information normally begin in the fourth grade. The ideal time to present a skill is when the individual pupil or group has need of it and will put it into immediate use.

The importance of primary instruction, elementary as it is, should never be minimized. True, at this age the attention span is very short and the reading skill undeveloped, but it is an excellent time for the children to learn good library manners, the appreciation and proper care of books, and library procedures so that these things will be automatic by the time

217

that their reading ability is developed for fullest use of the library.

It must be remembered that the library presents to these children a new vocabulary to be mastered — book truck, card catalog, book card, author, title, etc. Going from the known to the unknown seems the wisest course. Boys and girls know that their pockets will hold a myriad of things; they learn that a book pocket only holds a book card. The spine of a book helps the book to stand up straight on the shelf just as the human spine allows us to sit or stand straight (and right here you have to allow time for all of them to stiffen in their chairs). They like to know what book jackets are and why we use them on our bulletin board. All of the things we take for granted are new and wonderful to them.

We may talk about the kind of catalogs with which they are familiar and what they find in them. It is an easy step then to the different type catalog that contains cards telling us what books may be found in the library and who wrote them. While they cannot use the card catalog, they are quite impressed that they can read the letters on each tray. Of course there was one little boy who insisted that his grandparents had catalog syrup. Someone must have said can of Log Cabin Syrup none too plainly.

They learn to shelve books by matching letters on the book spine with those on the book shelves even before they can read. Having them decide which letter their book will be shelved under before they take the book to the shelf cuts down greatly on the confusion that can result there. If the lettering on the spine is not clear, they learn to look in that super "secret place" on the book pocket and card. Anything secret or special is a great help at this level. I find that I am continually having to keep my head down while a whole group comes in so quietly wearing their magic shoes or walking as silently as Indians going through the forest, in order that I may be completely surprised on looking up to find them there. They love surprises, so what difference if I know that they are scheduled to be there and if a few earth bound heels do drag the floor a little? The teacher and I have seen a beginning of self-discipline. It is certainly more effective and more fun than quiet signs and conduct lectures.

Then there are the golden gloves some children like to put

on before they come to the library, so that they will handle the
books carefully and with clean hands. In putting on their golden
gloves they say a word of the Golden Rule as they adjust each
finger of the glove. It works wonders. The librarian being a
Watchbird and giving a word of praise to those turning the pages
from the upper right hand corner brings hands quickly from the
center bottom of the pages; no feelings are hurt, and the books
last longer.

Rainy days may be looked forward to as being story days.
Choosing stories with varied types of illustrations helps them
to see and to value all of the little details that the artist has
put in to help them follow the story. One does not have to be
able to read to notice such things and at this age when reading
ability is negligible a sense of accomplishment in handling books
is especially important.

Teaching the difference between fiction and non-fiction, the
general arrangement of each, the basic use of the card catalog,
information file, and the use of some special reference books
begins in the upper grades. Where there is an encyclopedia in
each class room, the teacher does most of the teaching of its
use. The librarian can concentrate on showing both pupils and
teachers that by the use of the card catalog, the table of contents and indexes of the books to which the catalog refers them,
and by use of ephemeral material from the information file that
an encyclopedia is not the alpha and omega of reference work.
Certainly the basic information is in an encyclopedia. True, it
is easier to extract, but often the material that enlivens a
teacher's work and makes the subject come vitally alive to a
student is found elsewhere. A fact that is summarily treated
in the encyclopedia may be the subject of a completely delightful
chapter or an entire book. In other words, try to make library
instruction not an end itself but an instructional tool.

The use of over-size catalog cards facilitates instruction.

Whenever possible try to let the children see that the rules
and regulations of the library, the arrangement of the library,
the library "housekeeping" is all planned to help them. Point
out that replacing books properly is not so much a matter of
good housekeeping as that a book out of place is a "lost book."
Then, perhaps, present a hair-raising picture of their teacher
wanting a report before school is out only to find that the very

book that would save the day is "lost." They begin to get the point.

No attempt should be made to teach classification. Children soon learn the location of special interest. A portable blackboard is particularly helpful in showing the arrangement of books which are shelved by number.

When there is too much aimless wandering from the catalog to the non-fiction shelves, my pupils may suddenly find themselves talking about the importance of knowing where they are going. When they consider the results of being let out of a car four blocks short of their destination and having to walk the remaining distance, the numbers on the shelves begin to have more significance. We often play a game called, for lack of a better name, You Are Disqualified. The object here is for the student to move in the right direction when called upon to locate a given call number. The first time or two we use the "you are getting warmer, colder, burning up" device. Later any indecision in the direction taken disqualifies the player. There is no pupil resistance here. The children ask for this game.

Letters for the biographee on books in the biography section may be dramatized by asking a student what letter would be on the story of his life, written perhaps by his teacher. Each child is sure that the teacher really could write the story of his life, and it is all the more effective because at this age their own name and that of their teacher are most important to them. Washington, Lincoln, and others are just names.

Children often need the publication date of a book for their book reports and sometimes take the first date which they see. For some reason, it strikes them as very funny when I say that I never heard of anyone writing a book the year he was born. Reprints and new editions cease to be a problem when compared to mimeographed tests. The addition of new questions to such a test is plainly serious. A girl who made a dress by the patterns in a 1926 book or a boy who tried to find out about jet planes by reading a 1939 book may be used as extreme examples of people who were in trouble because they did not attach enough importance to the publication date.

The value of having pupil library assistants from the fourth grade on who can help instruct other children in the proper use of the library cannot be overlooked. There are times when one child can explain to another better than an adult can.

Teaching good judgment in the selection of a book begins with the very youngest child who must recognize the difference between books which he himself can read and those that will have to be read to him. Children who can read need guidance in selecting books on their reading as well as interest level, though, as one boy told me, "It's all right if this book has some hard words because that is the way you learn." Third and fourth grade students are apt to choose their books by size and weight. We do not choose our human friends that way, and it is even less wise to choose our book friends by this method.

Whatever approach you use, there will always be days when you are quite sure you have not taught a thing, but then some most unlikely child will save the day by proving you wrong, or a teacher will tell her children that they are learning things which she had to dig out for herself in college. Then "God's in his heaven and All's right with the world" once more, and library instruction again seems worth while and fun, and that is as it should be.

49. THE TEACHING OF LIBRARY SKILLS AND ATTITUDES

Helen Wheeler

As the extent of man's knowledge continues to expand at an increasing rate, the amount one person can possess about any one thing in proportion to the total amount known about it has become smaller and smaller. Where total knowledge is impossible, knowing where and how to obtain it is necessary. Those who have learned to use the library confidently and effectively have the key to almost unlimited knowledge, and they have, of course, also been given the means to better learning in school and self-realization out of school. The acquisition of library skills and attitudes is vital for everyone today.

There is also meaning here for educators; if attitudes are

to be shaped, this teaching should start in the elementary school;
the development of competencies should be emphasized in the
junior high school, where early adolescence is accompanied by
great curiosity and many new interests; mastery in later secondary school should be integrated with content learning; and,
teacher-preparation should support the whole concept.

The teaching of library skills and attitudes is a goal of education which is not now receiving adequate or appropriate attention. Its wording varies with authors, points of view, school-
level etc., and such terms as "library skills," " study habits,"
"reference skills," and "the use of books and libraries" are
also frequently employed. "The teaching of library skills and
attitudes," seems to be the most potent, since there is provision
in it for cultivation of a balance of feeling and knowledge. Although many factors are involved in the achieving of such a
goal, only the most specific characteristics of the program
necessary to give appropriate attention to the teaching of library
skills and attitudes will be described here. Such related-but-
controversial questions as the role of the library in the school,
the best type of set-up, the importance of materials collections
in relation to curriculum, the education and experience of the
librarian etc. will not be dealt with here.

Although much has been written about teaching the use of
the library, little objective investigation has been made. The
uniqueness of this area, by virtue of its close inter-relationship
with other areas and goals, should make the actual school situation the starting point. One would consider first such things
as the school program already in force, curriculum changes
in progress, the education of the teachers and their security
in relationship to library, etc. Specifically, it becomes necessary to operate within a framework of who (teacher . . . librarian . . . a combination . . .) is to teach; who is to be taught;
what is to be taught; when . . . how . . . why . . . We should
attempt to realistically characterize a program which would
be appropriate and adequate in terms of conditions which do
exist. Two specific points at which the teaching of library skills
and attitudes are especially vital have been selected for emphasis; junior high school and teacher preparation.

During the elementary school years, emphasis should be
placed by the teacher on developing library attitudes — the

child's experiences can be planned so that the library becomes a natural part of his life. He should derive personal pleasure from library experiences and begin to develop an awareness of his literary heritage; he should be guided in browsing and selecting books and in developing reading taste and interests; the part library citizenship plays in general good citizenship should be enlarged upon. The teaching of skills of independent library use should be begun by the sixth grade.

The importance of gaining competence in using a library during the junior high school years cannot be overemphasized. This time of early adolescence is marked by intense curiosity, by the awakening of new interests and desires, by a questioning attitude toward authority, by heightened imagination, and by the adoption of many new loyalties. A school-wide program of instruction in the use of books as an integral part of the class-work of various subject areas should be thoroughly detailed and carefully adapted to the school in which it operates. One such plan was prepared and tested recently and is described in INTEGRATING LIBRARY INSTRUCTION WITH CLASSROOM TEACHING AT PLAINVIEW JUNIOR HIGH SCHOOL, an imaginary school.[1] Characteristic are the facts that: each department has an outline of its library program made cooperatively by its members and the librarian; departmental plans insure every child a minimum of library experience and instruction in the use of books connected with the subject; allocation of responsibility for teaching certain understandings and skills is definitely indicated by the outlines of lessons; and all departments — not just English and social studies — participate. Such a plan provides for many periods of class attendance in the library. The class teacher and librarian cover the material involved; suggestions for classroom activities and homework assignments are included in the departmental plans. Seventh grade objectives, for example, may be summarized as:

1. to help children become independent in finding materials in the library;
2. to encourage reading for enjoyment;
3. to teach acceptable library behavior;
4. to teach library rules concerning the circulation and use of books; and,
5. to develop the ability to concentrate on individual work.

Specifically, the English Department seventh grade outline, as an example, provides:

First half . . . a minimum of twelve library periods
  1. orientation
  2. practice in the use of materials

Second half . . . a minimum of eight library periods
  1. program of personal reading
  2. instruction in note-taking
  3. reference tools for poetry
  4. reference materials and method of reference work for finding information about an author.

Each item is detailed for teaching purposes.

The growing dependence upon library materials in the teaching of secondary school curriculum has stimulated experimentation in methods of giving instruction. Three methods of giving library instruction are commonly used in secondary schools: a course integrated with the subject matter of the academic curriculum of the school; an independent course of library lessons; and unorganized instruction is informal, incidental instruction, usually given to individual pupils when needed.

A fully integrated plan means that the instruction is developed and offered to meet the pupils' felt need. It may lack a logical arrangement but it is directly related to the subject matter of the curriculum. The actual working out of practical problems introduced in the academic curriculum subjects, through the use of the library, results in the acquisition of knowledge and skills in the use of the library without the necessity of extensive formal presentation and drill. Advanced educational opinion appears to favor the fully integrated plan. (One study purports to present objective data pertaining to the relative merits of the three common methods of library instruction; the results indicate that organized instruction is definitely superior to unorganized, but that there seems to be no appreciable difference between the integrated method and independent lessons.[2] Both the independent course and unorganized instruction may be justified in the library-study hall situation, however.)

Since the teacher and librarian jointly plan the work of the integrated plan, there will be no failure because of lack of needed materials or waste of time from teacher and librarian working at cross purposes. While the teacher must take the initiative in directing the activities of the class because of intimate acquaintance with the class problems which have occasioned the visit, the librarian will be equally busy in his capacity of specialist-teacher and as host to the visitors. He will make the stay of each pupil as helpful and enjoyable as possible; the greater part of their instruction is given by the teacher, since the library tools to which they are introduced are employed in working problems set by him, and it is logical that the introduction be made by him at the time when it is most needed.

In general, acquisition of these skills and knowledge should be aimed at during the junior and senior high school years:

Grade 7	Grade 8	Grade 9
Library citizenship	Library citizenship	Library citizenship
Care and appreciation of materials	Care and appreciation of materials	Care and appreciation of materials
Locating library materials	Locating library materials	Locating library materials
Borrowing materials from school library	Borrowing materials from school library	Borrowing materials from school library
Discussing books	Discussing books	Discussing books
Reporting on books	Reporting on books	Reporting on books
Using an index and a table of contents	Using an index and a table of contents	Using an index and a table of contents
Using a juvenile encyclopedia	Using a juvenile encyclopedia	Using a juvenile encyclopedia
Using a card catalog	Using a card catalog	Using a card catalog
Borrowing books from public libraries	Borrowing books from public libraries	Borrowing books from public libraries
Taking notes	Taking notes	Taking notes
Using pamphlet and picture materials	Using pamphlet and picture materials	Using the pamphlet file
Using an atlas and a globe	Using an atlas and a globe	Using an atlas and a globe
Using an unabridged dictionary	Using an unabridged dictionary	Using an unabridged dictionary
Using World Almanac	Using World Almanac	Using World Almanac

Using poetry indexes	Using poetry indexes, etc.	Using poetry indexes, etc.
	Using Readers Guide	Using Readers Guide
	Using Guidance File	Using Guidance File
		Preparing book reviews
		Using special reference books

Grade 10	Grade 11	Grade 12
Library citizenship	Library citizenship	Library citizenship
Care and appreciation of materials	Care and appreciation of materials	Care and appreciation of materials
Locating library materials	Locating library materials	Locating library materials
Borrowing materials from school library	Borrowing materials from school library	Borrowing materials from school library
Discussing books	Discussing books	Discussing books
Reporting on books	Reporting on books	Reporting on books
Using an index and a table of contents	Using an index and a table of contents	Using an index and a table of contents
Using a juvenile encyclopedia	Using an adult encyclopedia	Using adult encyclopediae
Using a card catalog	Using a card catalog	Using a card catalog
Borrowing books from public libraries	Borrowing books from public libraries	Borrowing books from public libraries
Taking notes	Taking notes	Taking notes
Using the pamphlet file	Using the pamphlet file	Using the pamphlet file
Using an atlas and a globe	Using an atlas and a globe	Using an atlas and a globe
Using an unabridged dictionary	Using an unabridged dictionary	Using an unabridged dictionary
Using World Almanac	Using World Almanac	Using World Almanac
Using poetry indexes etc.	Using poetry indexes etc.	Using poetry indexes etc.
Preparing a bibliography	Preparing a bibliography	Preparing a bibliography

Using Readers Guide	Using Readers Guide	Using Readers Guide
Using Guidance File	Using Guidance File	Using Guidance File
Preparing book reviews	Preparing book reviews	Preparing book reviews
Using special reference books	Using special reference books	Using special reference books
Learning to evaluate and use magazines and newspapers	Learning to evaluate and use magazines and newspapers	Learning to evaluate and use magazines and newspapers
	Preparing research papers, including footnotes	Preparing research papers, including footnotes
	Developing a concept of library service outside of community, eg, LC, State Library	Developing a concept of library service outside of community, eg, LC, State Library

To carry out the foregoing program, a variety of materials is necessary for use by the teacher, librarian, and pupil, and for their joint use as well. They should be appealing, on all levels, related to aspects of the subject which will carry over into life both in and out of future schooling, and representative of all media. The present situation is not a bad one; it may seem so to some because they have not yet become acquainted with what there is nor how to go about locating or utilizing it. Revised and updated editions of some of the materials we have now are the major needs.

50. THE SCHOOL LIBRARY:
EACH TEACHER'S RESPONSIBILITY

Dorothy Roche

Recognizing the need for library instruction for all students, Belleville High School teachers assumed the responsibility of planning an effective program of library instruction. Principal and vice-principal gave the signal and it was "full speed ahead" in organizing a feasible course of study.

A committee of teachers representing all departments studied ways and means of helping students make more effective use of the school library. The committee felt, from its personal and classroom contact with the students, that there was a need for a thorough program of library instruction. How this could be accomplished — under crowded conditions and with the services of one librarian — was the problem.

The committee decided that the instruction planned by the librarian would be given in the English classes at all grade levels. The English teachers accepted the recommendation of this committee and made plans with the librarian to develop an effective program of library instruction.

In planning this course, the English teachers felt that they had an opportunity to continue the reading improvement program in which the entire faculty participated last year. Certainly teaching students how to use library tools effectively is important in all subject areas. All teachers share the responsibility for helping students to learn how to use the library tools in their subject areas.

A bibliography of materials and a list of the filmstrips to be used for this instruction were made available to every teacher. The basic course of study was outlined by the librarian and in parentheses after each main topic it was indicated who was responsible for the major teaching of the unit. Of course, this was a suggested procedure only; the teachers were free to arrange with the librarian if they wished any changes in the method of instruction.

RESPONSIBILITY

The freshman and sophomore classes received a very complete course in the use of the library. This instruction was begun by the librarian and continued by the English teacher and the subject teacher, using the text workbook, Exploring Libraries by Emmet Morris. All ten units in the text were covered in the freshman year. In the sophomore class special emphasis was placed on the uses of the card catalog and the Dewey decimal system and the special references. The junior instruction featured the use of the Readers' Guide to Periodical Literature and those other aids which would help them to prepare their term papers on careers. English 4 classes made extensive study for the preparation of a research paper and its bibliography, utilizing The Research Paper by Lucyle Hook and Mary Virginia Gaver.

At the close of the library instruction, each class made a trip to the public library.

Instruction of this nature will serve to promote good study habits in all subject areas; it will induce "free reading"; above all, it will give the student the "library habit."

LIBRARY INSTRUCTION OUTLINE

Introduction

The need for a thorough course in library instruction for each student is most evident. A good working knowledge of how to use the library tools available will benefit the student in many ways:

It will promote better study habits in all subject areas.
It will aid the student to solve his research problems.
It will help him to use these aids intelligently not only
    during his high school days, but also in his future life.
It will give the student the "library habit."
It will induce "free reading."
It will promote "reading."

With the cooperation of the English teachers and other members of the faculty, we hope to train all students in our high school to make the utmost use of our high school library.

Below is an outline of the <u>basic</u> program of library instruction. In parentheses after each main topic is indicated who is responsible for the major teaching of the unit. This is a suggested procedure, only; teachers are free to arrange with the librarian if they wish any changes in the method of instruction.

<u>Outline</u>

I. <u>The Book</u> (Classroom teacher)
    A. Origin of the book and early writing and printing of the book
    B. Parts of the book

II. <u>Dewey Decimal Classification</u> (Librarian)
    A. Main classes of books — Fiction and Nonfiction
    B. Ten major classifications
    C. Main subdivisions
    D. More specific subject areas
    E. These are again subdivided

III. <u>Card Catalog</u> (Librarian)
    A. Subject card
    B. Title card
    C. Author card
    D. Author, title, and subject analytics
    E. Fiction and nonfiction cards

IV. <u>Dictionary</u> (Classroom teacher)
    A. Abridged
    B. Unabridged
    C. Parts of the dictionary

V. <u>General Reference Books</u> (Classroom teacher)
    Encyclopedias

VI. <u>Almanacs and Yearbooks</u> (Classroom teacher)

VII. <u>Biographical References</u> (Classroom teacher)

VIII. <u>Readers' Guide to Periodical Literature</u> (Classroom

teacher or librarian at the request of the classroom
teacher)

IX. Periodicals
    A. Current issues
    B. Back numbers
    C. Newspapers
    D. Bulletins
    E. Reports

X. Gazetteers and Atlases

XI. Bibliography (Classroom teacher)
    A. Annotated bibliography
    B. Footnotes
    C. Abbreviations

Classroom teachers are free to request assistance from
the librarian at any time.

51. SIX POINTERS FOR TEACHERS

Louise L. Klohn

What use high school teachers make of the library depends
upon their understanding of the curricular needs of their students and upon their methods of instruction. If teachers think
of the high school as the educational interval during which students explore a wide variety of materials with curiosity and
keen interest, then they will recognize the tremendous advantages of the library in the school program. If they teach to
broaden and to enrich the textbook and the classroom, again
they will perceive the values of the library in the total program.
When this role of the library is accepted, teachers are
ready to employ techniques for effective library use. Here is

where the librarian can be of service. Some teachers become proficient library users by trial and error. They try a plan; if it succeeds, they incorporate it into their teaching; if it fails, they eliminate it. Often trial and error discourages the teacher when he happens upon too many procedures that fail. But the librarian knows what will prove successful and what will fail and should be the first point of contact.

What techniques assure a teacher a maximum of library service? Here are a few suggestions.

Use a bibliography to check availability of materials. Bibliographies should include surveys of the following types of materials: (1) books, supplying call numbers, authors, titles; (2) encyclopedias, supplying topics under which material can be located; (3) pamphlets, supplying subject headings for material; (4) magazines, supplying magazine titles, dates, pages; (5) filmstrips, films, records.

The compilation of these lists is the responsibility of the librarian. When she is busy, she may assign the work to members of her staff or request the teacher to send a superior student to help with the work. However, all bibliographies should be compiled under the close supervision of the librarian who should check their completeness and their final form.

A carbon copy of these bibliographies should be made so that one copy can be filed with the teacher, one with the librarian. Bibliographies can be kept up to date by the librarian by sending a mimeographed form listing new materials to the teacher from time to time. These forms can be stapled to the original copy.

Request the librarian to place materials on reserve when supply is limited. This is extremely important for effective use of the library. Students receive a negative impression when they are told to make a report on a topic for which they can not obtain materials. When a teacher assigns similar reports to five classes, a few students come to the library at once and draw out the books. When the majority appear after school, the librarian is forced to tell them that the references are gone. These students return to the teacher to say that their lesson is unprepared because of a lack of library materials. They feel no further responsibility. The teacher's plans are thwarted, and she too often forms a negative impression of the value of the library.

SIX POINTERS FOR TEACHERS

The request to reserve materials should reach the librarian before students are given the assignment. These materials should circulate only overnight.

Use student permits-to-the-library when materials are difficult or when supply is limited. Teachers will find that when only a few references are available or when the reading level of the materials is difficult, they can obtain best results by assigning topics to a few of the best students rather than to the entire class. The best students usually finish assignments sooner than others, and their work can be enriched by a visit to the library during class time to obtain information. By having them report to the class, all students receive benefit from the material.

Use page and chapter references when average students are sent to the library. Sometimes teachers will want students without exceptional ability to do reference work in reserve materials. Best results are obtained when the teacher specifies the book and pages to be read. Since many high school students have had very limited contact with reference work, they often are unable to locate information on a topic. By having it located for them, the teacher eliminates waste of time and assures completion of the assignment.

Have the librarian locate materials and place them at tables when classes are brought to the library. Some teachers object that students waste time and are noisy when they are brought as a class to the library to do reference work. These objections can be eliminated when the librarian has been asked ahead of time to make materials readily accessible. When materials have been placed where students are to sit, classes can settle down to work at once.

Successful class work in the library depends upon two additional factors: (1) sufficient materials; (2) separation of easy from difficult materials. When topics are too specific and too few, students have difficulty locating material. It is best to assign broad subjects and to permit the student to select a specific topic on his own initiative.

One device that works well, but is often unfamiliar to teachers, is to have magazines in the field placed on tables in sufficient quantities so that students can browse while making a selection. Pamphlets in a subject area can also be used in this way, as can collections of books selected for subject or for form. Short story, poetry, play collections are examples of the latter type. When classes vary widely in ability, the librarian can separate the easier materials from the more difficult so that teachers can assign poorer students to tables where he knows that they will find materials they can read.

Have library materials sent to the classroom when close supervision over an extended period is necessary. When library materials are needed for long periods of time, for example, a week or more, it is not always possible to avoid conflicts with other teachers who want to use the library. Sometimes the teacher wants to have students do their reference work under his close supervision. When these are the objectives, the teacher can secure best results by requesting the librarian to send the materials to the classroom. These materials are charged to the teacher and are used in his room. The disadvantage, of course, is that the materials are taken out of circulation. It is wise, therefore, not to use this method unless absolutely necessary.

Although these six techniques are simple and seemingly obvious, they are frequently disregarded. When they are employed, library usefulness increases immeasurably.

Teachers who have had unsatisfactory experience with using the library might pause to consider the following points:

There is no area of study for which it is impossible to obtain library materials.

The supply of library materials in an area depends upon the demands made by the teacher; frequent demand increases supply.

The teacher's attitude toward library reference work should be tolerant and flexible. In most instances this is the pupil's first contact with real reference work; skills must be developed. It is important not to expect too much too soon.

52. LIBRARY ORIENTATION FOR COLLEGE FRESHMEN

Georgetta Merritt Campbell

We are a small library in a newly integrated and rapidly expanding small liberal arts college.

Morgan State College had a record enrollment (1,811) this fall. Five hundred eighty-three freshmen arrived two weeks before the older students to begin a period of intense orientation. The library's role in this was quite different from all previous years, and now that we have seen the class complete the school year, we can say that this somewhat unusual role was extremely successful.

The reference librarian is the staff member who usually instructs new students in the use of the library. In previous years we have depended almost entirely on the instructors of freshman English to give a few hours of their class time to library orientation.

Sometimes the classes reached the library before the end of the first semester, but because of lack of time we were not able to accomplish very much even when they did. The less apt students often failed to take full advantage of library facilities early, probably because they were shy and afraid to experiment with the little library experience acquired before entering college.

We were at our wits end trying to teach the use of the reference tools, even the card catalog. Closed stacks were no help as space shortage prevented our following more modern trends. Then the administrators came up with the idea of a new orientation program for Freshmen.

Among the skills to be included in this period of training was the use of the library. Although much of the material to be covered was already contained in the "Student Library Handbook," the new approach to orientation demanded active student participation in the planned learning activities thus requiring material in addition to that in the "Handbook."

The training period was to be conducted by faculty members

235

meeting with small groups of students (four or five) two hours per day over a five day period. Use of the library was only one of the skills to be considered during the ten hours of study so that only the basic skills could be stressed at this time.

Every member of the faculty was to be involved in the endeavor and an in-service training program for faculty members had to be organized for them. In addition, the instructional materials had to be of such a nature that the average faculty member was able to use them with no more than a minimum of explanation.

Georgetta Merritt, reference librarian, was designated to work with Wilk Peters, assistant professor of Education, to organize the whole program. Two very competent members of the English department offered suggestions and edited the copy of the Workbook and Its Key, the instructional materials, which were typed, and mimeographed. The first job was to conduct the in-service faculty training, and then to act as consultants during the two week orientation period.

The Workbook contained five units — the card catalog and classification of books in a library, description and use of dictionaries and encyclopedias, periodical and book indexes, the use of miscellaneous references, and a review of how to know and use books. We made up exercises to follow each unit, trying always to use problems which should interest a new student at Morgan. Sample entries were taken from reference works, whenever possible, that would promote interest in the college's history and contribution to American life.

At the time of in-service training for orientation, we had the problem of convincing the faculty that they could teach the use of the library in spite of their subject specialization. Contrary to their doubts, they did an excellent job. We visited some of them during the period and watched them do a better job of the actual teaching than many professional librarians. With the smaller groups and knowledge and experience of teaching methods, they were able to produce results far superior to our former method of library instruction.

They had the use of the film Keys to the Library, which the college purchased especially for the orientation period. The Freshmen met in the auditorium to see the film and then divided into small groups of six to 12 for instruction. All during the day small groups drifted into the library. Large signs were there to guide them to the proper sources and almost every article of interest to them was labeled. Staff members were there to answer any other questions they might have, and often the groups, accompanied by the instructors, were given library tours. This has, incidentally, made many more students conscious of the material available in our closed stacks and impressed upon them the value and the necessity of knowledge of the card catalog.

For three or four days we had young visitors, then when school opened we had a library-conscious Freshman class. Circulation figures when compared with previous years showed a marked increase. We certainly are aware of increased use at the reference desk.

Many faculty members have also newfound library interests. This year no one had to write the heads of departments to remind them of our instructional services during the term. They consulted us often, sending their schedules and requesting special services at times when they were most needed. There have been requests from science teachers to have the use of Chemical Abstracts, Biological Abstracts, and the Current List of Medical Literature explained, a marked increase in the use of bound periodicals, indexes, and microfilmed newspapers. We have had to extend our library hours and open an additional downstairs reading room, and to keep pace with this growth, enlarge our staff.

Maybe all this is not a result of the little experiment, but we are sure it has had something to do with our unusual and interesting year.

I never before cared for freshman orientation periods as a time for library instruction. Having had this gratifying experience, I know now that with careful planning, preparation and study of a particular situation much can be accomplished.

53. CLASSIFICATION FOR THE NON-LIBRARIAN

Georgia Rankin Cole

Children in the elementary school can and do understand the Dewey decimal system and display great competence in using libraries. Since the libraries which they will use after leaving elementary school will be classified in this way, it seems advisable for the elementary library to follow the Dewey system, but there are situations when a simpler classification scheme is necessary if a library is to survive.

In many elementary schools, principals, teachers, and other persons untrained in library science are attempting to provide library service. Their other duties are not lessened to allow time for this work. Faculties and administrators in these schools feel that a central library is more valuable than a classroom collection even though the library has no librarian. Attempting to improve on Dewey's classification, spending hour after hour in the maze of cataloging, they grow weary, confused, and discouraged. The library frequently falls into disorder, and the books are returned to the classrooms. A simpler, less time-consuming system of organization is needed if these libraries are to survive.

One satisfactory method employs various colored dots and stars — of the variety available in ten-cent stores and office supply houses. Tapes available from library suppliers in colors and designs may be used also. Under this system, books are separated in groups by broad subjects selected by those who are organizing the collection. The ten large subject areas of the Dewey decimal system probably will be used, but others also will be needed to keep certain areas, such as the social sciences, from becoming too full for efficient use. The curriculum and the holdings of the library will help to determine the subject headings required. Examples of classifications which may be employed are: FAIRY TALES AND FOLKLORE, HOLIDAYS, SCIENCE, POETRY, FICTION, EASY BOOKS, AIRPLANES AND SPACE TRAVEL, HISTORY, BIOGRAPHY,

238

MUSIC, and ART. Instead of a classification number, a colored dot, star, or tape is assigned each subject heading. For example: holidays (red dot), poetry (blue star). The appropriate stars and dots can be glued to the spine, or to the book cover if plastic jackets are to be used. The books will be ready for circulation as soon as pockets and cards are added.

A prominently displayed "how to find it" chart will be needed. Subject classifications should be listed alphabetically, and the dot, star, or tape by which it can be located should be placed after each subject. A drawing of the shelving which indicates where each subject group is located will also prove helpful as will shelf labels with subject and classification symbols.

Dots instead of classification numbers could, of course, be carried to catalog cards. If the person in charge of the library has the time and skill for cataloging, however, he probably will be using the Dewey decimal system of classification. When untrained personnel attempt cataloging, the resulting index seldom is satisfactory. In addition, library service is curtailed or completely discontinued while the collection is being indexed. For these reasons, it probably is well not to attempt to catalog the library in this stage of development.

Even the smallest library should keep a record of its holdings. A shelf list is more practical than an accession book. Classification can be indicated in color on the shelf list card or can be typed in.

Obviously such a system of classification has disadvantages. Instruction in the use of their school library will not prepare children to use other libraries. Without a catalog they cannot be taught the use of this important tool, nor can teachers and children gain the fullest value from the book collection. There is no logical arrangement of the books on the shelves. The all-important services of the school librarian are lacking.

There are several advantages, however. Pupil assistants can help in every step of processing the books. Once the books have been sorted by subjects, a whole class may work at completing the project so that a great number of children have an opportunity to participate in the establishment of the library and have a special interest in it. The initial organization is accomplished quickly and without the necessity of closing the library for a long period of time. Since pupils can shelve books simply by putting all the purple dots together and books which are out of place are obvious at a glance, the time required for maintaining the collection is reduced greatly. Librarians who have employed paint, tape, shellac remover, and what-have-you to cover up or remove lettering on books will appreciate the fact that colored dots will interfere in no way with the lettering of these same books at some future date.

This plan of organization is suggested for elementary schools in which school officials cannot or will not add a librarian to the staff. Any time which is saved should be used to demonstrate to the school board and the administration the value of a central school library and the need for a school librarian.

54. CROSS REFERENCES MAKE CROSS READERS

George R. Ridge and Davy S. Ridge

"The Catalogers should be generous with references but should use them with intelligence."[1] The card catalog is a mixed blessing. It locates books and gives bibliographical data, and as long the user approaches it by title or author, his results justify the catalog. But once he tries to use it from the subject approach, he is bogged down in "red headings," "see references," "See also references," general references, and specific terms. Subject entries menace the subject approach, and as library collections grow — especially in research collections — the problems increase proportionately. Limited cataloging, use of Library of Congress cards, and the divided catalog are tentative solutions, but the fundamental problem is unsolved. The user cannot always utilize the subject approach meaningfully. Bibliography rooms, lists of subject headings, and even subject specialists do not strike at the root of the problem — the confusion about what a heading should be.

Maurice Tauber's The Subject Analysis of Library Materials is an excellent discussion of subject heading problems.

CROSS REFERENCES MAKE CROSS READERS

It presents problems discussed at an institute on subject headings in 1952 at Columbia University. It contains a summary of
studies in the use of the subject catalog by Carlyle Frarey,
who analyzes twenty-seven surveys made in the United States.
These surveys define problems in subject cataloging and sub-
stantiate other surveys by revealing that author cards are used
much more frequently than subject cards. For example, the
catalog at the University of California has been the object of
two surveys, both of which reveal that contemporary materials
are searched more frequently in the subject catalog and that
earlier works are located in subject bibliographies.[2, 3]
    Several studies in Frarey's summary underscore the value
of subject bibliographies in the research library, e. g., studies
at the Library of Congress,[4] Columbia University,[5] and the
University of Chicago.[6] The Chicago study on English literature
shows the advantage of the subject bibliography over the subject
catalog, and the Columbia work recommends selective subject
cataloging with heavy reliance upon the subject bibliography.
    Other catalog studies are based on interviews. One, for
instance, is based on questions asked college professors, most
of whom say they use subject bibliographies since they feel subject headings are outdated.[7] Another study concerns graduate
student use of the subject catalog.[8] The students believe the
subject catalog is inefficient and prefer periodical indexes
since they become impatient while searching the catalog. In
her survey of the college library subject catalog[9] Knapp maintains that students tend to use general rather than specific subject headings, look for the specific term rather than subdivisions of larger terms, look under place name rather than subject with geographical subdivisions, [. . .], use general headings which they do not pursue far enough, and look under form
rather than subject. In short, they are confused by a catalog
which does not fit their needs.
    Frarey summarizes the Symposium on Subject Headings
at the ALA meeting in July, 1952, at New York,[10] where the
same problems are discussed by many of the same librarians.
Included is David Haykin, who had recently published Subject
Headings: A Practical Guide and who defended the Library of
Congress Subject Catalog against the Hardy review. Haykin
advocates specific entries and maintains that the heading should

241

be as specific as the topic it is intended to cover.

Tauber also points out problems in the field in <u>Technical Services in Libraries</u>.[11] First, standard lists of subject headings are not comprehensive enough. Second, specificity itself is not "specific." Third, terminology must be either popular or scientific, not both. Fourth, the subject heading terms must be defined. Fifth, many subject terms are obsolescent. Sixth, multiplication of special subject heading lists creates further problems.

Moreover, the cross reference structure of the subject catalog has become so complex that it confuses rather than assists the user. Frarey agrees in his summary of catalog surveys: library users are quickly entangled with cross references.

What can be done?

The existing cross reference structure is the major cause of the user's confusion, and an evaluation of the need for cross references, as Tauber writes,[12] is mandatory. Little research has been done on this aspect of subject headings, and at present only problems of reference can be pointed out. The one obvious panacea, omission of all cross references, is drastic. Yet it may be warranted.

Haykin points out that <u>see also</u> references should be made from a given subject to more specific subjects or topics comprehended within it and to coordinate subjects which present other aspects or are closely related.[13] <u>See</u> references are from terms which are synonymous or closely synonymous to the terms under which the cataloger has placed the material. Haykin also states in an article:

> The true function of a see also reference is to bring to the attention of the reader the presence in the library of materials on related subjects and, what is perhaps even more important than this, to indicate to him that if he is really seeking material on a more specific topic he would find it under a correspondingly specific heading.[14]

Tauber states that <u>see also</u> references refer the catalog user from one heading to other related headings which are either more specific than the original term or equal in specificity.[15] Mann writes that see also references refer to or from terms where additional information may be found.[16] So much is clear. But while librarians define what references should do, the catalogers do not follow cataloging theory.

Catalogers tend to fail to approach the card catalog from the user's standpoint. McDonald believes that readers want to find materials through the exact topic they have in mind.[17] As examples he points out that readers look in the catalog for GHOST TOWNS instead of CITIES, RUINED, EXTINCT, etc., and for FEUDS instead of VENDETTA. Although see references are necessary, McDonald says that none were in the card catalog. He contends that in many cases librarians do not enter under the specific subject and fail to use see references for the user's benefit. Rogers, who writes from the scientific standpoint, states that in a scientific field see references from the synonymous for the main heading, and synonymous for the subdivision, with provision in inverted as well as chosen order, result in a complex cross reference system which is not worth the effort.[18] One library avoids recataloging old material by inserting a see reference which indicates that the subject headings was introduced at a certain date and that all books previously listed will be found in another place. Such practice inconveniences the user, who must consult two or three places, or more, to compile his bibliography.[19] A medical librarian comments that by using too many see references the cataloger condescends to his users, and the practice implies the cataloger's ignorance rather than the scientist's need.[20] Another medical librarian comments that most see references result from referral from obsolete and archaic terms largely chosen from dictionaries.[21]

Now this problem is essentially individual. It exists in a library, not in a theoretical vacuum, and hence must be solved individually in each library. But some librarians suggest more references while others say that too many now exist. There should be some theoretical guide — uniformity based on common sense. A copy of Sears might, for instance, be kept at the information desk,[22] and headings can be changed upon frequent request. Indeed a list of subject headings available near the card catalog helps the user to locate the subject under which he seeks material. Yet while catalogers can rectify some difficulties with more cross references, they can never teach people spelling or outguess their mental processes.[23] Thus all solutions are ultimately stalemated, and see references are at present in a quandary. Should the system be expanded, modified, or even omitted?

The see also reference presents even more problems than the see reference. The see also reference should be used to refer to related subjects, from the general to the more specific, and is useful for overlapping terms. Yet going from the general to the specific has gone much too far. In the Library of Congress Subject Headings there are seventy-seven references under INTERNATIONAL LAW, eighty-four under POLITICAL SCIENCE, and one hundred four under ETHICS. These lists result in confusion and great discouragement.

There are several remedies. For example, the noun approach to headings greatly reduces the need for see also references.[24] After all, it is impossible to foresee all significant relationships between headings.[25] It is also impossible to make all references suggested by subjects, and chasing see also references often becomes fruitless. See also references, in short, are frustrating at best.[26] One hundred nineteen subdivisions under English language combined with their numerous references not only result in confusion but also in absurdity. This does not mean the see also reference is always justified.[27] It means simply that the see also reference is so difficult to control that the entire matter should be reconsidered. In this connection simplicity should be the rule, like a card which states blandly:

> In addition to the books or articles listed on the following cards, other material related to this topic will be found under the headings listed below.[28]

Akers agrees that see also references should be used sparingly.[29] The new rule would state that the reference is unjustified unless the term used is one which everyone knows and unless the book definitely contains the material suggested.

Consider the absurdity of see also references in one university library. Many cards with their subdivisions lie beyond

MYTHOLOGY, and at the end of the section a <u>see also</u> reference directs the user to fifteen other headings. Tracing these headings shows the complete irrelevance of many <u>see also</u> references. ANCESTOR-WORSHIP offers little in connection with mythology but is rather concerned with Chinese culture and with Confucius. The books on ANIMAL WORSHIP are limited to BIRD WORSHIP, and the Argonauts are singled out as a separate heading though the cycles on Herakles and Cadmus, with typical inconsistency, are not. CULTUS reveals some books of use, and so does FOLKLORE. But HEROES contains many books which pertain to the Nietzschean <u>Uebermensh</u> rather than to mythology. Many of the books located in MYTHOLOGY are duplicated under RELIGION, PRIMITIVE, so that checking the reference is a waste of time. Several references hold one card each, and ART AND MYTHOLOGY holds a book for which a title card suffices. NATURE WORSHIP affords a book written from the theological standpoint. Thus at least seven of fifteen references can be eliminated: ARGONAUTS, DAWN, HEROES, MOON-WORSHIP, SUN-WORSHIP, and SWAN. And the other references all contain books which can be incorporated into the MYTHOLOGY heading.

This is a fair example of the condition of the average research catalog. It reveals an astonishing ignorance of the cataloger in referring to a subject which does not contain the material its heading claims. Moreover, the entire system of <u>see also</u> references is illogically and inconsistently developed. There is little that can justify it. Such a situation naturally results in the user's impatience and disgust.

The obvious solution is perhaps drastic, especially for the pursuit: it is to omit cross references entirely. One librarian did.[30] Cross references are undoubtedly used more often by the staff than others, and the librarian in question pulled all cross references from the catalog. The public was not notified of the change, and during a three year period not more than a dozen people commented on the change. A separate file of cross references was kept near the catalog for the user on request. The card catalog was greatly simplified to everyone's satisfaction.

Although research collections cannot omit all cross references, catalogers can certainly prune them and use them logically and meaningfully, as they have rarely done in the past. As Frarey says:

> I only maintain that something more revolutionary than simplified cards or more cross references is in order — perhaps a super-automat into which the patron can lisp his wishes and be rewarded with a jackpot of books pulled from the shelves by infallible robots. Something, I think, must certainly be done — in more than one age an enraged populace has arisen to burn the books, the libraries, and in all probability, the librarians too.[31]

Let librarians heed the warning. Let them prune all subject headings radically, omitting everything possible, including only the most necessary items with the strictest justification. Our present system of subject headings has resulted in confusion. If the system continues or is intensified, it will result in disaster.

55. FOURTH-GRADERS TO TO THE LIBRARY

Mary L. Connor and Ruth Ault

The library reading program for fourth-grade pupils at Horace Mann School in Indianapolis was undertaken to extend the reading experiences of pupils. The aims were to introduce them to the world of books and to create in them a desire to read. The procedures were (a) practicing story telling, (b) practicing oral reading with the idea of entertaining by dramatizing interesting parts of stories and making and giving puppet plays, (c) writing stories, (d) planning a summer reading program, and (e) pinning down interests. Plans included visiting the library regularly, scheduling special reading periods at school, and working out a few simple projects based on library reading.

FOURTH-GRADERS GO TO THE LIBRARY

The special reading period was to be used for silent and oral reading, for class discussion, and for book reports. Children could choose to tell the story, to read aloud, or to dramatize a portion of the book.

As a first step the teacher visited the library. She got application cards for the children and with the librarian planned for the children's visit. The library privilege application cards were sent home for parents' signatures, and the children discussed rules for travel to and from the library.

On the first visit to the library the librarian told the pupils about the rules for the use of the library. She discussed the care of books, behavior in the library, the number of books loaned to one child at a time, and how to use a card catalog. The children returned the application cards to the librarian. Each child browsed and selected the one book that was permitted to be withdrawn on the application card. Children who had previously obtained library cards checked out the regular number — four books and two magazines. Two librarians and the practice teacher assisted the teacher in guiding pupil selections. The books were checked out and the librarian, a gifted story teller, told the class the story, "How Pig Got His Curly Tail."

When the pupils returned from the library, they showed their books to other members of the class and they listed the names of the books on cards so that the teacher would have available a complete record of each child's library reading at the close of the library reading adventure. The class chose a regular reading period for each day.

Two weeks after the first visit to the library, the teacher's observations of some of the children were:

Mike does not read.

William paged thru his books, showed the pictures to others. He did not even read his <u>Mickey Mouse</u>.

Billy drew designs from someone else's books; he selected none for himself.

Picture books were most common with poor readers and those not interested. I decided to check to see who studied pictures only, who read with much help, who read his own books and borrowed books from others, and who read during spare moments.

Just before the second trip to the library, the pupils discussed the books they had read and those they would like to read. Then the teacher reviewed with them the travel and behavior rules, explained the meaning of shelf labels, and reviewed the librarian's suggestions for finding materials at grade levels.

At the library, on the second visit, one group of boys spent some time choosing biographies. Another group was interested in Popular Mechanics. A small group of boys and girls seemed fascinated by books at a primary level, such as Mickey Mouse. Some girls were interested in poetry and some in fairy tales. More than half of these fourth-graders used the card catalog on their second trip. The librarian gave pupils new library privilege cards, collected a fine for lost cards, and showed children how to fill out their own requests for books and checkout cards.

Following the second trip, the teacher's observations showed that pupils' interests were guiding the forming of their reading habits:

> Franklin, Clara Barton, and Jefferson are favorites.
> Poetry is being read and enjoyed by six girls.
> Travel picture books are wanted.
> Fairy tales are wanted.
> Favorite magazines are Popular Mechanics and Jack and Jill.
> Mike reads now during regular reading period.
> William pages thru the books and looks at the pictures.
> Billy draws pictures and dreams; he does not take books.
> Freddie reads to members of his family.
> Myrna just gets books.
> Jim reads once in awhile.
> Most of the children read during their spare time.
> Charlotte noted that a favorite illustrator did only good books.
> Patty, Carolyn, and James chose favorite authors; they followed an author's works.
> Vicki and Carolyn kept a book in reach, even when

on errands, for a quick read.

We have had several oral reading, story telling, and talking periods. Several children have illustrated their own books. The children are making puppets for telling particular stories. Plans are being made for a reading report in the form of a play.

Eight visits to the library were made during this semester of adventure with the library reading program. The full cooperation of the Indianapolis public librarians with the teacher and the practice teacher directing the project made progress possible with these fourth-grade pupils. The teacher is satisfied that her planned outcomes were at least partially achieved.

One value in such a program lies in interesting pupils in a worthwhile activity at a time in their lives when training of taste for good reading materials can easily be developed. A second and more immediate value is that interest in the summer reading program at the library is stimulated when this activity is undertaken during the spring term.

56. OUR LIBRARY IS A CENTER
FOR RECREATIONAL READING

Emily Harris and D. Richard Bowles

When a child really enjoys what he reads, half the mission of teaching him to read on his own is accomplished. However, he does not learn to read for pleasure solely by acquiring the desired reading skills. Often, a normal child who is diverted from reading by television, radio, and other distractions must have the door to the delights of reading pointed out to him, and perhaps even opened for him, until he has cultivated a taste for recreational reading. This taste for reading itself then serves to motivate the pupil to improve his reading skills. One of the aims of the library program at Brentwood is to stimulate just

249

such an interest in reading for fun. In order to understand how this aim integrates with the other aims of the library, a description of part of our school program is necessary.

Each elementary school in the Austin system is assigned one special teacher for every six teachers in Grades III to VI. This special teacher may be a librarian or a teacher especially trained in art, music, or physical education. The local principal and his staff decide what type of specialist should be engaged in a particular school. Usually, the first specialist chosen is a librarian because each of the Austin schools has a central library. Small schools sometimes choose a teacher qualified to serve both as a librarian and as a teacher in one of the other special areas.

Brentwood is large enough to have two full-time special teachers, a librarian and a physical education teacher. The schedule is arranged so that every pupil in Grades III to VI goes to the library or to physical education every day. Boys from two sections of a grade are grouped together in the library at a given period; girls from these two sections go to the gymnasium. On alternate days the schedule is reversed. (This plan provides the homeroom teachers in these grades with one period of unscheduled time every day.)

These periods are 40 minutes long. The number of such periods scheduled in the library varies from year to year. Ideally, the librarian should be left with enough time for administrative duties, and there should be time for unscheduled periods, preferably in the morning, when individuals and committees may come for research and reference work. At best, there probably should not be more than five periods scheduled for classes.

The minimum goal for library books in the Austin schools is about five per child. Once this goal is reached, it can be maintained and gradually increased by annually earmarking 60 cents per child out of the instructional budget for library books. In the first few years of a new school, it is necessary to supplement this amount with capital outlay funds so that the five-books-per-child goal can be reached in about four years. The librarian, together with the library supervisor and the principal, is responsible for ordering books to provide a balance between those needed to supplement the textbooks in social

studies, science, health, safety, and other subjectmatter areas
and books needed for recreational reading.

The librarian not only furnishes homeroom teachers with
books and vertical-file materials on the various units, but she
also provides each class with sets of books to be used for recreational reading in the homeroom. After a few weeks these
sets of books are returned to the library and exchanged for
others. The librarian also assists with the periodic visits of
the public library bookmobile.

Classes are specifically assigned to the library for supervised recreational reading. These periods are considered an
essential part of the whole library program as well as of the
whole school program. Their relationship to the program of
reading instruction is more than incidental; it is designed to
help the school obtain certain objectives.

In these days of comic books, movies, radio, and television, reading might take a back seat. But this condition may
have been with us for years. Judging from the dearth of solid
reading done in some homes today, yesterday's schools apparently did not do a good enough job of teaching people to read,
however well they might have done in teaching some how to read.
Of course, the regular reading instruction should teach pupils
more than how to read. But it never can be taken for granted
that children will find sufficient reasons for wanting to learn
to read outside their reading class. Acquaintance with fascinating stories will cause many children to want to improve their
reading skills. The recreational reading period in the library
can provide this acquaintance.

Attractive as our reading textbooks are, most of them still
have the appearance of having been "put together" for some
purpose other than reading for pleasure. But these basal and
supplemental readers may provide the pupil's only contact with
material written to be read for enjoyment, unless the school
has and properly uses a library. Simply having a library is not
enough. The pupils need frequent contacts with books which are
beautifully illustrated and printed, which tell an engrossing
narrative, which are written in good English and with good taste.

Only through such contacts, made in a pleasant and attractive atmosphere, can the pupil develop a discriminating taste
in the selection of his own reading materials.

Although a few children, like some adults, may abuse recreational reading, there are countless others who can find a wholesome release from tension in it. Even those persons who have relatively few emotional stresses need a change of pace in the day's routine. For example, the most interesting unit in social studies or science can be attacked with renewed vigor after a session with Charlotte's Web or The Biggest Bear. Many children and youth go through school without ever learning that reading is a kind of recreation. The period in supervised recreational reading can help children learn about this resource.

In the library an atmosphere that is pleasing to children helps to attain the foregoing named objectives. We attempt to make the library a center for many kinds of exciting activities, such as a doll parade after Christmas, a display of hobbies, and a flower show.

We also try to make each child feel that he is part of the library by encouraging different groups to plan and arrange bulletin boards, asking for suggestions as to what kinds of books they might like for us to include in our collection, and according each child in every class the privilege of assisting us with some phase of library work.

Before the library instruction can stimulate recreational reading, we must become acquainted with each child. Since we must learn to know some 400 children, we rely upon the classroom teachers for pertinent data such as reading levels, background information, and particular interest. We also consult the special reading teacher and cooperate with her.

In a typical library period, we may see as many different types of activities progressing as we have in any other classroom today. For instance, some children will be seated, reading books they had not completed in a previous period; others may be selecting books with the aid of another pupil; still others may be working out a dramatization in the workroom. Some pupils assist in checking out materials; this leaves the librarian free to guide pupils in their selection of books. We always like to allow each child who wishes to check out a book the time and opportunity to find just the right one.

We help pupils learn to select books independently, to evaluate what they read, to develop desirable reading habits, and to vary their recreational reading.

RECREATIONAL READING

Such a program, of course, is not free from pupils who have problems. Perhaps Donnie was one of our most obvious examples. When he first came into the library last fall, he told the librarian quite frankly, "I don't know why I'm stuck in here when you know as well as I do that I can't read them books." After checking with his classroom teacher, we found that he had been truthful; he could not read "them books" as he, a fourth-grader, was reading on a second-grade level. Besides having difficulty with reading, Donnie was not getting along well with his classmates.

As a matter of regular procedure, Donnie was referred to the special reading teacher. Meanwhile, we asked Donnie to help us check out books during his library period. This gave him a lift, for being permitted to stamp the books is a coveted position in our library. Also, we never lost an opportunity to call upon Donnie when someone was needed to deliver books or to check up on overdue books. Before long, we suggested that he might enjoy a picture book on cowboys. To our amazement, he took it to his seat and looked at the pictures for nearly 20 minutes — quite a feat for Donnie! As his work with the special reading teacher progressed, she and I both suggested books for him to check out. Today his teacher feels that he is making much progress in the classroom. We do not feel that the library solved all Donnie's problems or that he has completely adjusted himself to his group, but we can see that the library period offered him a steppingstone to other adjustments.

Certainly we realize that not all children will show as much progress as Donnie. Yet, as in all work with children, the successes are many when the children are given half a chance. We believe that the majority of our pupils are learning to read on their own.

57. PLAYGROUND FUN IN STORYLAND

Virginia Musselman

Storytelling is not an isolated activity. It runs through the entire playground program. It is found in games, particularly the singing and play-party games. It is found in music — in ballads, folk songs, opera. It is found in arts and crafts, sometimes clearly and sometimes through use of symbols. It is the essence of drama.

The playground should provide such a relaxed atmosphere that everyone feels free to talk about the daily happenings, the little excitements, the small events that play so large a part in life. It is the chief method of building up personal relationships.

There is no one place and no one time for storytelling on the playground. There will be a storytelling period, of course, set aside _primarily_ for that activity, but it goes on, and should go on, during _every_ activity. In rest periods after games, over the craft table or the drawing boards, on the hike, in the wading pool and sandbox, over the checkerboard, in the club meeting, at the picnic, talk goes back and forth while the tales of daily living, whether funny, sad, exciting, instructive, or inspiring, pass from one person to the other.

One of the chief duties of the playground leader is to foster such exchanges between individuals and to take a part in them, sharing freely _his_ experiences, opinions, thoughts, and information.

In the storytelling period — that time set aside in which stories can be heard on a special place on the background — storytelling becomes the _primary_ activity. It might include looking at pictures, or a little singing, or a little play-acting, or a little puppetry — but the story is the main thing.

Storytelling should be conducted in as quiet, comfortable and isolated an area on the playground as it is possible to find. In hot weather, there should be shade. The quiet and isolation may be provided by the schedule as well as the location.

PLAYGROUND FUN IN STORYLAND

The place might be almost anywhere — under a big shady tree; in the shade of an awning by the shelter house; on the steps of the shelter house; in a cool, grassy area; in a far corner. The area will gain more prestige if it becomes known by some special name, like The Story Tree, The Magic Ring, Story Steps, Make-Believe Corner. A nice name, however, will not make the story-hour a success. That requires good storytelling!

Unless the leader is a very skillful storyteller, the group should be kept small. Telling a story to more than 30 as a maximum is very difficult. Twenty youngsters make a better maximum.

They should be seated comfortably, fairly close together so that group reaction is easier, but with room for legs and feet to be comfortable. Everyone should be able to see the leader, and should be near enough to hear without straining.

The group should cover as small an age range as possible. When the age range is wide, the story should be suitable for the oldest, not the youngest. When the group contains boys and girls, the stories should be suitable to the mixed group. Girls will listen to boys' stories, but boys will scorn stories primarily suitable for girls.

As a general rule, the story hour should be long enough to include one favorite of the group and one story new to the group. If three stories are used, the first one should be dramatic enough to get and hold the attention; the second can be longer and more serious; the last one should be short and rollicking, leaving the group amused and happy.

Choosing the right story is the most important single factor in storytelling. There are stories for every mood, every age, every holiday, every situation, every interest.

First of all, the leader must like the story. No good storyteller ever tries to tell a story that he or she does not like.

Second, the story must have action. Long descriptions, no matter how beautiful, slow up the story. Descriptions should be brief, colorful, and incidental to the action.

Third, the story should not require explanations. It should be within the group's experience, understanding, and range of imagination.

Fourth, the story should not need any character analysis. The actions of the characters should speak for themselves.

The leader should make very sure that the story does not ridicule or cast aspersions upon any race, nationality, or religion. He must be conscious of this. Stories in which the Negroes or the Irish are always cast in the role of servants, the Chinese as laundrymen, the Japanese as Oriental spies, the Jews as cruel bargainers, should be avoided. Interracial and intercultural relations can be advanced or retarded through stories.

A few stories, particularly those with unusual or beautiful phrases, may be memorized, but usually it is wise not to rely on memorization. If a story has an especially interesting opening or closing line, it is likely to set the mood or the tone of the story, and can be used verbatim.

The most important principle in telling a story is for the leader to forget everything except the group and the story. He is giving them something he likes; they are sharing his pleasure, and so a very real bond is created between them.

The voice must be heard, of course, but it should not be loud, and above all, not monotonous. It should be relaxed.

Words must be enunciated clearly. Words are new to small children, and in most stories there are words unfamiliar to some children. Their meaning is made clear by the context, and they are added to the group's vocabulary with enjoyment.

Gestures can add greatly to the effectiveness of a story, provided they are natural and do not distract the interest from the story itself.

Mimicry, too, should be simple and subtle, never exaggerated except in the few stories in which it is the main ingredient. A change in voice indicating the different characters helps to distinguish them and facial expressions help to sustain the moods, but both lose their effectiveness if overdone.

Timing is very important. Perhaps rhythm is a better word. Every story has its own timing. Some of them gallop along swiftly, some march, some amble. The storyteller should present them in their individual timing, or part of their charm is lost.

The story should be told for what it is, not what it does. The storyteller should not point out a moral or a lesson in it.

256

If it's told well, the youngsters will get the point. Don't rub it in!

Once the climax is reached, the ending should follow swiftly, and the story should not be ruined by asking questions about it to see how much the youngsters remember!

58. GUIDING CHILDREN'S READING

Delta Jack

During the last twenty years the once narrowly confined world of children's literature has become a vast empire. Books are now written at every level of the child's ability to understand and appreciate the complex world in which he lives. Their latitude ranges from the very simplest of nursery rhymes and picture books to accurate and fascinating nonfiction, all important in emotional, social, and intellectual development.

Effective guidance on the part of the librarian necessitates understanding not only the developmental tasks of childhood and the factors which influence children's reading but also the developmental values in books and their use in personal adjustment and good citizenship.

Frances Henne in Youth, Communication and Libraries defines developmental values as

those elements in books which may aid the child in his choice of behavior. A book may produce stimulus situations for new behavior patterns or influence and reinforce desirable valuations and attitudes already formed by the child.

Alice Brooks, author of one of the chapters, provides an excellent classification of developmental values.[1]

Books for children have always contained developmental values but today many authors tend to overemphasize them.

Sometimes the moral rather than the story becomes the important factor and the book becomes "preachy." Children reject such books, as they read for the story itself.

The librarian is concerned not so much with the book itself as with the interaction which takes place between the book and the child, making effective teaching and learning possible. Children identify with book characters and the attitudes and values which the character expresses often become those of the child. Thus it is imperative that the librarian supply the right book for the right child at exactly the right time. Helpful aids are Patterns in Reading[2], an annotated list for young people, grouped according to reading interests, and Reading Ladders for Human Relations[3], annotated lists of books on specific developmental problems.

Reading needs and interests change as children grow. Early childhood is the time when humor and nonsense are most appreciated. The interests of small children center around people, animals, and everyday familiar happenings, but attention span is short and interest veers quickly from one thing to another. Picture books with rather brief stories answer their needs. Mother Goose is a constant delight, as are The Red Carpet, Frog Went a Courtin', Angus and the Ducks, and a variety of other simple tales.

Primary children have broader social interests and although they still like picture books, they enjoy realistic stories about home, school, and community. They, too, love humor and alliteration and delight in repeating with the reader the rhythmic phrases from Millions of Cats, Nothing at All, and Little Lamb. Since the child's stage of development involves learning how to get along with others, he sees the implications of sharing in Two Is a Team and comments upon them. His is a slowly developing world of social relationships which requires much help and patience.

The intermediate years bring a longer attention span and interest is centered in stories about other peoples, historical themes, folk tales, and stories in which grownups take part. Boys and girls, too, have an absorbing interest in horse and dog stories and in boy or girl stories. Both can enjoy Henry Huggins, Mr. Pudgins, and The Monkey with a Notion.

Preadolescence brings somewhat more specialized interests. There is a growing interest in the other sex, especially among girls. Boys are interested in sport stories, westerns, biographies of athletes, aviation, and hobbies. Girls like family stories, those dealing with ballet, cookbooks, and etiquette manuals — books which correspond with their developing needs.

In an attempt to meet all the needs and interests of children and to develop lasting attitudes, values, and learnings, the librarian must offer books to further specific teaching objectives, such as love of country and democratic ideals, understanding personal environments, a sense of belonging and prestige, belief in social equality and individual freedom.

In planning learning experiences the librarian must decide just what the needs of the group or the individuals are and how the experience will be of value in continued learning and development. It is important to relate the experience to something already known, appeal to present interests, and provide a problem which is real to the children — one which the situation can help solve. Questions will encourage children to consider what they might have done in similar circumstances and will help them transfer learning values to other situations which they may encounter.

In teaching love of country and democratic ideals the librarian makes use of current television interest in the development of the early West. Wyatt Earp, Gun Smoke, and similar programs provide a stimulus for biographies of such pioneers as Sam Houston, Daniel Boone, and William Cody. Group discussion of what makes a hero can extend through the entire field of biography and help stimulate reading interest.

Need for understanding personal environment is a vital one, for many children do not recognize the role they play in family relationships. All of a Kind Family, Two Log Crossing, My Mother Is the Most Beautiful Woman in the World, and Roosevelt's Letters to His Children are only a few of the books which interpret family life. Carefully planned questions bring to attention the things which create discord, reasons for anger, acceptance of responsibility, the effect of individual actions upon other members of the family, qualities and attitudes which are common and desirable in all family relationships.

The child's need to belong is answered in some degree by understanding and acceptance by the librarian but books such

as The Smallest Boy in the Class, A Sundae With Judy, and
Monkey Shines show how team work accomplishes what individuals alone could not do. Group discussion points up the benefits
to the group as a whole and to individuals.

Our American way of life is dependent upon our belief in
social equality and individual freedom. Unfortunately many
children enter school with definite bias and prejudice about
others. Reading aloud from such books as Shuttered Windows,
The Hundred Dresses, and Davey, the librarian attempts to
create sensitivity to the feelings of others. Discussion as to
whether the girl in Hundred Dresses deliberately lied will produce varying opinions and cause children to think about the
problems of others. For younger children the story of Charcoal
points out that external appearance is not a good criterion for
judging others. Through discussion the librarian attempts to
teach that differences in themselves are not bad but instead
often enrich the lives of others.

Girls reaching adolescence need book experiences like
those in Seventeenth Summer before their attitudes and values
have been formed. There are certain moments during which a
value must be taught if it is to be of use. If it comes too late
in a developmental stage, attitudes have already been formed,
often undesirable ones which are difficult to change. Role playing of a problem story helps to bring out the child's own attitudes and problems.

In the primary grades the stories which children enjoy have
happy endings, right always triumphs over wrong and the hero
overcomes all obstacles. As children develop, however, they
must learn to accept and evaluate the real world in which we
live, where not everything in life has a happy ending and where
there are handicaps and obstacles. The stories of Jane Addams,
Helen Keller, and others who have faced handicaps but have
built useful lives in spite of them, furnish a basis for understanding.

The use of biography, autobiography, personal interviews,
and observation helps both individuals and groups to recognize
and attempt to solve problems. Books like Caddie Woodlawn
help to show the recognition and acceptance of one's sex role.
Cassie of Peach Tree Island works hard to solve her problem
of gaining independence, and Adopted Jane presents the problem

of an orphan girl who has difficulty in finding the right kind of a home. These books present problems whose analysis suggest solutions. There are many ways to teach esthetic values and appreciations. Beautiful poetry and stories like Why the Chimes Rang, The Happy Prince, The Selfish Giant, The Egg Tree, The Country Bunny and The Little Gold Shoes enhance appreciation for fine literature and styles of writing.

Books about other lands, followed by questions pointing out similarities of activity, problems, and pleasures of people who are unlike us in some ways, help children in their understanding of others. The Chinese Children Next Door, Elin's Amerika, San Francisco Boy, and The Adventures of Wu Han of Korea all provide insight into the problems of the foreign-born. Suggestions from the children about ways in which newcomers to our shores could be helped to feel more at home often result in new attitudes. Discussion of the problems we might face in another country is most enlightening for the children.

Humorous books, providing entertainment and escape from the problems of everyday life, include nonsense verse and books like Paul Bunyan, Tom Sawyer, Angelo, The Naughty One and The Man Who Lost His Head.

All planned learning experiences require much thought, time, and research on the part of the librarian, but they are well worth the effort expended if they develop better attitudes, evaluations, skills, critical thinking, and real learning on the part of the children.

59. THE ART OF READING

Elizabeth Hodges

The reading program in the elementary school has a two-fold purpose — to teach the skills of reading and to encourage the art of reading. Responsibility for the former has tradition-ally been assigned to the classroom teacher; but accomplish-ment of the second goal is rarely possible without a school library to serve as a laboratory, and a librarian to give stim-ulation and guidance beyond what is possible in the classroom.

The more obvious purposes of the school library have been well publicized. It has been said again and again that the library is a materials center; that the librarian will acquire, organize, and circulate the printed and audio-visual aids need-ed to enrich the curriculum and to satisfy the interests of chil-dren; that through the library children will be taught the skills needed to find and use these materials. But too little emphasis has been given to the role of the library in helping children to grow into habitual and discriminating readers — readers who turn naturally to books for help and inspiration in everyday living, who recognize and choose worthwhile reading in pref-erence to trivia and "trash." In these attitudes and abilities lies the art of reading.

As reading instruction proceeds in the classroom, the practice of reading is carried on in the library. Here, the abundance of books, the warmth and friendliness of the atmos-phere, and the absence of grade levels encourage the child to believe that reading is a pleasant activity, offering rewards to all. The slow child sets his own pace and chooses the books best suited to his interests and abilities. The bright or average child explores, develops new interests, and meets new chal-lenges. The librarian's skill is severely tested as she offers guidance where it is needed, keeps hands off when independent action is desirable, and gives stimulation, encouragement, and instruction as required. Every day the school library gives children the opportunity to discover the satisfactions of reading;

262

every day it demonstrates its influence in developing in boys and girls the habits and appreciations necessary to the art of reading.

Tom was the school genius. Mature beyond his years and with an IQ of 190, he found work with a normal fifth grade class unbearably dull. His special aptitude in mathematics and science suggested to the school librarian that he might enjoy Hogben's The Wonderful World of Mathematics. This he devoured, and then went on to Plotz's Imagination's Other Place, that unique anthology of poetry related to science and mathematics. From these, Tom forged ahead on his own, finding many books worthy of his superior abilities in his favorite and related fields — and justifying the librarian's efforts to provide as adequately for the exceptionally bright child as for the slow learner.

At the other end of the scale was George. Ten years old and in the fourth grade (by way of social promotion), George could not read a word. Worse still, neither George nor his teachers expected that he ever would learn to read, for he came from a family of low intelligence, low morals, and low achievement. Like his older brothers, he was marking time in school until he could legally stop. His teachers did their conscientious best for him, but were discouraged by his low intelligence score (between 65 and 70) and his cheerful acceptance of the idea that he couldn't learn. To give him one more useful activity, his teacher allowed him to "help" in the library by straightening books, delivering messages, and replacing chairs. His visits gave the librarian a chance to win his confidence and to suggest that he could learn to read if he tried hard enough. She and George spent a few minutes each day finding interesting picture books and talking them over together. The classroom teacher learned of the experiment and responded with extra efforts to encourage and help George with his new interest. The combination of the right materials and individual instruction convinced him that he could learn, after all, and for the first time in his life he really tried to learn to read. By the end of the school year he was reading on a second grade level and was showing promise of making even further growth.

In one elementary library it seemed to be the fashion for poor readers among the older boys to resist all efforts to interest them in books. The librarian made a study of their backgrounds and abilities, and with the help of their teachers, chose a small group to form the nucleus of a reading club. In a relaxed and informal atmosphere, the librarian met the boys and set about learning their interests and finding simple reading materials related to those interests. By finding the right books and by taking a genuine interest in the boys themselves, the librarians showed the group that the library had something for them as well as for their more able classmates. Soon the boys were talking so enthusiastically about their "club" that their friends were applying for admission, and interest had replaced indifference as the popular attitude toward reading.

Jim was not exceptional — only exceptionally lively and curious about everything under the sun. Consequently his obsession with mystery stories was hard to understand. The librarian had resigned herself to letting him read his way straight through the entire mystery collection when he arrived one day to return The Grey Room, by Eden Phillpotts.

"This was a swell story," he said, "all about an antique bed that had belonged to Lucretia Borgia. Everybody who slept on it died. Who was Lucretia Borgia?"

Here was the golden opportunity! The encyclopedia was suggested to answer Jim's question, and curiosity did the rest. From the Borgias and their beds to a book on antique furniture was an easy step. Then came books on jewels and gems (another interest springing from the account of the Borgias), and finally, several books on fifteenth-century Italy. From then on, Jim never found time to return to his old love — mystery stories.

These incidents typify the happenings of a normal day in the school library. To the library come all of the children of all of the people. Here they are surrounded by the best in children's books, along with enough of the simpler and more popular books to satisfy the needs of those not yet ready for the best. Here they read, each at his own level, regularly and for his own purposes. Here they are introduced to the classics in their literature and encouraged to read the best books which they as individuals are capable of reading. Here they form habits which are bound to lead many to the public library for a lifetime of reading. The school which provides its children with a good library gives them the best opportunity to discover the joy of reading and to develop the tastes, habits, and appreciations necessary to the art of reading.

60. CENTRAL LIBRARY ON A LOW BUDGET:
WITH TIPS ON PLANNING, STAFFING — AND SHARING

W. Ambrose Kincaid and Mamie Ingram

An adequate library is just about indispensable for meeting the individual needs of all children in general and of the "gifted" in particular. The finest arrangement imaginable is a library of functional size and optimum staff in each elementary school. For 500 to 600 pupils it would include a library suite, 1,500 sq. feet in area, one full-time librarian and clerk, 6,000 volumes of literature and resource materials and audio-visual aids, if part of the library set-up. This arrangement, however, could range from $75,000 to $100,000 per school.

But Hempstead, New York has come up with a library program which it believes meets its elementary school needs very well indeed, and which costs only a fraction as much as the library-in-every-building plan. In the Hempstead plan the literature program is completely decentralized. That is to say, each home room has its own collection of 100 to 150 books for ready use by the pupils; these collections may be exchanged, in whole or in part, with other classrooms of the same grade or the next higher or lower grade level. Also, each home room from the 4th grade up has its own encyclopedia and certain other standard reference material.

To answer the need for supplementary enrichment materials for the boys and girls, Hempstead has established a Central Resource Library, which is administered by a full-time librarian aided by a full-time clerk. The district presently owns about 11,000 volumes and expects to buy 4,000 more before it will consider the job completed. Although the resource program has been in full operation for only a little over a year, it has already proved its value beyond question, at least in the eyes of the classroom teachers. To obtain 15 to 50 curriculum-supporting books, a teacher has only to send a request to the librarian for help on a given subject. The books are delivered on the following Tuesday, and they remain with the teacher and her children as long as needed.

As the school superintendent views the program there is only one "hitch." At the rate the service is growing it may be necessary in the very near future to provide a second librarian to take care of the demands. This, however, is a service that almost any school system with 2,500 to 3,000 elementary pupils can afford. While the Hempstead District owns about 10 books per pupil (in both home room and resource collections), it has only one library room (of 1,500 square feet) and presently only one librarian. Except for the books, the initial cost plus the operational cost is just about one sixth of that of the library-in-every-building program.

The Central Resource Library has fully justified itself in its first year of service. Over 7,500 books were circulated and many of them did double duty. For instance, where there were two teachers per grade within a building, one teacher might place a requisition for the two of them, if the children of both rooms were working on the same unit. The total number of teacher requests for resource aids was 488 from some 105 teachers.

Use of the central collection is growing monthly and appreciation for the enrichment it offers increases accordingly. In another year or so additional personnel is almost certain to be needed. But this is really a blessing in disguise, for more reasons than one. Among other things, it will provide time for the then head librarian to conduct workshops for both teachers and students in the use of resource materials. There will be time also to help principals and teachers select books for the home room libraries, and to assist teachers in story hour and literature appreciation periods.

And now for a bit of history about the Hempstead elementary school library program and how it has grown. The children's literature and standard reference home room libraries (total 15,000 volumes) were developed slowly over a long period of years. The Central Resource Library program now in progress will be completed in three years. For this latter program the necessary space was already available in one of the older elementary school plants; thus the initial outlay was held to a minimum. The first year's appropriation was $25,000; of this amount $20,000 went for the basic 8,000 volumes, and the remaining $5,000 for stacks and other equipment. Last year's budget provided for an additional 2,400 books and this year's budget anticipates still another 3,000. The remaining 1,600 volumes of the planned 15,000 will be added a few hundred at a time, to strengthen the collection and keep it up to date.

However, perhaps a couple of words of caution should be added. The launching of a resource library on such a large scale is a job for an experienced librarian. It requires a great deal of practical knowledge of the special kind that comes only through first-hand acquaintance with school library situations. It requires also an understanding of people and of how to enlist their interest and cooperation in developing the lists of books essential for backing up the schools' many courses of study.

The second caution concerns the amount of work involved in getting the basic 8,000 volumes ready for use. Nearly eight months passed between the day of the first planning conference with teachers and the day that the last book purchased was catalogued and shelved. Fortunately, Hempstead decided to withhold service until all books were ready. To have started when the first 2,000 books were catalogued would surely have led to chaos and given the program a poor send-off.

In its combination home room-central resource approach, this community has had a gratifying experience with an economical elementary school library program, which could work perhaps as successfully in your school situation.

61. THE ELEMENTARY SCHOOL LIBRARY AND THE GIFTED

Mildred P. Frary

Los Angeles has been experimenting with different programs to discover ways in which the needs of mentally-gifted children can be met in the elementary schools. In one area of our city, children from several schools meet with a special teacher for three hours each week for enrichment activities.

In another area, a reserve teacher is assigned to one school to work with the faculty in preparing projects or materials directed towards the gifted in each classroom. Other schools are conducting individualized interest and reading projects. School library service — varied and immediately available — has been essential to all types of programs.

Children and teachers have library books supplied to them through a dual service. Centralized libraries are functioning in 141 of our 400 elementary schools. About 30 libraries are added each year. In addition, the 8000 teachers may order classroom collections from the main Los Angeles City Schools Library and exchange them at any time. Six elementary librarians from the Library Section administer these collections.

One of these librarians is assigned to the gifted program as part of her regular duties. She attends meetings of the teachers and supervisors of the gifted and coordinates their planning with library materials. This same curriculum-library coordination is present in the planning for and service to teachers of Special Education and Remedial Reading.

Book selection for gifted children at this level is less of a problem now than it was a few years ago. Several fields of interest in non-fiction which have consistently reappeared in their requests can now be found in excellent titles bridging the gap to junior and senior high-school books. Archeology, history of mathematics and language, electricity, and chemistry are regularly requested subjects. Additional titles in art, music, travel, foreign languages, and government still need to be written for this age group.

Informal discussions of books and reading between children and librarians have shown the children reading and enjoying fiction at their own age level. While they may delve into their fathers' technical books, they are still children and relish the antics of Carolyn Haywood's Eddie and Ellen MacGregor's Miss Pickerell on her reluctant way to Mars.

Some activities have proved valuable to both the children and the librarians. Informal book discussions often bring out facets of a child's personality which formal testing does not reveal. By recording the discussions on tape, the librarian, the teacher and the counselor can return to the needed information. We learn where a child is in his reading and can go on from there. The child who is being pushed beyond his years, the child who is rooted to one subject, the child who hasn't time to read — all turn up as the discussion gathers momentum.

Some schools have gathered their high-index children into library clubs. They meet for book discussions, act as school library assistants, and review new books. They in turn share their enthusiasm with their classmates. In one school, the upper-grade children have become adept at storytelling and reading aloud to younger groups.

Continuing evaluations of the gifted programs usually point out in one way or another that success is based on books, libraries, and reading guidance unlimited!

62. THE SCHOOL LIBRARY HELPS THE GIFTED CHILD

Edith W. Dahlgren

In the past few years we have seen tremendous progress in the programs provided for the mentally retarded and handicapped children. However, this is only one segment of society which needs attention. Another group, namely the gifted pupils, have either gone unrecognized, been left to make their own way with the idea that they could take care of themselves, or been given a moderate amount of enrichment which depended on the vision of some observant individuals.

In larger areas it is easier to segregate and accelerate many of these able youth. However, something must be done everywhere for these pupils after their capabilities have been recognized and identified. How can regular schools leave the gifted with their regular groups, and yet keep the level of learning high, creative, and challenging?

There are many ways in which the school library with an enthusiastic librarian can help the superior child by training him to become a library assistant. The busy school librarian frequently finds young people can be trained to carry out many tasks. The gifted pupil, who is usually interested not only in books and materials but is curious about almost everything, can satisfy his inner urge to be useful, as well as render valuable service to the school.

If the school administrator can be shown that the work-experience opportunities which the library offers help in the growth and development of the individual, he may be willing to encourage teachers to excuse a few bright pupils from an occasional class, especially if the teachers can be sure that the program of library service is designed, as Mary Peacock Douglas points out in The Pupil Assistant in the School Library:

To give pupils an opportunity to broaden their personal experiences

To give pupils an opportunity to become more adept in the use of books and libraries

To provide opportunity to explore vocational interests through prevocational experiences

To provide opportunity for experiencing satisfactions inherent in service to fellow students and teachers

To promote cooperative attitudes between the librarian and students

To provide additional opportunities for democratic participation

To provide opportunities for developing and using special abilities and skills

To help provide increased and improved library service to the school community.

All assistants should know the general arrangement of the library, become acquainted with the classification system used, be familiar with the use of the card catalog and other reference tools, know the parts of a book, and know the rules and regulations of the library.

THE LIBRARY HELPS THE GIFTED CHILD

In addition, the brighter students will become acquainted
with the book collection as they charge, discharge, slip, and
shelve books. They receive much pleasure and information
from these materials, and learn the relationship of this library
to the over-all purposes of libraries in society, as well as
develop good work habits and the satisfaction of assisting in
an efficient organization. Room services such as housekeeping
duties, keeping periodicals in order, and arranging flowers
have numerous possibilities for many pupils. Book processing
alone gives youngsters a better understanding of what goes on
behind the scenes in a library. Assembling reserve materials
requested by teachers, opening and collating new books, clipping newspapers and magazines, mounting maps and pictures
give the bright pupil firsthand acquaintance with much material.

The curious mind that retains information is of invaluable
assistance in calling it to the attention of other pupils, classroom teachers, parents, and club members. It is a real joy
to watch a youngster spot a piece of information or a book
which challenges his imagination, and have him share it with
others. Youngsters take suggestions from their peers and follow them more enthusiastically than those assigned by teachers.

Publicity and public relations services such as planning
and arranging exhibits and displays call for resourcefulness
and ingenuity on the part of gifted youngsters. Articles in the
school paper, book reviews, assembly programs, radio or
TV skits, Book Week programs and quizzes give talented
pupils in art, writing, and dramatics a chance to be resourceful, original, and creative. Social leadership and human relations become an important part of all of these group activities
when different committees are responsible for various tasks.

Some of the recognized "bookish" children may be used
as "reference librarians" to prepare simple bibliographies
of teen-age books or vocation information, and to teach other
pupils who have not mastered the tools in regular library
classes. Others may be taught the principles of book selection
and reviewing which will help them judge, analyze, and prepare
oral or written reports.

Book repairing offers opportunities for youngsters to put
handicraft skill to practical use. They may be encouraged to
take pride in seeing the book collection in good repair.

The jobs relating to cataloging and order services, such

271

as preparing orders for printed cards, typing designated headings on printed catalog cards, arranging and alphabetizing and filing cards above the rod are exacting duties. Here is a chance for the gifted mature pupils who are easier to train and have learned to type.

The library training of pupils is one of the difficult aspects of the problem. Group instruction of a library club, which meets during activity or special period, is advisable; so, too, is use of a carefully constructed library manual. The bright pupil learns quickly and can soon teach others to handle those duties. The librarian must always be alert to challenge and inspire the talented ones, so they will not become bored with any one task.

For those who serve as library aids there should be some plan to rate and evaluate them on efficiency, cooperativeness, reliability, courtesy, industriousness, personal appearance, initiative, punctuality; and a cumulative record of this work-experience should be sent to the guidance counselor and deposited in the student's school record. Some kind of public or personal recognition of a pupil's service should be provided, such as pins, badges, or letters awarded at a school assembly.

Not only will these pupils broaden and enrich their work and reading interests, but working in the library will give them an opportunity to explore library service as a vocation, and provide experience helpful in securing summer positions in public libraries and part-time work in university libraries.

Another channel of interest for bright youngsters is the library club, with its many projects and committees providing constant stimulation and challenge to their imagination and resourcefulness, as well as an opportunity to work with others in a group. The increasing number of clubs and student assistant organizations offer opportunities for cooperation and leadership in student library circles even beyond their own school.

63. THE ROLE OF THE LIBRARIAN
IN THE READING PROGRAM

Reba Burtis

What is my responsibility toward improvement of reading in my school? I have a very definite problem to work out with the poor readers who have reached high school level. These students are confused with respect to reading by the difficulty of the books they are expected to read. Some are retarded because of mental ability; others would improve if given the proper remedial procedures and proper guidance in the selection of their reading material. Since these students cannot do the reading expected of them they lag behind in their work. This leads to confusion and frustration, the major causes of the discipline problems I face in the library.

I feel that the library has a special contribution to make to the reading lives of these young people. The library can be a teaching agency, giving pupils instruction in the use of the library and its tools. It can help the student to get pleasure and profit out of the available materials, and it can be a factor in the direction of study, helping the student to become self directing and developing independence in his study habits.

Some of the things I have used to interest the slow, indifferent, or reluctant reader include book talks, exhibit cases, hobbies shared, games, and contests. Storyhour, dramatizations, and opportunities to share and discuss books increase the pleasure of the school library and its book collections. The bulletin board is always a source for creating interest. It has proven an effective way to introduce new books or books that need to be read and enjoyed. By changing the board at least once a week interest in it is kept alive. I have tried to interest slow readers by giving them opportunities to handle the books by doing chores in the library. Some of these chores include arranging the books, dusting, and mending magazines. These tasks give them a feeling of importance and lead them to feel the library is for them, too. For some of the very slowest

273

readers I have borrowed books from the elementary school library. Every book read, no matter how simple, I feel is a victory won! Through constant and happy experience with books reading becomes interesting and fun.

For these slow readers, I have included in my book collection many books of high interest with low ability level. I plan to add to this list each year for there must be enough material so that extensive reading may be done. These books must be interesting or the reading will be half done and will produce a dislike for reading. Little benefit will be derived if the reading is too hard. Some books must be easy enough for the poorest reader to read rapidly.

There are many benefits to be derived from easy reading. The recognition of common everyday words is speeded up. The second benefit is the enlargement of vocabulary. It must be remembered that only easy reading will improve the eye movement habits. Not only do we get increased reading ability, but improved reading taste is the result of much easy reading.

It has been both interesting and gratifying to note some of the results of my efforts in helping these students with their reading problems. Some of these include grade improvement, happier student-teacher relationships, better discipline, and above all the students feel pride of achievement.

64. BUILDING A VOCATIONAL INFORMATION FILE

Marianne Schmidt

From the time a child first hears the question "What will you be when you grow up?" until he is launched on a career, the one which is eminently right for him, there is no more important question he has to answer. And in today's specialized society, none more difficult.

Fortunately vocational literature has kept pace with the growing complexity of the vocations themselves. It is fortunate too, considering the budget limitations of most libraries, that a great amount of useful vocational material in pamphlet form can be gathered for the price of postcards.

There is little danger that a vocational information file will not find users. High school teachers assign papers on vocational topics. Counselors and journalists offering advice customarily point the bewildered youngster to his public library. The adult who feels he might be more satisfied in another job finds his way there too.

This article, describing arrangements at Dearborn Public Library, may be helpful to those small and medium-sized libraries which are planning to set up a vocational file or who are, as we were last spring, dissatisfied with present arrangements.

Our collection of vocational materials includes books. These are designated by a "V" before the call number and are shelved on top of the file which holds the pamphlet material. Nearly all of these books have a copyright date within the last ten years. Changes in salary estimations and in the fields themselves make it necessary to keep a vocational collection, books and pamphlets, well-weeded. An exception we make to the ten-year rule of thumb is the United States Department of Commerce series on establishing and operating small businesses, which contains practical, specialized material not found elsewhere. Although these were assigned call numbers when we received them, they could as well be treated as pamphlets. Most pamphlets are considered to have served their purpose within a five-year span.

Our vocational information file contains newspaper clippings as well as pamphlets. One of the local newspapers has a regular question-and-answer feature about vocations. Articles about shortages of workers in certain fields, about vocational courses being conducted in the area, about persons who have been honored as outstanding in their professions provide file material, also.

Our vocational pamphlet file is a supplement to the general vertical file and the color green is used to set it apart. Pamphlets are kept in folders marked by a green gummed star label before the subject heading. A green star, this one penciled in, also appears before the subject heading on each item to facilitate refiling. Labels on the drawers containing the material and the one-card catalog tray containing the index to the collection are green, too.

We have found that subject headings in the form of the name of the worker rather than the field of work are more useful because this tends to be the form in which the patron asks for information and also because it provides for natural subdivisions of material. Our folders containing material on Engineering, for example, were overloaded. We still have a heading Engineer, which takes care of general material, but the card labeled Engineer in the vocational file index refers the patron to fourteen specializations in the field, from Aeronautical engineer to Petroleum engineer.

We have switched therefore from the old Science Research Associates headings (their present headings also use name of workers) to those used in Occupational Literature; an Annotated Bibliography by Gertrude Forrester, New York, Wilson, 1953. (A new edition appeared October 1958.) These headings are a useful distillation of those appearing in the U.S. Employment Service's two-volume Dictionary of Occupational Titles, which may, however, be used to supplement it. Aside from the obvious advantage of having a limited number of headings to work from, the bibliography listed under the headings serves also as an explanation of the heading, in cases in which two headings seem to be equally appropriate. Many of the cross references used in it can also be borrowed for the card catalog index to the file, an inevitable appendage unless the file is going to be severely limited in size.

We followed this procedure in changing headings:

weeded file
gave material which was retained a heading from
    Forrester and checked the heading in the book
sorted material and made new folders — pages can
    do this
made a card index

Cards were stamped Pamphlets and clippings on this subject will be found in the vocational information file, a subject heading placed above this, and any see also references below.

BUILDING A VOCATIONAL INFORMATION FILE

This card file also analyzes vocational book material, but gives only a brief description of the book since it appears also in the public catalog.

Because the subject headings, unlike those of the general information file, did not have to conform with those of the public catalog — or Forrester either, for that matter — consistency was sacrificed for practicability wherever necessary. The "official" headings <u>Manager, Retail food</u> and <u>Manager, Retail floral</u> were changed to the more direct Grocer and Florist. It should be noted, however, that nearly all of the headings in Forrester take one directly where he wants to go. He may consult material, for example, by checking <u>Sailor</u> rather than U.S. Navy what-have-you.

We retained some of the old Science Research Associate headings which had proved their usefulness, headings for material which is of general nature: <u>Job Hunting</u>; <u>Job satisfaction and success</u>; <u>Occupations, choice of</u>.

Some few headings were improvised. <u>Automobile dealer</u> was a concession to the special interest of this area. <u>Laborer</u> was added as a catch-all for miscellaneous information about skilled and unskilled jobs for which we had little material and little demand.

After we weeded our three file drawers, there was barely one drawer of pamphlet material left. Now, with new material, we have four drawers nearly full.

Most of the material was free. The government, industry, professional organizations, trade unions, colleges and universities provide gratis most of the answers that even the most foresighted and demanding patron can ask. We sent postcards with this message:

> We are building up a file, as complete as possible, of vocational material. This will be used particularly by young people who are in the process of choosing a vocation. If material is available on your profession, we would like to include it.

These cards, signed with the name and address of the library, were duplicated in quantity.

Our first group of cards went out to likely-looking

organizations listed in Encyclopedia of American Associations: A Guide to the Trade, Business, Professional, Labor, Scientific, Educational, Fraternal and Social Organizations of the United States, Detroit, Michigan, Gale Research Company, 1956. This is particularly useful for its listing of professional organizations. It was evident from our replies that ALA is not the only organization busy with recruiting.

Typically, the scientific organizations seem to be best organized in their approach to vocational material. The National Science Foundation, Washington 25, D.C., sent "Sources of Information about Scientific Careers," a mimeographed sheet which permits an easy approach to collecting information about scientific professions. "Encouraging Future Scientists: Keys to Careers," rev. ed. 1956-1957, available from the National Science Teachers' Association (1201 16th St., Washington 6, D.C.), contains a good bibliography of free and inexpensive material on science-related fields.

Most large businesses and industries in the country can be counted on for some good material about their own field, and a number have a series on vocations as a public service. Second to none is the New York Life Insurance Company whose ads "Choosing Your Occupation" have become familiar. A set of these articles, and the hard-bound Guide to Career Information: A Bibliography of Recent Occupational Literature, Harper, 1957, was sent to us in return for a post card addressed to New York Life Insurance Co., 51 Madison Avenue, New York 22.

It is impossible to list here the sources of good free material, and of course vocational interests vary with the community. I wonder if Dearborn is typical in this: it appears that the teen-age girls who are not going to become models are planning to become airplane hostesses! Incidentally, Glamour magazine's Job Department, 420 Lexington Avenue, New York 17, sent us gratis a good summary description of this field, and a lot of others too.

It is important to provide a balanced picture of a vocational field. For an objective view of many occupations get the United States Bureau of Labor Statistics' Occupational Outlook Handbook; Employment Information on Major Occupations for Use in Guidance, 1957. This is for sale by the Superintendent of Documents for $4. Commercial publishers also present an objective view of a vocation. Watch dates on these publications, however, to keep from ordering material that is already out-dated. Careers Research Monographs, for example, does not include dates on their listings, except in response to a request for it. A good source of information about such publications-for-a-price is Fifty Sources of Occupational Information, available free from the State Department of Education, Division of Vocational Education, 220 South Parsons Avenue, Columbus 15, Ohio.

To anyone building a vocational information file many helping hands reach out. It is not difficult for libraries to collect good material, and to make it available is well worthwhile, considering the importance of the decision it is helping to shape.

65. THE LIBRARIAN AND THE GUIDANCE PROGRAM

Aurelia Davis

"I don't know what I'd do without our librarian," said a high school counselor recently. "I would never get to do any professional reading if she didn't keep up with the new books and periodicals in the field and order them for our library. She sends them to me and to the other staff members upon arrival so that we may have up-to-date material. She's the best press agent the guidance program has."

Many guidance programs have had their beginnings through the efforts of some far-sighted school librarian such as the one described above. Certainly such programs could not develop and progress in a desirable way without the help of librarians who are guidance-minded, well-informed, and interested enough to be alert for opportunities to assist both staff and students. Many such opportunities are possible from day to day.

In the area of educational guidance the librarian renders a real service by having a complete file of catalogs, bulletins, pamphlets, and leaflets from colleges and trade schools. It should be possible for the student to check this material out so that he and his parents may study and discuss it together. Also clippings about schools and former students now at college should be displayed. The librarian might prepare posters or bulletin board displays showing locations or offerings of various schools and colleges. During a recent College Day program there was on a library bulletin board a pen sketch of a bewildered senior looking at a map on which were located many colleges. On the shelves below were featured such books as The College Blue Book, How to Pass College Entrance Tests, Choosing the Right College and So This Is College.

There is much that a librarian can do in providing occupational information and vocational guidance. Clippings, leaflets, booklets, and periodicals can be collected and occupational files kept up to date. Current materials should be ordered as new vocations come into being. Frequently displays on various occupations with preparation needed for each are attractively arranged in the library or on bulletin boards elsewhere. Jackets of both fictional and non-fictional literature are often used to attract attention to new books in this area.

By being observant and by working with the counselor in learning the interests and abilities of individual students, the librarian can render invaluable aid by helping students select the right books in their interest areas and on their ability levels. She can also show her personal interest in a certain student by passing on to him a clipping or leaflet about his chosen vocation.

Providing books and other materials including audio-visual aids to teachers, classes, and individual students for use in a unit study on occupations is a real service. The librarian can help prepare a traveling library that can be moved from room to room as a convenience as well as a stimulant to interest.

Librarians can serve as speakers on Career Day programs, assemblies, or class programs. These occasions afford opportunities to stimulate interest in librarianship as a career. Recently in a large Negro high school on Career Day those people interested in becoming librarians met in the library where attractive displays had been arranged depicting Negroes who had excelled in various vocations. Many of the students in the group were library assistants and members of the Library Club. The librarian was present and participated as a member of the group under the leadership of an outside speaker, a well-known librarian.

The librarian better than anyone else perhaps has the opportunity of helping students to develop good reading habits and tastes, and a wise use of leisure. This must be a cooperative undertaking on the part of the teacher, counselor, and librarian. Never has there been a time when the wise use of leisure has been so important as in these times of cheap literature, comic books, poor television and radio programs, and unwholesome activities that may help to contribute to the alarming increase in juvenile delinquency. The responsibility for stimulating interest in the reading of worthwhile literature and in other wholesome activities is therefore a very great one.

The Library Club has value both vocationally and personally. Students interested in becoming librarians belong to the club under the sponsorship of the school librarian. Also those interested in reading as a hobby or in working in the library as assistants often like to belong to this club. Sue was a painfully shy girl who found it almost impossible to overcome her self-consciousness sufficiently to make any friends at all. She became increasingly withdrawn and self-centered despite all efforts on the part of students and teachers to make her feel a part of the group. The librarian noticed that Sue came to the library at every opportunity — study periods, and before and after school. Sue showed intelligence in the choice of books and appeared to enjoy reading. Finally, the librarian asked Sue to become her assistant which she did. As this girl helped bewildered and shy boys and girls select books for reference work and leisure reading, she began to forget herself and to get interested in helping others. Before long she was an officer in the Library Club and participated in other group activities in school and out. This is only one example of how a school librarian helped a student in overcoming personality difficulties.

Ronnie was the problem boy of the freshman class. He had ability but appeared to have no interest at all. Test data, former school records, interviews with parents and teachers and even with other students revealed very little as to what his interests might be. The teachers did notice, however, that

Ronnie frequently asked for permission to go to the library. Naturally this permission was always granted as teachers are glad to have peace in the classroom. Ronnie was a problem to everyone except the librarian who found him a model person. She observed that this boy always selected books relating to animals. One day she engaged him in conversation and learned that he had gathered a wealth of information on animals, and that he was planning to become a veterinarian. When this fact was passed on to his teachers, Ronnie soon ceased to be the boy without interests and became known as an authority in his chosen field.

Librarians can assist counselors by observing students with a view toward noting personality traits such as day-dreaming, dawdling, worrying, and reading difficulties. They can help a great deal by guiding the boy or girl in selecting books and materials, either fictional or non-fictional, that will give him an insight into his problem. There is much that may be done in the realm of bibliotherapy, and it is here that librarians and counselors may be of mutual help.

In the area of group guidance the librarian becomes the counselor. She may explain to faculty, parents, or students the use of educational and occupational materials. She may discuss library work as a career. She may discuss the value of reading as a hobby. She may also review books that would be of interest to adults in an effort to understand their youth, and to young people in understanding themselves and others.

The librarian in the elementary school has perhaps an even greater responsibility in the guidance program than the high school librarian since there are fewer counselors at the elementary level and the teachers naturally look to the librarian for help. With an increased interest in identifying children with personality problems as early in their school life as possible, there has been an increase in the number of publications for both parents and teachers. The elementary school librarian is in a position to make these materials available and to help in preparing programs and literature for Parent-Teacher Study Groups. She might well be chairman of the Guidance Committee because of her contact with all age levels and all staff members. The librarian often organizes Reading Clubs both during the school term and during the vacation months. Here again one can gain an insight into the interests and abilities of individual children, knowledge which is of great value to the teacher.

The counselor and librarian in their effort to render service to all students, staff members, and parents have much in common and are interdependent. We as counselors like to feel that the librarians are our "press agents." We hope that we in turn are helpful to them.

66. COOPERATION OF COUNSELOR AND LIBRARIAN

Helen F. Faust

There are the obvious and usual ways for the librarian and the counselor to cooperate: referral by the librarian to the counselor of children who seem to need intensive, individual help, and referral by the counselor to the librarian of pupils with particular intellectual, vocational or recreational interests who need help in using books more advantageously. These opportunities we use and surely could use more frequently and with more discrimination. However, this sort of cooperation will inevitably grow out of our mutual recognition that our bond is deeper than this reciprocal use of each other's service.

The real bond between us is that we both have the opportunity to work with individuals as individuals. For that reason, I thought perhaps it might be useful to speak briefly of a few of the concepts which are fundamental to good counseling and have bearing in all relationships with young people.

These four or five concepts will not be new to you, but in both our groups they may be so obvious that their importance is lost in the pressures of our busy days.

One of the basic facts about youth, and particularly adolescents, is their tremendous potential for change. The contrast between students from the time that they are in 10A and the time that they graduate provides a vivid illustration of the enormous changes occurring in adolescence. The pudgy, smooth-faced, transparently moody little boy in 10A becomes in three years a tall, well built, poised young man. One such boy who had many, many problems in growing up and who stormed and wept his way through three years in and out of the counselor's office came in a few days before graduation and with great dignity asked the counselor — "How are things with you today, Mrs. Smith?", thus indicating a mature capacity for being concerned about others.

A firm belief in growth as a positive life force and as the biggest asset to educators is a vital one for us to have, not just as a stray physiological fact, but as a basic article of faith.

We tend to take growth for granted and consider more carefully the pattern that we, consciously or unconsciously, wish to impose. You want to make the child a good reader. I may want him to attend school more regularly or study harder, and we both struggle to compel him to accept our convictions. Right now the whole country is clamoring for the schools to make young people better scientists, better mathematicians and better behaved citizens.

There is great danger in all this clamoring demand that we may forget a second concept — namely, that the direction of this change will be determined largely by the individual's choice. We may be able to help him find a more positive direction, but we cannot make him be anything he does not choose to be. Try to make a chronic truant who hates school become a good student. We may take him into court; we may fine his parents; we may penalize him for breaking the law by committing him to a correctional institution; but he can forever resist our demands that he do well in school.

In working with youth, it is vital that our second article of faith be the recognition that the individual's goals, his direction and the amount of energy he puts into pursuing them, will ultimately depend on his own will and motivation.

Once we accept in all sincerity the validity of these two concepts: the inevitability of change, and the dominance of choice as the factor determining that change, then we necessarily become curious about what are the things which will affect his choice. Why does one boy choose to be an earnest student and another of equal ability to be a playboy? To generalize very simply, each chooses in order to meet his own pattern of

needs — physical, intellectual and emotional. This leaves us
with the complex task of trying to understand the pattern, which
is a varying one. For example, while the baby's needs are to
be cared for, to be loved, fed and made comfortable, probably
the most important one for an adolescent is his need to discover
his own identity as a person. "Who am I?" "What am I?" "What
will I be?" are the most pressing questions for the adolescent
who is deeply troubled because he actually has so many important choices to make.

A few years ago, a group of very superior students in one
of our senior high schools were asked to submit anonymously
any problems about which they were so deeply concerned that
they would welcome discussion of them by a psychiatrist. I have
a copy of the list of questions — which are sometimes humorous
and sometimes poignant, but always searching. Let me quote
a few which illustrate this third point I wish to make — that adolescents are searching to understand themselves and to find the
pattern of their maturity.

"At times I act stupid in front of my parents and relatives.
However, when I am out with friends I act older and more serious. Is this normal?

"What makes some boys and girls shyer than others, and
how can this be prevented?

"I have no special goal in life. Just take things as they
come."

"How can I get out of the shadow of more intelligent relatives?"

"Why is it that when I work in my father's store the customers always ask for other salesmen?"

The questions of these boys were predominantly questions
of this sort, revealing their concern about themselves and their
desire for inner security.

Moreover, their search is not simply an intellectual process. Emotional reactions, conscious and subconscious, are undoubtedly the more powerful factors. Adolescence is a highly
charged emotional period. Whether he appears inarticulate,
or brash and noisy, there is in the adolescent a kind of quiver-
ing sensitivity in his responses to life. If we wish to be helpful
in his development and education, we cannot ignore the fact that
feelings vitally affect the child's functioning. Help offered in

counseling and in all direct relationships with youth must take into account the quality of those feelings.

Let me illustrate this concept by quoting from a boy's high school composition which explains his choosing to be in a gang. First, he tells about his loneliness in living with a grandmother who worked, drank and ignored him.

"This made me feel as if I wasn't wanted, and it also gave me a feeling of insecurity. Every human being, no matter how good or bad he or she may be, has a desire to love and be loved. I was no different from anyone else in the world.

"When I was younger I used to sit and daydream about those lucky individuals who had a mother and father. Sometimes I would put myself in their places. These thoughts filled my soul with rapture.

"Some of the boys in the neighborhood started a gang. I was asked to join, and this I did. In this gang I found the love and security for which I looked for so long."

This excerpt states dramatically in a few sentences all that I have been trying to say: the boy's awareness of his own change and development, his search for status and security — a place in the sun, his awareness that he himself chose the gang, and his recognition that emotional factors were largely responsible for his choice.

Our adolescent pupils, changing, groping, uncertain of themselves and highly emotional, invite strong reactions from busy adults. We are apt to shift between downright antipathy when their behavior annoys us to a sentimental sympathy in our more nostalgic moments. These young people need adults, and they need us to hold firmly to a midpoint that is neither unfriendly nor sentimental. A group of high school teachers were talking with our psychiatrist about how to establish a favorable emotional climate in the classroom. He proposed a formula which he called the 3 F's — friendliness, fairness and firmness. Friendliness and fairness are natural outgrowths of understanding, but these are not enough without the third ingredient.

A fifth concept which is useful both to librarians and counselors is that of the importance of clear-cut limits maintained by understanding adults. These limits — rules, authority, discipline or simply adult strength — are effective controls on all this emotional power of the searching youth. A library has to have rules, so does a counseling office, so does the total school. These rules we normally think of as being useful to keep order or to be sure that the books are used to the best advantage, but there is another even more important point to rules. We want youth to develop under controls; but to help them learn how to do this, we need to define rules clearly and then hold to them firmly. Without this firmness, understanding is apt to be a flimsy thing. There was a family once who knew all about the importance of healthy emotional development and about the mysteries of psychological phenomena. These parents became very unhappy because their children developed a habit of throwing their toys out of the second-floor window. So perturbed were they, that they went to a psychiatrist for help with this problem. After listening to their sad tale, he looked at the parents sternly and asked, "Did you ever tell them to stop it?"

These are not new concepts to any of you, but what do we librarians and counselors do with them? First of all, knowing them with our heads is not enough. Conviction about their validity needs to permeate our thoughts and feelings to such a degree that our relationships with young people are intuitively sound whether they develop in a series of interviews about complicated personal problems or whether they are limited to brief interviews about very concrete situations.

There is considerable evidence that school problems are basically personality problems. If this is so, it becomes imperative to introduce a mental hygiene approach into the school. Such an approach has been resisted because to many it connotes a lowering of standards which school personnel rightly defend. Handling a pupil with knowledge and consideration of his feelings has been confused with coddling him. Many of you handle the pupils who come to you with generous portions of warmth and intuitive understanding without sacrificing standards. Miracles are accomplished, but they are not enough. In order to help pupils overcome personality difficulties and learn more readily, school personnel must be equipped with current knowledge relating to the growth of the healthy personality.

In the beginning I said that a good relationship between the counselor and the librarian is a logical one because we both work with individuals. I have tried to suggest a few concepts we both use in helping pupils. These concepts are implicit in

287

the mental hygiene approach. One thing more we share is the opportunity to demonstrate the strategic role of school personnel in helping with personality problems. We have the responsibility of more intensive work, while you have a natural role with great numbers of students and the very important function of making available the excellent published material in this field.

67. GUIDANCE THROUGH BOOKS

Virgil M. Howes

Books are effective tools for guidance when utilized to help youth face and solve the varied problems of growing-up. Although they do not necessarily alter or improve behavior and attitudes, they do provide teachers and librarians with valuable resources for developing youths' insights and understandings of personal situations.

All children, as they grow and develop, meet a continuous series of adjustment problems. Some are related to physical and mental growth, others arise as youth make attempts to cope with the environment, to meet societal expectations, and to develop and use their talents and capabilities wisely. Reading experiences focused on these needs are a valuable part of a teacher's guidance program.

Role of the Librarian

Librarians assist teachers to provide guidance of this kind in various ways. With their special skills and knowledge of children's books, they can help select materials appropriate for reading level, interest level, and content. They can prepare guides which classify books into general problems categories and which annotate specific values, relationships, and childhood problems portrayed. For example, materials might be roughly grouped into four categories:

Books about learning to live in the family (brother
and sister relationships, parent-child relationships,
family responsibilities, the only child, etc.)

Books about learning to live at school (getting along
with others in work and play, adjusting to school
rules, using time wisely, etc.)

Books about learning to live in the neighborhood and
the community.

Books about learning to live with one's self (fears,
physical handicaps and attributes, using one's abilities, etc.)

Annotations of books provide teachers with still further
clues. Comments may indicate book content, such as: illus-
trates problem children face in moving to a new school or community; shows how pupils make a new class member feel welcome; discusses brother and sister relationships; points up the
importance of rules for group living and working. Other notes
can suggest specific uses. For example, materials which may
help: children who are continually quarreling; an early maturer
having difficulties accepting rapid physical growth and body
changes; a child who resents both size and appearance; students
having difficulty with social adjustments; and, smaller boys
who find competition with larger boys difficult.

Such specific values of books are numerous. Sometimes
books help by illustrating different solutions to a problem, by
showing that the problem is common to others, or by presenting needed information and knowledge. At other times books
help children verbalize pent-up feelings, discuss problems
more freely, understand their own personal capabilities better,
appreciate efforts of others, enlarge fields of interest, or understand and accept attitudes and expectancies of the cultural
group. Through books, the reader may be guided toward a constructive course of action and begin to develop deeper insights
into behavior motivations of himself and others.

Developing Plans

Using books to help students solve developmental problems is sometimes called bibliotherapy. As Russell and Shrodes define it, bibliotherapy is:

> a process of dynamic interaction between the personality of the reader and literature — interaction which may be utilized for personality assessment, adjustment, and growth. This definition suggests that bibliotherapy is not a strange, esoteric activity but one that lies within the province of every teacher . . . . It does not assume that the teacher must be a skilled therapist, nor the child a seriously maladjusted individual needing clinical treatment. Rather, it conveys the idea that all teachers must be aware of the effects of reading upon children and must realize that, through literature, most children can be helped to solve the developmental problems of adjustment which they face."[1]

Successful attempts to guide children's reading depends a great deal on knowledge of the pupil's personal problems. Interest inventories, anecdotal records, autobiographies, creative writing, home visits, talks with teachers and librarians, and parent conferences are all techniques useful for obtaining needed data. Such information helps the librarian and teacher select appropriate materials and plan for their maximum use.

Bibliotherapy can be a part of the regular school program — during language-arts, social studies, or even physical education periods since many of youths' problems center around personal appearance and dramatic body changes. Selections directed toward students' personal needs provide a setting for further activities — group discussions, role playing, writing, art, debating, and panel or symposium presentations. Through these extended activities, youths are helped to relate and apply acquired principles to their own problems or situations.

Procedures and steps for developing guidance experiences through books are frequently clarified through written plans. Some teachers use a plan sheet similar to the following example.

GUIDANCE THROUGH BOOKS

Plan Sheet for Bibliotherapy

Grade:_____ Number in Class:_____

1. Description of class or individual problems:
2. Statement of objectives or purposes:
3. Story title: (Note: The librarian may suggest possibilities, especially if the completed plan sheet is shared.)
4. What parts or situations of the story are particularly appropriate?
5. Will you use the complete story or only parts?
6. Class period where you will use the story: language-arts _____, social studies_____, reading_____, literature_____, other_____
7. Use of story planned for: total group_____, specific individual_____, small group_____, total group but for an individual _____, other_____
8. Plans for presenting the story: read aloud_____, have student(s) read silently_____, tell it_____, other_____
9. Related activities planned: class discussion_____, role playing_____, art_____, writing experiences_____, panel discussion_____, other_____
10. Specific questions you might use to help students relate reading to personal situation: (Examples — in what ways did feelings make a difference? What would you have done? How would you feel? What other things might he have done? Have you been in such situations?_____)

Evaluation

11. Questions, comments, or reactions made by the group or individuals regarding this story. (Note especially how children reconstruct the story.)
12. Suggestions for changes in planning or approach for further use of this book.

Written plans provide an excellent record of activities and outcomes. One teacher looking over the work of the preceding month noted an increase in the amount of discussion on questions raised as the program progressed. Students seemed eager to write down their thoughts, to share opinions with others, and to talk about some of the problems they faced. Such reviews will help teachers and librarians to improve their skills and to make their program of bibliotherapy more effective.

Opportunities to use books as guidance tools are almost unlimited. Librarians with their knowledge of children's books, their understandings of youths' developmental problems, and their appreciation of the values books have for children can stimulate and encourage such programs and provide valuable services to teachers and youth.

68. MENTAL HYGIENE AND BOOKS: BIBLIOTHERAPY AS USED WITH CHILDREN AND ADOLESCENTS

Richard L. Darling

A survey of the literature dealing with bibliotherapy soon reveals that two different techniques are referred to with the one term. Indeed, one could point out more than two techniques to which the term bibliotherapy is applied but the bibliotherapy which consists of giving physically ill patients books to take their minds off their ills is not of direct concern to us here. Rather we are concerned with bibliotherapy insofar as it involves the use of books to help solve emotional problems of the emotionally disturbed. In this area fall the two kinds of bibliotherapy with which this paper is concerned.

The first technique is that in which a psychiatrist or some other person attempts to solve a child's or adolescent's emotional problems by bringing him a similar experience vicariously through books. Through recognition of the problem and its solution in literature the individual gains new insight into his own problem and presumably is then able to take a step toward solving it.

The second technique is often called preventive bibliotherapy, though this would seem to be somewhat of a misnomer.

The theory involved here is that all children and adolescents are apt to face certain types of problems. By developing a sane set of attitudes through literature the youngster is prepared to make a satisfactory adjustment when a similar problem actually arises in his own life. The obvious analogy here is with the inoculation to prevent the contagious disease. A little vicarious injection of experience with a problem in a book is to prevent a hard case of this same kind of experience in the young reader's development.

In September and October 1950 David H. Russell and Caroline Shrodes made an exhaustive survey of the contributions of bibliotherapy to the language arts program. I have used their findings as a starting point. Though their analysis is particularly concerned with implications for language arts teaching, it is general in its coverage. They say:

> Bibliotherapy may be defined as a process of dynamic interaction between the personality of the reader and literature — interaction which may be utilized for personality assessment, adjustment, and growth.[14]

The first half of their definition is, to some extent, a definition of the act of reading literature in any situation, not merely a bibliotherapeutic one. It is in the second half of the definition that the implications for bibliotherapy lie, for it is actually in an adjustment of personality that any therapeutic effect must lie.

The therapeutic effect itself, they find, is usually explained in terms of identification, catharsis, and insight. Identification is fairly easily explained since this is an almost universal experience of readers, especially of young readers. Surely everyone has at one time or another identified himself with some real or fictional character in literature, or has recognized the traits of a parent or friend in a character he has read. It is through this affiliation with a character or with a group that therapy can have its beginning. Once identification has taken place it is possible for the second elementary in the process to come into action.

When the reader has identified himself with a character in

a book, he is then prepared to gain a cathartic effect from reading about a situation that parallels his own. As the character with whom he has achieved identification works through his problem and releases his emotional tension the reader is able to relieve his tensions also. Like a cathartic, the book's solving of the emotional situation provides a purge for the emotions of the reader. This certainly is an ancient and respectable theory for it is the basis of Aristotle's explanation of the effect of tragedy on its audience. Unfortunately there is very little concrete evidence to back it up, though the individual testimony is formidable. Aristotle's explanation, and the explanation of the contemporary writers on bibliotherapy, is that the release of tension comes about "through symbolic gratification of socially unacceptable urges."[14]

Insight, the third component of the process, is dependent upon the first two. When the reader realizes his identification with the book character he is able to see the motivation of his own behavior more clearly. Purged of some of his own emotional tension the way is cleared to make a more intellectual approach to his problem. The result is that "some sort of integration of intellectual perception and emotional drive takes place."[14]

Russell and Schrodes report that the majority of the writers surveyed take a similar approach to bibliotherapy though some give a more detailed explanation. Appell for example lists six ways in which bibliotherapy can help the individual:

(1) to acquire information and knowledge about the psychology and physiology of human behavior, (2) to live up to the injunction "know thyself," (3) to be ome extraverted and find interest in something outside himself, (4) to effect a controlled relief of unconscious difficulties, (5) to use the opportunity for identification and compensation; and, (6) to clarify difficulties and to acquire insight into his own behavior.[14]

Basically they boil down to the three elements: identification, catharsis, and insight.

Though much of the writing was enthusiastic, Russell and Shrodes found a number of writers were cautious about the claims they made for bibliotherapy. In fact, Russell says,

"evidence of the positive effects of reading is largely lacking."[14]
In addition there are certain other recognizable drawbacks. To
begin with, the person who is to be helped by bibliotherapy must
be a reader, and a good reader, for only when a wide variety of
suitable material can be used will there be much hope for helpful results. The poor reader, who must struggle with the simple process of reading, will be ill equipped for the necessary
processes of identification, catharsis, and insight, since he
must devote all his energies to mastering the words and sentences and will have little energy remaining for a deeper understanding of the situation.

In addition each reader brings to the situation his own complex of prejudices and needs and may completely misinterpret
a given situation to bolster his own shaky ego. One writer suggests that an adolescent's individual attitudes may completely
prevent the enactment of the response desired and may instead
provide a response that will have an effect the opposite of therapeutic. This raises the question of what kind of book ought to
be provided for what kind of difficulty. Is the best kind of approach a direct one or an indirect one? There seems to be no
unanimity in the answers, although there have been attempts
to compile booklists based on the assumption that certain kinds
of books containing certain kinds of ideas will be effective in
solving certain kinds of problems.

Dr. T. V. Moore of the Catholic University of America has
written a great deal about bibliotherapy with children and young
people. Indeed Catholic library and school periodicals show an
unusually high proportion of interest in bibliotherapy. Most of
this writing shows a characteristically Catholic point of view.
Dr. Moore believes that psychiatry and psychology have put too
great an emphasis on the emotional elements in the human psy-
che and too little emphasis on the importance of intellectual
ideals in determining human conduct. The intellect, he feels,
has a great deal to do with determining conduct. If we can give
children and young people proper principles of conduct, we can
alter their behavior and make it more desirable. One of the
best ways of altering their conduct is by implanting desirable
ideas gained from books. He reports a boy whose deep jealousy
of a sibling has been modified by ideas gained from reading
Skidmore's Hill Doctor, in which the boy recognizes as admirable

doing things for others. A girl in her early teens was helped to a satisfactory adjustment concerning the problems of dating and parental attitudes toward dating by reading Maureen Daly's Seventeenth Summer. A necessary part of the process of gaining help from these books was the discussion of them with Dr. Moore in which he helped the youngsters to see the application of the situations in these books to their own problems.

With this emphasis on the intellectual element in bibliotherapy it is easy to justify a kind of preventive bibliotherapy which might well be practiced by teachers, librarians, or guidance officers. In fact Dr. Moore says:

> Bibliotherapy is a kind of therapy that can be practised by anyone with common sense and the warm personal interests in the welfare of children.

If a school cannot afford, as most of them cannot, a psychologist or psychiatrist on the school staff, then the librarian, Dr. Moore feels, is a logical person to undertake bibliotherapy, provided he can find fifteen or twenty minutes a week for a quiet talk with the youngster. The librarian must know a good deal about the child's problem, of course, but this can be gained from talking to the child, to other teachers, and to parents.[12]

Dr. Moore considers bibliotherapy chiefly as a way of getting to the problem child, and in his introduction to Kircher's Character Formation Through Books he describes two ways in which books may aid in treating the problem child. The child:

> Obtains psychological relief by giving vent to pent up emotions by identification with characters suffering trials like his own.
> Gains principles for governing his conduct.

These two, he says, are frequently mixed and may proceed simultaneously even though the child may not immediately apply the principles he gains. He describes four steps in the therapeutic process:

> Principle is perceived and admired.
> It remains dormant in the mind for an indefinite

period and has apparently nothing to do with conduct.

An occasion arises in which the student sees a relation between the occasion and the principle and with more or less effort on his part the principle determines conduct.

A period of development in which the principle more and more consistently determines conduct until the correct response to the situation follows as if by reflex action.

Bibliotherapy should only be begun, however, after a good rapport has been established between the child and the therapist. Above all, the therapist must know the library with which he works. The work he describes seems to have been with children who were not seriously maladjusted and does seem to have been effective. There is no possibility, however, of determining whether the book or the psychiatrist was more effective in solving the youngsters' problems.

Kircher praises the work done and reported by Cole as positive evidence of the value of bibliotherapy, but when I followed up her citation I could find little in Cole's report to justify her enthusiasm. The report deals chiefly with the results obtained from the Washburne Social Adjustment Inventory.[3] Insofar as it deals with bibliotherapy it states what they hoped to do rather than what they accomplished. Cole outlines the case histories of several boys but ends at the point at which bibliotherapy is about to begin. I have not been able to discover any report of the actual results of his work.

Hartley[7] recognizes the lack of established evidence from research and experiment but maintains her faith in bibliotherapy nevertheless. She acknowledges that most of the evidence is testimonial and admits that there are drawbacks to testimonial evidence, particularly that most testimonial evidence is based on hindsight rather than an awareness at the time that a book was providing a therapeutic effect. Many people read

. . . not to explore and examine with open mind and honest experience but rather to select and reinforce their own traits, aversions, unrealities, and so to perpetuate their immaturities, or lacking concern

with the issues encountered they remain immune to
any potential influence from what they read.

The one experimental project which she reports, a project in
which Hartshorn-May honesty tests were given to a control
group and to an experimental group before and after reading
stories concerned with honesty, appears on the surface to be
damaging to the theory of bibliotherapy. However, it must be
recognized that the numbers involved were too small to give
much weight to the experiment and other factors, such as the
pressure for higher grades as the semester drew to a close,
were obviously involved.
She feels that literature can help a student achieve a "mature personality," which she defines as a personality that has
outside interests, an objective view of itself, and a unifying
philosophy of life. Her description of the way in which literature helps to create a mature personality parallels the way in
which bibliotherapy is reported to operate. Literature does its
part, she says, by:

> Awakening perceptions, heightening sensitivities,
> awareness of values, a setting of goals and a definition
> of purposes, and a widened range of understandings.
> Relieving emotional tension by universalizing ex-
> perience.
> Giving an undistorted view of reality.

Though her emphasis is a little different and her explanation
of the cathartic process as the result of "universalizing experience" introduces a new element, yet basically it does not differ
from the explanation in Russell and Shrodes.
Lindahl and Koch[11] report on their work in the middle elementary grades. Again they have more hope than proof that they
are achieving the desired results. They include a short annotated bibliography of the books they are using which provides
some insight into their methods. Other lists that have been prepared for bibliotherapy are those by Alice Brooks,[1] by Kircher,[10]
and by Heaton and Lewis.[9]
Heaton and Lewis provide a lengthy introduction in which
they set forth steps in class discussion of reading in order to

alter attitudes and behavior. The steps should include:

> A retelling of what occurred in the story itself.
>
> A probing into what happened in feeling, in shift of relationship and change of behavior.
>
> A stimulation to identify similar incidents drawn from the experience of the students or from other stories.
>
> An opportunity to explore the consequences of certain behaviors or feelings.
>
> A chance to come to a conclusion or generalization about the consequences of certain behaviors or feelings.

In many ways this is probably the most effective setting forth of a method of using books for preventive bibliotherapy with groups, though it should be pointed out that this bibliography is more concerned with social attitudes in modern society than with emotional problems, though these are included in such areas as family life, adjustment to new places and situations, differences between generations, and how it feels to grow up.

It is difficult to draw any sound conclusions about bibliotherapy. Faith in it as a means of solving certain emotional problems is great, yet the concrete evidence for its effectiveness is small. Dr. Moore and other Catholic writers, as well as many non-Catholics, have presented bibliotherapy as an excellent tool for dealing with problem children, yet much appears to depend on the skill of the therapist, so that it is difficult to gauge the extent of the book's influence, though unquestionably the book is an essential part of this technique. There seems to have been little attempt to use bibliotherapy with the deeply disturbed so that we are not in a position to judge how far bibliotherapy may extend.

The most promising bibliotherapy seems to be the preventive variety since this can be used with groups. Calling it bibliotherapy does seem to be a misnomer, however, since there is little difference between bibliotherapy as we have described it in this sense and teaching in the classroom and reader guidance in the library. Certainly it is mental hygiene but it lacks the basic requirement of therapy which seems to require that an illness be present to treat. It seems unlikely that anyone would actually want to describe growing up, even with all its problems, as an illness that requires treatment. No one would deny that children and adolescents should be provided with standards of behavior and with attitudes which will help them to adjust to whatever problems they meet. This seems to be what "preventive bibliotherapy" provides.

69. SMALL FRY NEED GOOD BOOKS

M. Elizabeth Leonard

The venture into the field of children's books today is bound to be a thrilling one either for the child or for the grown-up interested in the child's reading. Most who have attempted to fashion that world have bent their efforts towards making it instructive and inspiring. Authors, illustrators, and publishers contrived to add to it further interest and beauty and succeeded beyond all hopes in the task. Parents and teachers are delighted in it, and the children are happy in their inheritance. It has become such a crowded world, however, that guidance is needed for the best selections to enrich a child's world, as far as reading is concerned.

Skill and taste in the selection of literature for primary grade children depend upon sympathetic understanding of children and their interests and activities, as well as familiarity with the literature that has genuine appeal for them. It is vital to provide the book that will be read, for the older practice of presenting the books that ought to be read too often deprived children of finding any natural companionship with books, of feeling that books are their very best friends.

Books for the youngest children must, of course, be picture books. There are today several children's illustrators, men and women of considerable artistic talent, who are publishing charming picture books of distinct educational value. Most of these books have a few printed words near each picture and children often learn to read from spelling out these words.

Picture books should be true to life in color and form, and should be drawn in broad outline with not too much detail. Pictures of airships, animals, automobiles, houses, and other children fascinate little tots.

The shape of the picture and the arrangement of the picture with respect to printed words are also important. For example the great popularity of the "Peter Rabbit" series among the very young children is due as much to the way it is printed as to its content. The pictures tell the stories, and the stories explain the pictures so well that the effect upon the child is greatly enhanced.

It is not necessary to give the child a great number of picture books. A few will keep him happy for he is, after all, very little and dependent upon them for his "reading." There is generally someone in the family who will read to him.

Mother Goose is the starting point from which mankind begins its knowledge of books. The novelist, whose name is in the mouths of the multitude, probably gained his first notion of fiction on his mother's knee from the somewhat highly colored story of the old woman who swept the cobwebs out of the sky; the poet's first pastoral was "Little Bo-Peep," his first tragedy, "Ding, Dong, Bell." These nursery rhymes have trained the ear and stirred the imagination of generations of children and are worthy of adult consideration not only because of their venerable antiquity, but also because of their peculiar fascination for the child mind.

As we look over the history of these old rhymes we are filled with wonder at their vitality. Century after century has passed over them, and they still find a place in every nursery, a corner in the heart of every child. Mother Goose rhymes are a little child's introduction to poetry. To learn to listen to the music of great verse is the beginning of a love of poetry. Many verses for children have been written in modern times which to the adult mind seem more melodious and attractive, but the child looks upon them with more or less coldness. They may amuse them for a time; but, after all, it is his Mother Goose that he takes to bed with him. He does not know why he likes it; he simply likes it.

LEONARD

The child takes little thought as to what any of these verses mean. There are perhaps four elements in them that appeal to him: first, the jingle, and with it that peculiar cadence which modern writers of children's poetry strive in vain to imitate; secondly, the nonsense, with just enough of sense in it to connect the nonsense with the child's thinkable world; thirdly, the actions, for the stories are quite dramatic in their way; fourthly, the quaintness. Many of the objects which are referred to are entirely strange and beyond his horizon, and perhaps this quality of mystery also adds to them a certain charm. No child knows exactly what it was that Little Miss Muffet sat on, and it is an interesting experiment to get from a dozen average children their ideas on this subject. The conceptions range all the way from a rocking chair to a mushroom, and I have observed that the artists who illustrate Mother Goose are as far apart in their views as the children.

Consideration of children's reading preferences show that young readers are notoriously conservative in their demand for simplicity in stories. The little child lives in the immediate present. His everyday world is a place of such marvels and mystery to him that living for him is exploration of the actual. It follows quite naturally that he prefers to hear about the things that belong to his environment, that have to do with whatever he sees or hears or handles. What he likes best is to hear his own experiences reproduced exactly as they have happened to him. Stories based upon such experiences and containing the expressions used by children meet with enthusiastic response. Stories of cats, dogs, rabbits, and in a lesser degree, farm animals now hold tremendous interest for the child. We should not forget the peculiar interests of our metropolitan child who is charmed with the stories whose patterns embody city sights and sounds and the magic of modern machinery.

During the child's first two years at school we can help him best to an appreciation of the imaginative by keeping close to what is actual to him. Doing this we shall avoid the blunder of bringing the fairy tales too early into the child's experiences for his fullest enjoyment. The marvels of the fairy world are appreciated with greater zest by the children whose sense of objective reality is strong enough to help them to realize that there is a fairy world. They enter it freely and joyously and

302

SMALL FRY NEED GOOD BOOKS

without the bewilderment that often makes it remote or fearful
to children whose experiences with the actual have been few or
unsatisfying. It is every child's right to enter the magic land
of elves and pixies, enchanted princes and princesses, giants
and dragons, and flying carpets.

Development of a love of reading is dependent, to a great
extent, on exposure to books in early childhood. If the child
finds himself in an environment of books and, moreover, is
encouraged by an interested person to read books, he will come
to realize what wonderful companions books can be to him.

70. JUNIOR HIGH SCHOOL LIBRARIES MUST BE DIFFERENT

John A. Ratliff

Junior high-school libraries must be different if they are
to serve the needs of junior high schools because junior high-
school pupils are different. They are different from the children they just were because they are putting behind them childish things and ways. They are different from the adults they
will become because the pattern of their adulthood has not yet
taken form. Their horizons are extending amazingly fast and
far, and their vision is not yet limited by reality. Their courage
is so high that they dare dream and even plan deeds of wonder,
grandeur, and service. Their curiosity makes them thirsty for
knowledge and hungry to know the reasons why. The tenuous
nature of the early adolescents' world and their sensitivity
create an urgent need for a dependable, friendly, and confiden-
tial place where they may find answers to their thousands of
questions about themselves and other people. Their quest for
a pattern of living requires the safety of vicariously experiencing many ways of life and being many kinds of people. They
need to think the great thoughts of great people, to feel the en-
nobling emotions of loyalty, devotion, humility, and pride that
are found in great literature. They need to face the situations

that require courage and sacrifice, to feel the lift of beauty in
words and pictures that are all contained in books.

Junior high-school pupils are interested in everything.
Their range of interests can be nurtured only by a library of
broad dimensions and extensive depths. One area of increasing
interest is vocational. In junior high school, the pupil first
begins to think seriously about what he will do to make a living.
Many studies indicate that this is one of the chief concerns of
adolescents. Changes in economic organization, increased
specialization, and bigness in business have increased the ser-
iousness and the complexity of choosing a vocation. Household
technology, increase in divorces, cost of living, and other
factors have made it essential that girls give serious thought
to the possibility of a vocational future. The future subject
choices and the degree of excellence of performance in school
will be influenced by the wisdom with which pupils think of their
vocational futures. A feeling of progress and satisfaction will
accompany the growth toward vocational astuteness. A good
junior high school will have an abundance of current and reliable
vocational materials.

Junior high-school pupils seem possessed of boundless
vitality, and they respond best in a place that is vital with life.
For these pupils a library should not be just a book repository
or a place where things are kept. It should practically jump
with life, and a pupil should feel better just for having been in
such a library. Healthy growing plants should be in evidence;
the common varieties will help, but the more bizarre plants
have a special value. Charts and maps should be openly displayed to take the pupil's mind places, help him identify and
find places, or give more reality to the stories he reads. There
should be beauty in art and art objects to uplift his spirit, and
collections to challenge his imagination. Special arrangements
of timely materials will stimulate his inquiry and give him help
in maintaining status. Tropical fish, models of rockets, cos-
tume dolls, shells, butterflies, things from foreign countries,
and all sorts of clutter should be skillfully made a part of a
junior high-school library.

From long practice, a system has evolved that makes better and more efficient use of all the resources in a library. At
the beginning of a pupil's junior high-school career, he should

be taught about the system, and how all the materials in the library and other libraries are organized. The use of the devices and materials the library has as tool materials should be a planned part of his library experience. The process of running down a problem or project should be cooperatively planned by his subject teacher and the librarian. Training in library usage is a definite part of the junior high-school library program.

Many of the differences in the needs of junior high-school pupils are differences in degree only. These are the differences that are the most apparent and are thus likely to be looked upon at this stage of growth and maturity as an interval in a continuum. It is this, and because it is a particular interval in the developmental processes, the needs and interest are different. However, early adolescence is more than a place in a growth continuum. There are important, complex and potent changes occurring in pupils from twelve to fourteen. Orientation and re-orientation to many things are necessary. At this stage, pupils are particularly sensitive to their environment and, because of their quest for self-hood, they are in a state of readiness and vulnerability which will not prevail again. One might think that Brutus had these pupils in mind when he said:

> There is a tide in the affairs of men,
> Which, taken at the flood, leads on to fortune;
> Omitted, all the voyage of their life
> Is bound in shallows and in miseries.

The tide is surely at the flood in junior high-school years — the pupil is at his most receptive and impressionable age. This and the succeeding generations of pupils must be educated as no other pupils before them. The times into which we are inducting them cannot afford the luxury of misfits, too narrow specialization, or the neglect of special talents. If in each pupil there is a seed of greatness, who can say at this age in what direction that seed may grow. A library rich in resources, stimulating in atmosphere, and challenging to be in is needed to produce vigorous, balanced growth. These pupils will grow up as all youth have, but they are so important that how they grow up is important. The nurturing media must be rich in all the elements needed for full and proper maturing.

The unique quality of a junior library depends upon specific things. The lingering childhood and approaching adulthood require books suitable for each and capable of helping to ease the transition from one to the other. The rapidly expanding horizon means books of great diversity and dimensions. There are more dimensions in a good junior high-school library than in any other. The junior high-school pupils' fancies may carry them far, but their need for proving themselves in actual try-out manipulations means that books of the how-to-do-it type should be available in almost every field. All the things in nature suddenly need exploring and classifying. From atoms to the universe, from birds to rocks, from fish to stars, from antiquity to infinity — all these and many more topics will be subject to search by junior high-school pupils.

Yesterday is history, and tomorrow never comes to junior high-school boys and girls, so there must be an abundance of current materials, and the best current materials are in magazines and pamphlets. The arrogant inquisitiveness of these pupils will cause them to open any door. The library must furnish many doors.

Because of their in-betweenness, the junior high-school pupils need to learn more about themselves and more about themselves in relation to other people. This area of their curiosity is so fraught with emotion and so powerful in its compulsiveness that the answers are sought shyly and often secretly but persistently. The junior high-school library should have available materials which are easily accessible and even expendable. Pupils need to know about their changing bodies and the accompanying changes in their responsibilities. They need to know that they are normal people and that their differences are alike in that they all have them. It gives pupils confidence in their library to find that it helps them in such personal and important problems.

Each junior high-school pupil must shape his own pattern and make his own set of values compatible with those of his culture. To do this, he will need, in manageable form, the patterns of many admirable lives. He will need, from frequent reminders and from a variety of approaches, to become familiar with the values society holds dear and which have long endured. Many books of good, courageous, and valuable lives should be where they can readily be found and on levels of difficulty so they can be used by all pupils. Tales that are inspiring, thought provoking, and enticing enough to evoke empathetic responses in right and good ways will be a part of a good junior high-school library.

No one learns just by reading. The more one is involved, the more one grows in reading strength; so a good library will use all the audio-visual devices it can obtain to help enrich and intensify the experiences obtained in the more conventional ways. It is more than a repository for records, tapes, filmstrips, films, pictures, scale models, and other such materials. It instructs in and motivates their use.

A junior high-school library may be organized and equipped bountifully on a basis of the unique characteristics and needs of the pupils it serves and still not be functional. It requires a junior high-school librarian to make it work. Since the function and organization of the library are unique because the pupils it serves are unique, a special kind of person is needed. He should have all the technical skill, endurance, and good housekeeping abilities of any other school librarian, but, because he is a junior high-school librarian, he will need more than these.

One of the important qualities of a junior high-school librarian is that he be interested in what he can bring to the pupils of junior high-school age through his management and coordination of the library and the people who need to use it. He must care for the materials, but not save them. He will be expensive, because materials will be used up. He will have to be robust because he will have few opportunities to sit at a desk. He will need to be aggressive to the extent that teachers who never had a chance to get the concept and spirit of a junior high-school library will need to be interested, taught, and helped by experience in good library teaching. He will need to know not only what to do with library materials but also what the contents are.

A good junior high-school librarian will have a real human and professional interest in the pupils. Their fads, their crushes, their interests, their feelings, and their problems will all have implications for work. He must be shock proof and noncommittal at times and enthusiastic and curious at others. He must be sympathetic and patient at times, but firm and demanding at other times. The confusion, enthusiasm, optimism, pessimism, boldness, shyness, handicaps, talents, and all the other inconsistencies of junior high-school pupils must be handled expertly, tactfully, and productively.

A good junior high-school librarian should be curious and enthusiastic about the many special interests and projects of his pupils. He will know about hobbies, and about the more common ones. He will very likely have collecting and doing hobbies of his own and will certainly encourage, by display and materials, the hobbies with educational implications.

A good junior high-school librarian makes wise use of the pupils who are available to help in the library. He instructs them in the library skills necessary to help them extend the usefulness of the library. He uses them as resources to keep up with what is going on in the junior high-school world. He uses them to help get the word out about what is new and what is going on in the library.

The good junior high-school librarian is a good teacher. He knows the courses of study. He knows how the best kind of teaching is organized. He teaches pupils and teachers how to use all the resources available to find the best possible answers. He has the teaching concept of evaluation so that he is able to measure his effectiveness. Anything taught can be taught better if the resources of the library are made a part of the learning experience.

Time is of little importance to the good junior high-school librarian. He will come early and stay late. He will often use his weekends to develop his work. On vacations, on shopping trips, and even while thumbing through magazines, he will be looking for ways and materials to make his library a more attractive, stimulating, and interesting place.

If the junior high-school library and librarian are the kind needed for the unique purposes and possibilities of the junior high school, they will make a very important contribution to the school. The whole school will have a different spirit, and learning will become an enthusiastic experience on a level of research and scholarship that we can only imagine. If this kind of library is not in existence and if the librarian does not have this concept of his place and the place of the library, the pupils are not likely to reach the level of attainment of which they are capable or will society realize the values they have to give.

APPENDIX

APPENDIX

Because intelligent selection of books is the cornerstone of successful library service, each school librarian should be willing to choose materials in an orderly and unprejudiced fashion. The two schedules reprinted here may help him to do so. The first presents standards for making a book selection policy; the second is a thoughtful implementation of the standards. Both schedules are reprinted, with permission, from a statement published by the American Association of School Librarians in 1961 (JN 24663). This and other materials, including the authoritative Standards for School Library Programs (American Library Association, 1960), are available from the American Library Association, 50 East Huron Street, Chicago 11, Illinois, and taken together provide a guide to the building of better libraries.

POLICIES AND PROCEDURES FOR SELECTION
OF SCHOOL LIBRARY MATERIALS*

The following statement of policy-making with regard to materials selection for school libraries is offered as a guide to those wishing to formulate a policy. It is believed that such a policy should be formally adopted by each school district as a basis for consistent excellence in choice of materials and as a document that can be presented to parents and other citizens for their further understanding of the purposes and standards of selection of school library materials.

Patterns of Policy Making

The governing body of the school is legally responsible for all matters relating to the operation of that school. It is recommended that assumption of responsibility and the delegation of

---

*Approved by the Board of Directors of the American Association of School Librarians at the ALA Midwinter conference, February 3, 1961.

APPENDIX

authority be stated in a formal policy adopted by the legally
responsible body.

Selection Personnel
Materials for school libraries should be selected by professional personnel in consultation with administration, faculty,
students and parents. Final decision on purchase should rest
with professional personnel in accordance with the formally
adopted policy.

Types of Materials Covered
There should be criteria established for all types of materials included in a library collection. Such criteria should be
available in written form.

Objectives of Selection
The primary objective of a school library is to implement,
enrich and support the educational program of the school. Other
objectives are concerned with: (1) the development of reading
skill, literary taste, discrimination in choice of materials, and
(2) instruction in the use of books and libraries.

The school library should contribute to development of the
social, intellectual and spiritual values of the students.

Criteria for Selection
1. Needs of the individual school
   a. based on knowledge of the curriculum
   b. based on requests from administrators and teachers
2. Needs of the individual student
   a. based on knowledge of children and youth
   b. based on requests of parents and students
3. Provision of a wide range of materials on all levels
   of difficulty, with a diversity of appeal and the
   presentation of different points of view.
4. Provision of materials of high artistic quality.
5. Provision of materials with superior format.

Selection Tools
Reputable, unbiased, professionally prepared selection aids
should be consulted as guides.

APPENDIX

Challenged Materials
    A procedure should be established for consideration of and
action on criticism of materials by individuals or groups. The
School Library Bill of Rights, endorsed by the Council of the
American Library Association in July, 1955, is basic to this
procedure. [The School Library Bill of Rights is presented in
full on text page 82 of this volume. — ed.]

BASIC PRINCIPLES FOR THE SELECTION OF MATERIALS
FOR THE EAST GREENBUSH CENTRAL SCHOOL DISTRICT
SCHOOL LIBRARIES
Adopted at a meeting of the Board of Education
March 22, 1954

    It is the policy of the East Greenbush Central School Dis-
trict to select materials for our libraries in accordance with
the following:

    1. Books and other reading matter shall be chosen for
       values of interest and enlightenment of all the stu-
       dents of the community. A book shall not be excluded
       because of the race, nationality, or the political or
       religious views of the writer.
    2. There shall be the fullest practical provision of
       material presenting all points of view concerning
       the problems and issues of our times, international,
       national, and local; and books or other reading
       matter of sound factual authority shall not be pre-
       scribed or removed from library shelves because
       of partisan or doctrinal disapproval.
    3. Censorship of books shall be challenged in order
       to maintain the school's responsibility to provide
       information and enlightenment.

    Interpreting these principles in selection of reading material
more specifically, the following will apply:

    1. We believe it is the right and responsibility of
       teachers and librarians to select reading

313

material which is carefully balanced to include various points of view on any controversial subject.

2. Since materials are selected to provide for the interest and needs of the school community and the school program, therefore, they will be selected cooperatively by teachers, principals, and librarians, sometimes with the assistance of students.

3. Selection of materials will be assisted by the reading, examination, and checking of standard evaluation aids; i. e., standard catalogues and book review digests.

4. Two basic factors, truth and art, will be considered in the selection of books and other library materials. The first is factual accuracy, authoritativeness, balance, integrity. The second is a quality of stimulating presentation, imagination, vision, creativeness, style appropriate to the idea, vitality, distinction.

5. Materials for the school library shall be examined to select those in which the presentation and the subject matter are suitable for the grade and the interest level at which they are to be used. They will be considered in relation to both the curriculum and to the personal interest of pupils and teachers.

Books and materials meeting the above standards and principles will not be banned but books or materials of an obscene nature or those advocating overthrow of the government of the United States by force or revolution shall not be recommended for purchase.

Criticism of books that are in the library should be submitted in writing to the Superintendent. The Board of Education will be informed. Allegations thus submitted will be considered by a committee among the faculty which will be appointed by the Superintendent. This committee will be in the subject matter field of the book or material challenged and the challenged book or material will be judged by the committee as to its conformity

APPENDIX

to the aforementioned principles. The books or materials involved will be suspended pending a decision in writing by the above committee. Appeals from this decision may be made through the Superintendent to the Board of Education for final decision.

NOTES

2. HOW WELL WILL THE SCHOOL LIBRARY SERVE

1. N. E. A., Research Division. The Secondary School Teacher and Library Services. Research Monograph 1958 M-1. Washington D. C.: the Association, November 1958.
2. A. L. A., American Association of School Librarians. Standards for School Library Programs. Chicago: the Association, 1960.
3. Certain, C. C., Chrm. Standard Library Organization and Equipment for Secondary Schools of Different Sizes. Report of the Committee on Library Organization and Equipment. In Proceedings of the National Education Association. 1918. Pp. 691-719. Washington, D. C.: the Association, 1918.

4. LIBRARIANS WORK AT THEIR PROBLEMS

1. Mrs. Grace Dunkley, Coordinator of Curriculum Materials, Bellflower (California) City Schools.

9. SCHOOL LIBRARIAN: COORDINATOR

1. W. C. Olson, The Packet (D. C. Heath)

14. HOW WILL THE NEW SCHOOL LIBRARY STANDARDS AFFECT HIGH SCHOOL LIBRARIES?

1. Endorsed by the Council of the American Library Association, July, 1955.
2. James B. Conant, The American High School Today (New York: McGraw-Hill, 1959), p. 77.

NOTES

19. AIDS TO BOOK SELECTION

1. Hazard, Paul. Books, Children, and Men. Third edition.
Boston: Horn Book, 1948. 176 p. $3.
2. Haines, Helen E. Living with Books. Second edition. New
York: Columbia University, 1950. 610 p. $5.
3. Strang, Ruth; Gilbert, Christine; and Scoggin, Margaret C.
Gateways to Readable Books. Second edition. New York: H. W.
Wilson Co., 1952. 148 p. $2.75.
4. Munson, Amelia H. An Ample Field. Chicago: American
Library Association, 1950. 122 p. $3.
5. Arbuthnot, May H. Children and Books. Chicago: Scott,
Foresman and Co., 1947. 626 p. $5; school edition, $3.60.
6. Smith, Lillian H. The Unreluctant Years. Chicago: American Library Association, 1953. 193 p. $4.50.
7. Norvell, George W. The Reading Interests of Young People.
Boston: D. C. Heath Co., 1950. 262 p. $3.50.
8. Giles, Ruth, and Cook, Dorothy E., compilers. Children's
Catalog. Eighth edition, revised. New York: H. W. Wilson Co.,
1951. 919 p. Price on application.
9. Hurley, Beatrice D. Children's Books for Seventy-Five
Cents or Less. Bulletin No. 36. Washington, D.C.: Association for
Childhood Education International, 1951. 55 p. 50¢.
10. American Library Association. Book Evaluation Committee. Inexpensive Books for Boys and Girls. Third edition. Chicago:
the Association, 1952. 25 p. 65¢.
11. American Council on Education, Intergroup Education in
Cooperating Schools. Reading Ladders for Human Relations. Revised edition. Washington, D.C.: the Council, 1949. 115 p. $1.25.
12. Library Journal. Recommended Children's Books of 1953.
New York: R. R. Bowker Co., 1954. 100 p. 50¢ for cash; $1, if
billed. (Reprinted from Library Journal)
13. Library Journal. Starred Books from Library Journal.
New York: R. R. Bowker Co., 1954. 120 p. 50¢ for cash; $1, if
billed. (Reprinted from Library Journal)
14. Library Journal. R. R. Bowker Co., 62 West 45th Street,
New York, New York. Semimonthly September thru June; monthly
in July and August; $7 per year.
15. Center for Children's Books, University of Chicago. Bulletin of the Children's Book Center. (5750 Ellis Avenue, Chicago
37, Illinois) Monthly except August; $2.50 per year.
16. Child Study Association of America, Children's Book Committee. "Books of the Year for Children." Child Study 31:26-40;

NOTES

Winter 1953-54. Reprint available from Child Study Association, 132 East 74th Street, New York, New York. 25¢.
17. Children's Reading Service, 1078 St. John's Place, Brooklyn 13, New York.
18. Carpenter, Helen M. Gateways to American History. New York: H. W. Wilson Co., 1942. 255 p. $2.25.
19. Horn Book Magazine, 585 Boylston Street, Boston 16, Massachusetts. Bimonthly; $3.50 per year.
20. Grade Teacher. Educational Publishing Corporation. Darien, Connecticut. Monthly except July and August; $4 per year.
21. Parents' Magazine. Parents' Institute, Bergenfield, New Jersey. Monthly; $3 per year.
22. English Journal. National Council of Teachers of English, 704 South Sixth Street, Champaign, Illinois. Monthly September thru May; $4 per year.
23. New York Times Book Review. New York Times Co., Times Square, New York 36, New York.
24. New York Herald-Tribune Book Review. 230 West 41st Street, New York 18, New York.
25. Cundiff, Ruby E. 101 Magazines for Schools; Grades 1-12. Revised edition. Nashville: Tennessee Book Co. (126 Third Avenue North), 1954. 27 p. 30¢.
26. Martin, Laura K. Magazines for School Libraries. Revised edition. New York: H. W. Wilson Co., 1950. 196 p. $2.75.
27. National Council of Teachers of English, Committee on College Reading. Good Reading. Revised edition. New York: New American Library of World Literature, 1952. 35¢.
28. Stefferud, Alfred, editor. The Wonderful World of Books. Boston: Houghton Mifflin Co., 1953. 319 p. $2.

21. COST OF CATALOGING VERSUS PRINTED CARDS IN THE SCHOOL LIBRARY

1. Costs shown are for Wilson printed cards with subject headings and classification numbers. Cost of Library of Congress cards will differ somewhat; also processing time.

28. AN ORGANIZED CLUB OF STUDENT LIBRARY ASSISTANTS

1. L. Hunter, "Library Clubs in Florida Secondary Schools," Wilson Library Bulletin, 28:200, October, 1953.

NOTES

2. Mary Peacock Douglas, The Teacher-Librarian's Handbook, Second Edition, (Chicago: American Library Association, 1949), p. 26.
3. California has such a program for the northern half of the state. San Jose State College has recently provided space to set up a permanent headquarters and mailing address for The Student Library Assistants of Northern California.

29. TRAINING CIRCULATION ASSISTANTS

1. For a discussion of the relative merits of full-time versus part-time workers, see William Jesse. Shelf Work in Libraries. Chicago, American Library Association, 1952, 1. 61-62.
2. For a discussion of orientation and its value, see Francis R. St. John. "In-Service Training." In Lowell A. Martin, ed., Personnel Administration in Libraries. Chicago, University of Chicago Press, 1949. Also Alice I. Bryan. Public Librarian. New York, Columbia University Press, 1952, p. 236-242.
3. For a detailed discussion of shelf training, see Jesse, op. cit., p. 63-66.
4. Edward C. Heintz. "Industrial Training Applied to Libraries." Wilson Library Bulletin 21:353-7, January, 1947. Also Nathaniel Stewart. "Library In-Service Training." Library Journal 72:146-8, January 15, 1947; and St. John, op. cit., p. 144-5.

36. THE LIBRARIAN AS PERSUADER

1. cf. Stryker, Perrin. "Motivation Research," Fortune, June 1956. A useful introductory article.

38. THE SMALL AND MEDIUM SIZED COLLEGE LIBRARY

1. Branscomb, Harvie. Teaching with Books. Chicago, American Library Association, 1940, p. 84.

42. LIBRARY ACTIVITIES FOR AN ELEMENTARY SCHOOL

1. Grade Teacher, April 1956.
2. Underhill, Charles S. "Sketch for a Picture Collection," Wilson Library Bulletin 30:539-42, March 1956.

NOTES

44. THE LIBRARY: KEY TO CURRICULUM COOPERATION

1. Cincinnati Public Schools: Central High School, Teachers' Manual of Procedure, Cincinnati, Ohio 1955-56, 1955.

49. THE TEACHING OF LIBRARY SKILLS AND ATTITUDES

1. Berner, Elsa. Integrating Library Instruction with Classroom Teaching at Plainview Junior High School. Chicago, American Library Association, 1958. P. iv.
2. Chrestien, Lucy E. The Relative Merit of Selected Methods of Teaching the Use of Books and Libraries. New York, Columbia University School of Library Service (MS thesis), 1945.

54. CROSS REFERENCES MAKE CROSS READERS

1. Margaret Mann. Introduction to Cataloging and the Classification of Books. Chicago, American Library Association, 1952, p. 139.
2. Anne E. Markley. "University of California Subject Catalog Inquiry . . ." Journal of Cataloging and Classification 6:88-95, Fall, 1950.
3. Leroy C. Merritt. Use of Subject Catalog in the University of California Library. Berkeley, University of California Press, 1951.
4. C. Sumner Spalding. "The Use of Catalog Entries at the Library of Congress." Journal of Cataloging and Classification 6:95-100, Fall, 1950.
5. Wesley Simonton. "Duplication of Subject Entries in the Catalog of a University Library and Bibliographies in English Literature." College and Research Libraries 11:215-21, July, 1950.
6. Raynard C. Swank. "The Organization of Library Materials for Research in English Literature." Library Quarterly 15:49-74, January, 1945.
7. Willis H. Kerr. "The Professor Looks at the Card Catalog." College and Research Libraries 4:134-41, March, 1943.
8. Emily K. Brown. Use of the Catalog in a University Library. A.M. Essay, University of Chicago, 1950.
9. Patricia B. Knapp. "The Subject Catalog in the College Library, the Background of Subject Cataloging." Library Quarterly 14:108-118, January, 1944. Also Patricia B. Knapp. "The Subject

321

NOTES

Catalog in the College Library, an investigation of Terminology."
Library Quarterly 14:214-228, July, 1944.
    10. Carlyle J. Frarey, Editor. "Symposium on Subject Head-
ings." Journal of Cataloging and Classification 8:131-58, Decem-
ber, 1952.
    11. Maurice F. Tauber. Technical Services in Libraries.
New York, Columbia University Press, 1954.
    12. Ibid., p. 172
    13. David Judson Haykin. Subject Headings: A Practical Guide.
Washington, U.S. Government Printing Office, 1951, p. 14.
    14. David Judson Haykin. "Subject Headings: Principles and
Development." In Columbia University. School of Library Science.
The Subject Analysis of Library Materials: Papers Presented at
an Institute, June 24-28, 1952 . . . Edited, with an Introduction
by Maurice F. Tauber. New York, Columbia University School of
Library Service, 1953, p. 51.
    15. Tauber, Op. cit., p. 155
    16. Mann, Op. cit., p. 114.
    17. Gerald D. McDonald. "Application and Limitations of Sub-
ject Headings: Humanities." In Columbia University. Op. cit., p. 60.
    18. Frank B. Rogers. "Application and Limitations of Subject
Headings: the Pure and Applied Sciences." Ibid., p. 78.
    19. Frarey, Op. cit., p. 132.
    20. Frarey, Op. cit., p. 141.
    21. Frarey, Op. cit., p. 150.
    22. Henrietta Quigley. "An Investigation of the Possible Re-
lationship of Interbranch Loan to Cataloging." Library Quarterly
14:333-38, October, 1944.
    23. Columbia University. Op. cit., p. 147.
    24. Frarey, Op. cit., p. 136.
    25. Frarey, Op. cit., p. 141.
    26. Frarey, Op. cit., p. 143.
    27. Frarey, Op. cit., p. 151.
    28. Henry Black. "Experimenting with Cross References."
Journal of Cataloging and Classification 6:58, Summer, 1950.
    29. Susan Grey Akers. Simple Library Cataloging. Chicago,
American Library Association, 1954, p. 37.
    30. Black, Op. cit., p. 59.
    31. Carlyle J. Frarey. "Studies of Use of the Subject Catalog."
Columbia University. Op. cit., p. 149.

NOTES

58. GUIDING CHILDREN'S READING

1. Alice R. Brooks, "Developmental Values in Books," in Youth, Communication and Libraries, ed., by Frances Henne and others. Chicago, American Library Association, 1949. pp. 58-59.
2. Carolyn Jean Roos. Patterns in Reading. Chicago, American Library Association, 1954.
3. Margaret M. Heaton and Helen B. Lewis. Reading Ladders for Human Relations. Washington, D.C., American Council on Education, 1955.

68. MENTAL HYGIENE AND BOOKS: BIBLIOTHERAPY AS USED WITH CHILDREN AND ADOLESCENTS

1. Brooks, Alice R. "Integrating Books and Reading with Adolescent Tasks," School Review, LVIII, 4, pp. 211-219 (April 1950)
2. Candell, Lucy. "Story Hour in a Neuropsychiatric Hospital: With a List of Picture Books Used." Library Journal, LXX, 805-807, (September 15, 1945)
3. Cole, D. M. "Bad Boys and Their Books," Wilson Library Bulletin, XVI, 532-536, 543 (March 1942)
4. Craig, L. P. "Boys and Books Get Together," The Child, XVI, 89-101+ (March 1952)
5. De Boer, John J. "Literature and Human Behavior," The English Journal, XXXIX, 76-82 (February 1950)
6. Hall, Elvajean. "Personal Problems of Children," 5th ed. Boston: Personal Book Shop, 1952. 4 p.
7. Hartley, H. W. "Developing Personality Through Books," English Journal, (April 1951) XL, 198-204.
8. Heaps, W. A. "Bibliotherapy and the School Librarian," Library Journal, LXV, 789-792 (October 1, 1940)
9. Heaton, Margaret M. and Lewis, Helen B. Reading Ladders for Human Relations. American Council on Education, 1955.
10. Kircher, C. J. "Bibliotherapy and the Catholic School Library." Vol. 2, pp. 173-184. In Martin, David, brother, editor. Catholic Library Practice. Portland, Ore. University of Portland Press, 1950
11. Lindah, H. M. and Koch, Katherine. "Bibliotherapy in the Middle Grades," Elementary English, XXIX, 390-396 (November 1952)
12. Moore, T. V. "Bibliotherapy." p. 140-148 in Institute on

NOTES

the Elementary School Library, Catholic University of America, 1944. The Catholic Elementary School Library: Proceedings of the Institute. . . . June 27-29, 1944. Washington: Catholic University of America Press, 1945.

13. Russell, D. H. "Reading and the Healthy Personality," Elementary English, XXIX, 195-200 (April 1952)

14. Russell, D. H. and Shrodes, Caroline. "Contributions of Research in Bibliotherapy to the Language Arts Program." School Review I. LVIII, 335-342 (September 1950) and II. LVIII, 411-420. (October 1950)

15. Witty, P. A. "Reading to Meet Emotional Needs." Elementary English XXIX, 75-84 (February 1952)

THE CONTRIBUTORS

FRANCES H. ADAMS is Publications Consultant to the Los Angeles County Schools, Los Angeles, California.

ELEANOR E. AHLERS is Executive Secretary of the American Association of School Librarians, Chicago, Illinois.

ROBERT L. AMSDEN is Principal of Columbia High School, South Orange and Maplewood, New Jersey.

RUTH AULT teaches at Horace Mann School, Indianapolis, Indiana.

ROY D. BAKER is Librarian of the Tahoe-Truckee Unified School District, Truckee, California.

HELEN B. BALDWIN is Librarian of the Buffalo Public School System, Buffalo, New York.

JUNE BERRY teaches in the Brigham Young University High School, Provo, Utah.

ALBERT J. BIGGINS is Librarian at Contra Costa County Library, Martinez, California.

D. RICHARD BOWLES is Assistant Director of Instruction, Austin Public Schools, Austin, Texas.

REBA BURTIS is Librarian of Madisonville High School, Madisonville, Texas.

FAY J. BUTTLE teaches at Brigham Young University High School, Provo, Utah.

GEORGETTA MERRITT CAMPBELL is Assistant Librarian, Bloomfield Senior High School, Bloomfield, New Jersey.

THE CONTRIBUTORS

JAMES H. CHERRY is General Assistant Superintendent, Joliet Township High School and Junior College, Joliet, Illinois.

GEORGIA RANKIN COLE is Director, Division of School Libraries and Teaching Materials, Indiana Department of Public Instruction.

MARY L. CONNOR is Principal of Horace Mann School, Indianapolis, Indiana.

EDITH W. DAHLGREN is Librarian, Samuel Gorton Junior High School, Warwick, Rhode Island.

RICHARD L. DARLING is Coordinator of Library Services, Livonia Public Schools, Livonia, Michigan.

AURELIA DAVIS is Director of Services for Exceptional Children, Atlanta Public Schools, Atlanta, Georgia.

MARY PEACOCK DOUGLAS is Supervisor of Libraries, Raleigh Public Schools, Raleigh, North Carolina.

RAYMOND G. ERBES, JR. is Librarian of Reavis High School, Oak Lawn, Illinois.

VEDA FATKA is High School and Junior College Librarian, Estherville, Iowa.

HELEN F. FAUST is Assistant Director, Division of Pupil Personnel and Counseling, School District of Philadelphia, Pennsylvania.

AMY FENNER is Supervisor of Work With Young Adults, City Library Association, Springfield, Massachusetts.

MILDRED P. FRARY is Supervisor of Elementary Libraries, Los Angeles City Schools, Los Angeles, California.

JOHNNIE GIVENS is Assistant Librarian, Austin Peay State College, Clarksville, Tennessee.

BESS GRAY is Librarian of Condit School, Houston, Texas.

THE CONTRIBUTORS

BEN M. HARRIS is Assistant Professor, College of Education, University of Texas, Austin, Texas.

EMILY HARRIS is the former librarian of Brentwood School, Austin, Texas.

BERTHA D. HELLUM is County Librarian, Contra Costa County Library, Martinez, California.

FELIX E. HIRSCH is Librarian and Professor of History, Trenton State College, Trenton, New Jersey.

ELIZABETH HODGES is Supervisor of Library Services, Baltimore County Board of Education, Towson, Maryland.

VIRGIL M. HOWES is Administrative Assistant, Department of Education, San Diego County, San Diego, California.

LAWRENCE R. HUBER is Librarian, Gallia County District Library, Gallipolis, Ohio.

MAMIE INGRAM is Librarian, Hempstead Public Schools, Hempstead, New York.

DELTA JACK is Librarian of O. W. Holmes Elementary School, Detroit, Michigan.

W. AMBROSE KINCAID is Superintendent of Schools, Hempstead, New York.

LOUISE L. KLOHN is Librarian of Bryant Junior High School, Minneapolis, Minnesota.

IRVING E. LANE is Principal of East Bakersfield High School, Bakersfield, California.

CHRISTOPHER A. LEGGE is Librarian of Bradford Junior College, Bradford, Massachusetts.

M. ELIZABETH LEONARD is Teacher-Librarian at Daniel Boone Elementary School, Chicago, Illinois.

THE CONTRIBUTORS

I. T. LITTLETON is Chief of Technical Services, North Carolina State College, Raleigh, North Carolina.

WALTER R. LUND is Librarian of Central High School, Cincinnati, Ohio.

DAVID McALLISTER is a teacher-training advisor with the USOM, Resht, Iran.

VIRGINIA MUSSELMAN is with the Program Service of the National Recreation Association.

PHILIP S. OGILVIE is Director, Roanoke Public Library, Roanoke, Virginia.

JEAN PARRISS is Librarian of the Beaches Branch, Toronto Public Libraries, Toronto, Ontario, Canada.

FRANCES PERSKE is Librarian of Andrew P. Hill High School, San Jose, California.

VIOLET E. PETERSON is Librarian of Montclair Academy, Montclair, New Jersey.

BERNARD POLL is head of the Children's Department, King County Public Library, Seattle, Washington.

GLADYS L. POTTER is Deputy Superintendent of Schools, Long Beach, California.

GERALD RAFTERY is Librarian, Lafayette Schools, Elizabeth, New Jersey.

JOHN A. RATLIFF is Principal of Pershing Junior High School, Houston, Texas.

DAVY S. RIDGE is the wife of George R. Ridge.

GEORGE R. RIDGE is Associate Professor of French, Georgia State College, Atlanta, Georgia.

DOROTHY ROCHE is Librarian of Belleville High School, Belleville, New Jersey.

328

THE CONTRIBUTORS

JOHN C. ROMAN is Coordinator of Curriculum, Central High School, Cincinnati, Ohio.

HELEN R. SATTLEY is Director of School Library Service, New York City Board of Education.

MARIANNE SCHMIDT is Reference Librarian, Dearborn Public Library, Dearborn, Michigan.

JOSEPH F. SHUBERT is State Librarian, Nevada State Library, Carson City, Nevada.

JULIE SILAGYI is Librarian of the Joint Junior High School, Portage, Pennsylvania.

LYNN L. SOLOMON is Librarian, Stockton Elementary School, Chicago, Illinois.

ALMA N. STANLIS is Coordinator of Libraries, Riverview Community School District, Riverview, Michigan.

DONALD E. STROUT is Professor of Library Science, University of Illinois, Urbana, Illinois.

MARY L. TARBOX is Library Consultant to the Jamestown Public Schools, Jamestown, New York.

VIRGINIA TOZIER was, at the time of the writing of "What Motivates Secondary School Voluntary Reading?", Librarian of Edgemont High School, Scarsdale, New York.

STANLEY D. TRUELSON, JR., is Librarian of the Upstate Medical Center, State University of New York, Syracuse, New York.

EDWARD C. WERNER is Head Librarian and Director of the Audio-Visual Department, New Mexico Western College, Silver City, New Mexico.

HELEN WHEELER is Librarian of Chicago City Junior College, Chicago, Illinois.

BENJAMIN C. WILLIS is General Superintendent of Schools, Chicago, Illinois.

THE CONTRIBUTORS

JOSEPHINE WORTHAM is Librarian of Casis Elementary School, Austin, Texas.

LOIS E. WRISLEY is Librarian, Stranahan High School, Fort Lauderdale, Florida.

SYLVIA ZISKIND is Librarian, Bellflower High School, Los Angeles, California.

AUTHOR-TITLE INDEX

AUTHOR-TITLE INDEX

A NOTE ABOUT THE EDITOR

CHARLES L. TRINKNER is Chairman of the Library
Services Division of the Pensacola Junior College, Pensacola,
Florida. He is a graduate of the University of Florida and of
the Louisiana State University from which he received the
M. S. L. S. in 1954.

He has been a teacher and librarian in the Florida public
schools and has held positions in Texas and Arkansas. During
the summer of 1955 he was a visiting professor of library
science at Texas Woman's University. He served with the U. S.
Marine Corps during the Second World War and participated
in the Battle of the Coral Sea and the Battle of Midway.